Praise for
Reversing the Weight Gain Spiral

"The first account that bridges the biological cause of overeating with a novel approach to maintaining weight. *Reversing the Spiral* is one of the most important weight management books available."

–Kenneth Blum, Ph.D.
Former Professor and Chief
Division of Addictive Diseases and
Laboratory of Pharmacogenetics
University of Texas, Health and Sciences

"*Reversing the Spiral* is an excellent application of relapse prevention principles to the problem of compulsive overeating."

–Terence T. Gorski
President, CENAPS Corporation
Relapse Prevention Specialist

Consultants: Lisa Havens, RN, NCACCII
Stephen W. Emerick, Ph.D.

Reversing

the

Weight Gain Spiral

The Groundbreaking Program for Lifelong Weight Control

Merlene Miller
and David Miller

HP Harrison Plublishing

ISBN-0-9661604-0-1

Cover illustration by Donna Diamond
Cover design by Richard Hasselberger

Manufactured in the United States of America
First Edition: 1994, Ballantine Books
Second Edition: 1997, Harrison Publishing

10   9   8   7   6   5   4   3   2   1

For

Irene Dowler and Anne Welch,

with love and appreciation

Contents

Foreword

Merlene and David Miller have made many important contributions to the field of addiction therapy. This book of theirs addresses the problems of people who repeatedly gain, lose, and regain weight. The authors draw on the experiences—both successes and defeats—of individuals from every walk of life. Their stories depict the perseverance and the power, when well informed and motivated, to change.

The Millers have a mission: to help people discover that they *can* change. Often our inability to change unwanted behavior is couched in indecision and fear. Looking at the causes and stages of the weight spiraling syndrome, readers can at last identify the nature and causes of their actions that have seemed overwhelming in their resistance to reform. Having highlighted those features, the authors offer equally specific ways to recover, to reverse the regression spiral, allowing physical well-being and self-esteem to soar.

Not only does this program recognize the need for self-care, it also shows us how to prevent a regression from recovery—how *not* to get caught up again in the vortex of the weight spiraling syndrome; or how, when a regression isn't altogether preventable, to interrupt it at an early stage by recognizing that we have the power to identify and to choose constructive behavior. In showing us ways of doing that, the authors counsel even the use of anxiety as a tool for constructive change. That approach affirms the adage that many problems in life can be seen profitably as opportunities rather than feared as obstacles.

The authors are seasoned writers who have made distinctive contributions to the understanding of relapse and relapse prevention. Merlene is known for her work with Terence T. Gorski, including their jointly authored book *Staying Sober.* *Learning to Live Again*, a book by the Millers and Gorski, has touched the lives of many; this popular work on facing addictive behavior has supported the reversal of many downward-spiraling lives. Through his professional counseling David has helped people with confused and painful lives see the upward way and to take those first steps.

Merlene and David detail a way that is based in practicality, yet is inspiring. They address us warmly and often humorously; they spin a tale to make us laugh—and to make a point, memorably. They make the complex simple to grasp and show that sometimes the seemingly impossible is achievable. Their partnership in life has become a light for many who had given up hope.

> Diana W. Guthrie, R.N., Ph.D.
> Professor
> University of Kansas

Special Acknowledgment

W ith love and gratitude we thank our friend and colleague Anne Barcus for all her contributions to the development of the spiral model of regression prevention and for many of the concepts set forth in this book. For several years she has used the spiral model with her clients recovering from addictive disorders. She has applied regression prevention principles to the treatment of people who have relapsed with a variety of conditions. Anne has generously shared her experiences and her ideas to help develop and expand the model presented in *Reversing the Weight Gain Spiral*. She helped with our initial organization of material for this book, and some of the personal stories recounted here and have come from her clients. Anne has gathered innumerable anecdotes and illustrations that she's passed along to us over several years, for use not only in these pages but in other materials we have written. It would require another book to convey fully the extent to which her efforts and insights have contributed to this one. We can only say thanks.

Acknowledgments

W e thank Terry Gorski for his friendship and his work in relapse prevention, from which some concepts in this book have emerged. We also appreciate the support of Richard Guthrie and Diana Guthrie, who have applied the spiral model in their work and have given us feedback and encouragement. Other colleagues who have applied the spiral model and allowed us to benefit from their experience with it are Alicia Buckley, Mary Muncrief, Lisa Havens, and Carol Cummings. We thank them, as we thank Linda Moore for her suggestions that we have applied in the manuscript. Ken Blum, whose research in neurochemistry has been a valued resource, has willingly shared information and given us support. Joel Robertson has also contributed to our understanding of the connection between weight spiraling and brain chemistry. We appreciate Bob Mesle's sharing of ideas, especially about power, reflected in the thoughts expressed in this book. Marilyn Shank, our friend and assistant, has contributed countless hours in manuscript preparation, as have Merle and Cleona Guthrie. We also appreciate the assistance and suggestions of Jean and Lloyd Hurshman. We appreciate all that Clark and Kathy Sloan have done to lighten our load to allow us to write. We thank Jack Fahey and our editor at Ballantine, Cheryl Woodruff, for what they have done to make this book possible. Of course, we thank all those who have shared their experiences of weight spiraling, especially Donna, Kristy, Christene, Dave, Dan, Frankie, Barbara, Sharon, Garlena, Monica, Bill, Rod, Irene, and Anne. Finally, we send love and appreciation to our parents, our sons, our daughters-in-law, and our grandchildren, all of whom give us continuing support and encouragement.

Introduction

Perhaps no problem has received more treatment or mistreatment than that of weight gain. There seems to be no end to the many weight loss gimmicks, plans, and books, as the very existence of this one tends to confirm.

A major tendency in the treatment of excess weight has been the focus on only one aspect of a condition that affects most people physically, mentally, emotionally, and socially. Most plans apply their "truth" to part of the problem and do not address the needs of the whole person suffering the effects of a misunderstood and baffling condition. Most programs are based on the assumption that if the fat goes, so will the other problems.

Others are based on the idea that once we understand the emotional problems that cause us to overeat, we won't need to overeat anymore. Such programs seem to imply that a magical meltdown of the physical problem will follow upon the resolution of psychological issues. Solving emotional problems is an important part of creating a healthy life; but without understanding the physical condition that contributes to the problem, most people continue to be overweight despite good mental and emotional health. This is as unrealistic as expecting blood sugars to become normal as a result of treating the emotional problems that accompany being diabetic. Certainly emotional health affects diabetes, but addressing psychological issues alone will not result in a miraculous recovery. The same is true of a weight problem.

Neither will addressing the physical condition alone ensure a long, healthy life. It's true that the conditions that cause a person to gain weight easily, lose weight slowly, and regain weight rapidly are largely physical. But weight loss programs that advocate eating less (and, sometimes, exercising more) as the entire solution are missing the mark. Eating less and exercising more will usually result in weight loss.

But what is it that causes a person to *stop* eating right and exercising—and to regain lost weight?

The issues that lead a person to stop exercising and eating a certain way are often psychological. They are related to the shame, the despair, and the anxiety that accompany a weight problem. Unless these issues are addressed, weight loss is only temporary, and the shame, despair, and anxiety increase (along with the tendency to continue the pattern of losing and gaining).

In this book we refer to the condition of repeatedly losing and gaining weight as the *weight spiraling syndrome*—a physical condition that affects and is affected by psychological and social factors. We offer no magical cures or "quick fix" answers. We hope to increase understanding both of the physical nature of weight spiraling and of the thinking and the feelings that contribute to the problem. This book reflects what we have learned from people who wrestle with weight spiraling and who have found some answers, not by cleaving to any one approach but by addressing the needs of the whole person.

In working with those who struggle with the weight spiraling syndrome, we have found people who carry an undeserved burden of shame. Many experience the body-image shame of being overweight and have also accepted society's inappropriate perception of overweight people as weak-willed and lacking in self-discipline. The more ways they have tried without success to solve their problem, the greater their shame, and the more strongly reinforced their belief that they possess some basic character flaw that prevents them from doing what it takes to attain their ideal. We hope that a better understanding of the nature of the weight spiraling syndrome will allow those who carry this burden of shame to lay it down and break free of the restrictions that society has put on them (and that they have put on themselves) because of incorrect information and prejudice.

Our work with relapse prevention began with addiction clients using the CENAPS model developed by our colleague, Terence T. Gorski. Several years ago, in cooperation with Dr. Diana Guthrie and Dr. Richard Guthrie (specialists in diabetes), we modified the CENAPS method to use with diabetes patients and then with people with weight problems.

The term *relapse* seems less appropriate for weight spiraling than for an addiction to alcohol or other drugs. With a chemical addiction, a more definitive line—use of the addictive substance—identifies a relapse. Not so when we are dealing with food. Compliance with a program of appropriate eating is a matter more of degree than of absoluteness. The term *regression* better describes this process; a gradual spiraling away from a program of self-care to which there has been a full and honest commitment. Regression prevention is what we do to prevent or interrupt the regression spiral.

This book is divided into four parts. Part One, *The Weight Spiraling Syndrome*, discusses all aspects of the problem of weight spiraling—physical, psychological, and social. Part

Two, *Choosing Recovery*, discusses recovery and what it takes to live healthily despite having a condition that causes one to gain weight easily. Part Three, *Reversing the Spiral: Regression Prevention*, provides guidelines for preventing regression into ways of thinking and behaving that interfere with ongoing recovery. Part Four, *There Is More to Life Than Not Gaining Weight*, is about the need to go beyond a focus on weight to a focus on living fully.

The personal stories are experiences of real people. In order to protect their privacy, we have changed many details; in some cases, we've combined details, so that a story may actually be a composite of more than one person.

We've placed self-application exercises throughout the book to aid you in applying the information to yourself. We suggest you get a notebook and allot one section of it to each part of this book. At a glance, the exercises may sometimes appear simplistic or childish, or you may feel you're being asked to repeat dutifully the information you've just now received and can't so quickly have forgotten. But the act of writing does help you plant a fact or an idea in your mind, and the focusing effect of actually setting words on paper may help you clarify your own thoughts. The exercises are not requisites to your success in tackling the weight spiraling syndrome, but we believe you will get more from the book if you do them.

As a word of caution, we would suggest that anytime you find that reading a description of a certain food triggers a craving for that food you may want to take a break from your reading and come back to it when you are less vulnerable.

See the end of this book for a list of other books and resources that you can draw from to further assist your recovery. Agencies offering treatment or seminars based on "Reversing the Spiral" principles are listed there for those who may wish more help in using the ideas discussed in the pages ahead.

Part One

The Weight Spiraling Syndrome

Chapter 1

Commitment to What?

*For thirty-five years Pamela's weight controlled her life.
She was overweight as a child and still remembers
the pain of hearing people say, "She has such a pretty
face." Throughout her childhood, adolescence, and adulthood, her life revolved around feeling the pain of being
overweight and eating to assuage that pain. She always knew what would ease it—her tried-and-true
friend, food.*

*The first time she went on a diet her doctor told her
that she could eat anything as long as it contained
no white flour or white sugar. She immediately went
home and baked a lemon meringue pie using brown sugar
and whole wheat flour. Needless to say, it wasn't as good
as the "real" thing, but she soon got used to the
taste—and rapidly gained five pounds.*

*Later that year she decided to take the bull by the
horns and just quit eating. The scale kept her going for
four days; it was saying great things. When her
mother pleaded with her to be more sensible, she got
out the cottage cheese, took a few bites, then reached
for the cookies.*

Diets came and went, each beginning with strong determination and ending in despair. She would do almost anything for the elation of stepping on the scale and seeing a number lower than the one that had mocked her the day before. She says, "For years and years I let the scale determine whether or not I was a person of worth."

Pamela tried commercial programs, liquid protein, diets of the stars, diets of her friends, hypnosis, and fasting. Each time she started with the best of intentions. She would plan her menus, read diet magazines, and talk weight loss with her family. Diets controlled her life. She knew all the foods not to eat, the kind of exercises she needed to start doing, and precisely how many calories she should cut back.

Many times, she lost weight. Once—to her delight and that of her family and friends—she lost 116 pounds and weighed what the charts said she should. She told herself, "If I can do this, I can do anything." She felt invincible. The world was her apple and that apple would always be eaten raw, never again in a pie. She would do whatever it took never to let one regained ounce tarnish her hard-earned victory.

Through two years' vigilant self-deprivation and icy determination, she kept the weight off. Then the ice began to melt and the vigil ended. She watched the weight come back as though it had a life of its own; again, the scale controlled her. Pamela was never a quitter, so periodically she'd get out her diet books, rejoin a weight loss organization or a health club, inform her family of her intentions, and brace herself for the siege before her. Each time she would be successful, success being measured by what the scale said to her each morning.

And each time the unfairness of her plight, the burden
of never-ending vigilance and feelings of deprivation,
overwhelmed her. Eating would win out, leading to
her gaining even more weight than she had lost most
recently.

The worst part of this battle was living with the hopeless,
helpless, guilt-ridden messages that kept replaying
in her mind: You're a failure and always will be. You
have no willpower. You will never change. And with those
old recycled tapes playing in her head, she would reach
for her old friend, always there to soothe and comfort
her—food.

If Pamela's story is familiar to you, we have bad news and good news. The bad news is that you probably have a condition that makes it more difficult for you to lose weight than it is for some other people. This condition also sets you up to easily regain weight you have struggled to lose.[1] The good news is that even though it's not your fault that you have this condition, you can free yourself of its devastating effects in your life. That the efforts you've made in the past haven't worked does not mean that yours is a hopeless condition. New understanding and a commitment to recovery, rather than to weight loss, have given hope and a new way of life to many.

Weight management requires a commitment, a commitment that most of us make over and over again. We make an honest commitment to doing what it takes to be thin—and we do lose weight—but one day we look around and realize that we are not thin and we are no longer doing what we made a commitment to do. What happened? How did we get to this place again? How did we fail? Was all our effort for nothing? Are we hopeless?

Even our best friends question the honesty of our commitment; they say we just didn't want badly enough to be thin. But we know we honestly intended to make it this time. Are we just incapable of following through? Was our commitment to something that could not work?

Perhaps it is *what we are making the commitment to* that is setting us up for failure.

Most people who lose weight commit themselves to reaching a goal. They commit to doing specific things for a certain number of weeks or months or until they have lost a specified amount of weight. They have the illusion that the need to eat differently (diet) will have an end, that when they reach their goal they will be transformed into a person who will "never have to do this again." We can do almost anything for a while. And that is the commitment we make: to restrict ourselves until we come to the end of the need to restrict ourselves.

Most rapid weight loss plans are not roads to health but cul-de-sacs that lead us back to where we started. This painful process is not only emotionally demoralizing, it is physically damaging. We buy diet book after diet book. We try one plan after another, only to fail and try again. Many of us have given up hope, not of losing weight, for we have done that many times, but of maintaining the weight loss permanently.

Exercise

Answer these questions as honestly as you can:

How many times have you attempted to lose weight?

How many times have you gained back more than you lost?

This book is not just about weight loss. Helping anyone lose weight is not our major goal. Weight loss may be important;

we encourage anyone to lose weight who needs to, especially when excess weight threatens one's health. But it will do no good to lose weight without learning how to keep the weight off, without learning to live differently.

Sometimes we break our honest commitments to managing a weight problem because we really don't know *how* to manage it. We don't lack commitment; we lack knowledge. We have learned only how to "hang on" for limited periods of time. We know only what not to do, not what to do. Our commitment, although real, has been misconceived: We've been trying to remain dedicated to *restricted* living rather than opening ourselves to *enriched* living.

Let's remove the word *diet* from our vocabulary. When we think "diet," we have in mind a limited amount of time; the diet will end. We then go back to our old eating habits. We also think "deprived." Being on a diet suggests restricted eating, doing without.

For those of us who have a weight spiraling problem—we have lost weight and gained it back numerous times—there are no short-term answers. There is no "transformation." Weight loss is only a temporary solution to a long-term problem.

Underlying conditions predispose us to weight spiraling. They include a metabolism that causes us to burn calories slower than the average person; a low energy level that causes us to get less exercise; an imbalance in brain chemistry that causes cravings for certain foods or for larger quantities of food. A person who has a problem with weight spiraling may have any one or all of these underlying conditions.

The conditions that cause some people to regain lost weight rapidly—the weight spiraling syndrome—do not go away when short-term goals are achieved. A commitment to losing weight does not produce a permanent solution. A permanent solution requires learning to live with a lifelong condition that does not go away when a goal weight is attained.

Having the tendency toward weight spiraling is very much like having any other chronic condition, such as diabetes or arthritis. People with these problems still have them even when they are not experiencing the symptoms. People with diabetes can eat in a prescribed manner, exercise, and take insulin or medication to control the symptoms of their illness. But they cannot do these things for a period of time and have their diabetes go away forever.

The weight spiraling syndrome is not a visitor we can send home after a certain period of time. It is a family member that will live with us for the rest of our lives. Like a marriage, it requires a lifelong commitment. It requires that we make peace with it rather than fighting it or running from it. It means accepting the unpleasant aspects of managing the situation just as healthy families learn to accept the unpleasant aspects of living together. It takes a commitment for life, one day at a time.

We would like to believe those weight loss advertisements and commercials telling us that we can lose weight, and so work magical transformations in our lives. But the problem behind weight spiraling is not solved when we lose weight. A commitment to recovery from the weight spiraling syndrome is a commitment to a way of life. It is accepting this lurking condition as a permanent part of us, and bringing it home to live.

Exercise

Complete this sentence at least five ways:

Accepting weight spiraling as a condition I continue to struggle with means . . .

Commitment to Recovery

Recovery begins when we accept reality. The weight spiraling syndrome cannot be vanquished by a succession of short-term measures; dieting is not going to make it go away; being thin is not the solution; weight loss is not going to fix us.

This acceptance brings with it the knowledge that what we have been doing can, at best, bring about only short-lived relief—followed by more intense pain. We recognize the need to break the cycle of weight loss and weight gain by relinquishing our attempts to dissolve the condition. We recognize the need to stop trying to *cure* the weight spiraling syndrome and learn to *manage* it.

In the past we have wanted to believe that if we just try harder we can change reality. We have wanted to believe that at some point we can overcome the tendency to be overweight and leave it behind us, forever.

Oh that this too too solid flesh would melt, thaw and resolve
itself into a dew. William Shakespeare
Hamlet

Exercise

Ask yourself some questions:

How many times have I started a "diet" in the past five years?

What is my weight now compared to what it was five years ago?

How many pounds have I lost and regained in that period of time?

What is the longest time I have maintained weight loss before I started regaining?

How many different wardrobe changes have I made? Do I
have "fat" clothes and "thin" clothes (or "fat" clothes
and "not so fat" clothes)?

What do your answers tell you about your pattern of
losing and gaining weight?

Some of us have believed that if we ignore reality it doesn't
exist. We're not overweight, just underheight. If no one sees
us eat, the calories don't count. We can starve ourselves down
to 98 pounds, believing that being so small will make us like
someone who has never weighted above 110.

If, rather, we recognize reality for what it is, whether or not
we like it, we can adapt to it and put our energy into what can
be changed. There is no serenity in retreating from reality.

. . . you have only one life to live. If you don't accept what
reality has to offer, you have only fantasy to support you,
which is about as satisfying as the hole in the doughnut
in the long run.   Abraham Twerski[2]

There is power in acceptance. It frees us to function in the
real world, helps us set ourselves onto the path to a better way
of life.

There comes a time when we must ask ourselves: Do we
want to continue to believe that if we can just be thin everything will be all right? Do we want to keep trying over and
over again, and failing over and over again, to *make* something true that is just not true? Or are we ready to give it up?

When we've looked honestly at reality—and in the looking
have managed even to see—we realize we have two options:
take it or leave it.

Recovery begins when we give up our old way of living, its futility all too repeatedly proved, and accept a new way. We come to recognize that to achieve any kind of peace or serenity we have to let go of trying to fix something that (we now see) we don't have the power to change.

Becoming aware of our limitations, we accept them; accepting them, we become free to move beyond them, to look at new options for meeting our needs. When weight loss is the goal, then our only possibility for reaching it is exercising more while eating less. That's it. But when recovery is our goal, in addition to losing weight, we open up an array of possibilities for living fully and abundantly. For feeling good.

Giving up the old allows birth of the new.

Exercise

Complete this sentence at least five ways, each time differently, remembering that awareness can be physical, emotional, mental, or spiritual:

I am beginning to be aware . . .

Chapter 2

Why Dieting
Doesn't Work

"I am so sick of hearing people say, 'The main exercise
you need is to push yourself away from the table,' "
Sharon groaned. "If I have heard that once in my
life, I've heard it a thousand times. No one knows how
infuriating that is except people like me who have pushed
away from the table hungry so many times we should
weigh ninety pounds by now. I know I should have
more willpower because I've been told that so often, but
I don't know where to get any more."

Even though Sharon feels angry when people tell
her she's weak-willed, she herself believes it: Lack
of willpower is her problem, she thinks, and if she could
just get more of it she could get thin and stay thin. She
has believed that if she can work up enough determination, she can endure the misery. And she has
lost weight by clenching her teeth and hanging on; she's
done it enough times to prove that everyone's belief is
the truth: She just needs more willpower.

Contrary to popular opinion, willpower—and character
traits in general—have little to do with our tendency to

gain weight. The predisposition to put on pounds too easily is a condition that some of us were born with[1] or that we developed through behavior we did not realize would harm us. We who gain or regain weight easily often have slow metabolism, low energy, and/or brain chemistry imbalances that cause us to experience cravings that we use food to satisfy. These conditions relentlessly set us up for seemingly endless cycles of losing and regaining weight; we call this effect the weight spiraling syndrome.

The syndrome issues from an impairment in the body's ability to regulate weight so that weight easily spirals upward, out of control. This condition is *what we have, not what we are*. We also may have green eyes and brown hair. These are characteristics, not our identity. We are not overeaters, compulsive eaters, relapsers, or yo-yo dieters. We struggle with these things; we ourselves are not these things. We may be fat or skinny, but these are only characteristics we have; they do not describe who we are. It is important that we not label ourselves and that we not accept labels from others.

Sometimes, making this change in attitude can help us begin to think better of ourselves. Improving our opinion of ourselves is, in fact, necessary to recovery from the weight spiraling syndrome. We must think better of ourselves, regardless of our size, regardless of how many times we have lost and regained weight.

Exercise

Take time to write a few words, or a few pages—whatever comes to mind—in response to the following incomplete sentence:

> When I think that weight spiraling may not be a willpower issue, I feel . . .

Although weight spiraling is often accompanied by a tendency to use food as a way to feel good and to relieve physical and emotional pain, the syndrome has nothing to do with willpower. It is not a character flaw. It is more than "mind over platter." Most of us have had the willpower, over and over again, to lose weight or at least to try diligently to do so.

We've used all kinds of methods. We have had the self-discipline to limit our food consumption to grapefruit and cottage cheese, to live on liquid formulas (powder mixed with water that tastes like powder mixed with water), to go for periods of time without eating at all (often with the notable effect being that seven days of fasting made one week). Some of us have been so committed to weight loss that we even had our jaws wired or our stomachs stapled.

We agree with Ziggy that "a waist is a terrible thing to mind," but we keep trying.

We do not lack commitment, self-discipline, willpower. Once we truly believe that, freeing ourselves of the labels we've borne, we have taken the first step in choosing to live a satisfying life despite the continuing nature of the weight spiraling syndrome.

A number of conditions may be a part of the syndrome, some inborn, others created by our behavior. A strong genetic basis for being overweight has been substantiated; but in most cases, heredity mainly sets the stage for other factors favoring weight gain.

Many of us grew up in families where eating was encouraged as a balm for life's discomforts (eat, you'll feel better). Or where being a "good eater" was a source of pride (did you belong to the Clean-Plate Club?). Besides, we live in a world that loudly promotes both eating and being thin (eat eat eat; just don't swallow). This is a setup for weight spiraling. Eat the pizza, the burgers, the fries, and the ice cream. But be thin. Eating is what we do to have fun, and dieting is what we do to be thin.

Exercise

List some of the messages you have heard that have contributed to mixed feelings about your eating habits.

Emotional trauma, low self-esteem, and shame mean inner pain, and, very often, eating relieves that pain. Food may even become our only source of comfort. The side effects of this self-medication, however, are weight gain and eventually the weight spiraling syndrome. The social stigma of being overweight adds to our emotional trauma, low self-esteem, and shame, increasing the need to eat for comfort.

Regardless of how they developed, a variety of symptoms make up the weight spiraling syndrome. Some of us experience certain of these symptoms; some of us have all of them together. As you'd suppose, cohabiting symptoms intensify one another. Here are the main troublemakers.

Slow Metabolic Rate

Metabolic rate is the rate at which the body burns calories, or uses energy. We are not born equal when it comes to rate of metabolism. Some people burn calories slowly; they gain weight easily. Many of us have suffered repeated indignities because of the common belief that everyone burns calories at the same rate given the same activity.

When Sharon was in high school, she and her friend Diane (who wasn't overweight to start with) decided to go on a diet together. They ate about the same

*things, the same number of calories. Diane lost five pounds
in two weeks, Sharon lost two. Their friends said
Sharon must be cheating, but she knew she wasn't. She
cut her calories even more, but still Diane lost faster.*

*After four weeks Sharon and Diane both went back
to their regular eating habits. Sharon rapidly regained
the weight she had lost, Diane didn't. A couple of years
later and ten pounds heavier than before, Sharon consulted
a doctor. He handed her a 1,000-calorie exchange
diet. The first week she lost two pounds; the second
week she lost none. Her doctor insisted she had been
cheating even after she denied his charge. "The body
burns more than 1,000 calories a day," he said. "So
if you have been eating less than that, you would
have lost. You are eating things you are not aware of."
His insistence made Sharon feel a little crazy, so she
didn't go back.*

Some people are born with a slow metabolic rate.[2] Others
lower their rate of metabolism with very-low-calorie diets that
severely restrict nutritional intake. Most of us weight spiralers
combine these characteristics. We were born with a slower
than average metabolic rate, so we have a tendency to gain
weight. And in order to counteract that tendency, we have
gone on very-low-calorie diets that have further slowed metabolic rate. The more we diet, the more easily we gain weight.

A drastic restriction of caloric intake (especially when it's
imposed over and over again as we repeatedly lose and gain
weight) slows the body's calorie-burning rate and impairs its
ability to regulate weight. When we reduce our calorie intake,
the body, reacting as though it is being starved, attempts to
conserve energy by burning even more slowly the calories it
does get.[3] When we increase our calorie intake, the body, hav-

ing adapted to the lower rate, continues to burn calories slowly, and we rapidly regain weight. Every time we go on another very-low-calorie diet, metabolic rate is further lowered, until, after dieting for a few weeks, all we lose may be a few weeks. In addition, when we lose rapidly, we encourage muscle loss; when we regain, we risk replacing the lost muscle with fat.[4] The higher the percentage of muscle to fat, the faster we burn calories. People who are more muscular are fast fat burners; people with more body fat are slow fat burners.

Low Energy

Some people have more energy than others. Of course, active people burn more calories than their more sedentary neighbors do. They weigh less even when they eat the same amount as people who are less active. By nature some people prefer activities that do not require a high expenditure of energy.

Walking is something Sharon used to do mainly to get to the kitchen and the garage. She enjoys reading, watching television, going to movies, sewing, and playing the piano. She likes to slow dance, but does not enjoy fast dancing of any kind. Once when she was dieting, she ran two miles every day and hated every minute of it. "Low energy has affected my life," Sharon says. "I really don't understand why people want to bowl or play baseball or volleyball. Lack of participation in physical activities has affected my social life. I have started walking because it increases my metabolic rate and helps me feel better, but I always walk with a friend. The conversation is what I enjoy and what keeps me doing it."

People who have low energy may wish that Henry Ford was right when he said, "Exercise is bunk. If you are healthy, you don't need it; if you are sick, you shouldn't take it." But he *wasn't* right. And thinking as he did can contribute to weight spiraling in a number of ways.

Paradoxically, movement increases energy; lack of activity reduces energy. The less we move, the less we want to move and the fewer calories we burn. Some people think that exercise is counterproductive because it just makes us hungry. But studies show that physical activity actually reduces appetite, especially for the sorts of "forbidden" foods (low in nutrition and abundant in calories) that a great many people tend to crave.

Physical activity reduces stress, so it makes us less likely to eat in order to relax or calm ourselves. It lifts our mood, so we are less likely to eat because of depression. It increases the production of brain chemicals that are natural tranquilizers, so we have less need for foods that produce these "mellow molecules."

In addition, of course, exercise allows us to eat more without gaining weight and therefore to live on a less restrictive nutrition plan. Exercise also raises the metabolic rate. Research has shown that we burn calories at a higher rate for up to twelve hours after we exercise.[5] So, if the news on slow metabolic rate has discouraged you, take heart from these good words about exercise.

If we let lack of energy cause us to live a sedentary life, we increase our risk of eating to feel good, or of feeling deprived because of restricted eating. The lower our level of physical activity, the fewer calories our body uses to maintain itself—and hence the more calories it stores as fat in our fat cells.

Fat Cells

The body stores fat in fat cells. People with more fat cells or large fat cells gain weight more easily than other people. As a result of his research with overweight people, Kelly D. Brownell, of the University of Pennsylvania School of Medicine has this to say about obesity and fat cells:

> Obesity runs in families. A child with no overweight parents has less than a 10% chance of being overweight. If one parent is obese, the chances increase to 40%. With two obese parents, the odds are 80%. This could, of course, reflect the tendency of families to pass along their poor eating and exercise habits to children. However, we have known for years that animals can be bred to be fat. The meat you buy at a supermarket is from an animal bred to have a certain percentage of body fat. Recent studies with humans suggest that there may be a stronger genetic component to human weight problems than was previously thought. . . . The body accumulates and stores fat in fat cells. Some people have too many fat cells, while others have a normal number but their fat cells are too large. Still others have both types. People who were overweight in childhood or are very heavy tend to have excessive numbers of fat cells.[6]

Altered Brain Chemistry

Every feeling we have, every thought we think, everything we do produces a chemical reaction in the brain. Brain chemistry levels have a lot to do with our mood, our energy, our thinking. Many chemicals work together in the brain to produce thoughts and feelings and influence behavior. Our supply of brain chemicals is highly dependent upon genetic makeup, but brain chemistry levels are also affected by thoughts, emotions, behavior, and—significantly—by what we eat. Brain chemicals are made from amino acids and vitamins in food.

Studies show that brain chemistry plays a significant role in appetite and in control of eating behavior. Imbalance of brain chemicals involved in the system that regulates food intake and energy expenditure can result in obesity.[7]

Research indicates that some people are born with brain chemistry imbalances. Deficits can also be created by trauma, mood-altering drugs, inappropriate nutrition, and extreme behaviors or emotions.[8] Our knowledge about the permanence of brain chemistry imbalances is scant, but we do know that deficits can be modified (at least temporarily) with proper nutrition, exercise, laughter, sleep, love, medication, and meditation.

Different brain chemicals produce different effects. *Endorphins* and *enkephalins* are the brain's natural pain relievers.[9] When the brain's supply of these chemicals is low (whether because of hereditary or environmental factors), we feel incomplete and uncomfortable. Certain foods, physical exercise, love, and laughter can increase the release of endorphins and enkephalins, creating a feeling of calm, even euphoria.

Dopamine is the brain's energizer. An inadequate supply of this chemical results in lack of energy or drive. *Serotonin*, produced from carbohydrates, is an emotional stabilizer; when it is low, we may feel down and irritable for no apparent reason. A low level of serotonin induces our hunger for carbohydrates.[10]

These are only a few of the many brain chemicals that transmit thoughts and feelings. The balance or imbalance of these chemicals affects our mood and our thought processes. Alterations in brain chemistry, whether due to heredity or environment, alter our thoughts and feelings and, therefore, our behavior.

Brain chemicals are produced from amino acids that come from food. Whatever we consume affects the balance of brain chemistry. Nutrition and malnutrition can alter brain chemistry levels on a long-term basis.

> *You are what you eat. So, I'm a piece of chocolate cake.*
> Judith Light as Angela on "Who's the Boss"

Eating certain foods may produce immediate pleasure or relief but can, in the long run, have damaging effects on brain chemical levels (as well as overall health). Eating large amounts of foods high in fat may, for example, produce brain chemistry changes that create pleasant short-term feelings. But over time, a diet disproportionately high in fats may deprive the brain of an adequate supply of other nutrients necessary for balanced brain chemistry.

People who have the weight spiraling syndrome often have a brain chemistry imbalance that creates a craving that they use food to satisfy. Studies show that the amount of food we eat, how often we eat, and how much we eat are influenced by our brain chemistry levels.

In some people overeating produces brain chemistry changes that feel pleasurable. Eating large quantities of food (bingeing) calms them by increasing the release of enkephalins. People with certain brain chemistry deficits may get a desired response from specific mood-elevating foods. Chocolate, for example, produces a brain chemical referred to as PEA, which induces a contentment similar to the warmth that comes of feeling loved.[11] When feeling lonely or unloved, the only thing better than a chocolate brownie is ten brownies.

Cal actually gets "high" from binge eating. When he allows himself to eat large quantities of food at one time, he becomes euphoric, feeling intense pleasure and release. For him, binge eating results in the release of certain brain chemicals, very much like the effect of a mood-altering drug. Sharon does not get that response from bingeing, but certain foods (especially ones high in fat, sugar, and chocolate) give her what she calls a "zing." She describes this as a sort of rush. Her favorite zing food is chocolate brownies.

Stress can cause brain chemistry alterations that create food cravings, usually for carbohydrates. The stress of not being thin in a thin-oriented society, the stress of struggling to lose weight, the stress of feeling continually deprived can create emotional distress that increases the compulsion to eat for relief. Unresolved guilt and shame also result in stress that interferes with healthy brain chemistry balance.

Dieting deprives us of the only way many of us know to relieve the discomfort of deficient brain chemicals. We can talk about willpower and self-discipline all we want, but let's face it: Anyone feeling uncomfortable "long enough" (a variable period of time) looks for ways to relieve the discomfort. We do not grit our teeth and bear it indefinitely. We want relief. If eating is the only way we know to get it, we will eat. The only alternative is learning other ways to feel good.

Many activities can replace eating as a way to produce feel-good chemicals in the brain. But when our goal is weight loss and our method of achieving it is very-low-calorie dieting, we experience discomfort and cravings due to insufficient levels of those chemicals in the brain. All diet roads lead to the refrigerator. The only way out is to give up both overeating and dieting—and to find other ways to alter our brain chemistry.

L.B: When I have set my mind to it I have always been able to lose weight for a while because I substituted the good feelings of losing weight for the good feelings of eating. Every time I went down a size in my clothes I felt so good. The high of having people tell me how good I looked kept me going for a while. But after I got to a certain point people stopped talking about it. It wasn't exciting anymore. And I didn't have my old comfort, eating, either. So I didn't have any way to feel good. Now I am learning that there are ways to change my brain chemistry besides eating or getting praise for losing weight. I wish I had known that a long time ago.

Cravings and Trigger Foods

Brain chemistry deficits create cravings for certain foods.[12] Rather than satisfying us, the foods that some of us choose in response to these cravings create a desire to eat more, intensifying the craving and setting up a compulsion to overeat or binge.

These trigger foods are not the same for everyone. But the most common trigger foods are high in both sugar and fat. Studies at the University of Michigan, UCLA, the University of Washington, and MIT suggest that *the basic craving is for fat* and that sugar just enhances the taste.[13]

Sharon had always thought that sweets were her trigger foods. She never thought about fat being her problem; she prefers brownies to potato chips. And if she can't have too many chocolate chip cookies, she will do without. But when someone suggested that it might be the fat in the cookies rather than the sugar, she started to notice her physical reaction. Hard candy—sugar, no fat—has no appeal for her. She does not crave it, and

if she eats it, it does not trigger a craving for more or
a compulsion to overeat. But sweet foods that are also
high in fat set up a craving so intense that once she
begins to eat them the only way to stop is get com-
pletely away from them. Recently a friend baked a
fat-free cake. After eating a few bites, Sharon said, "I
miss the 'zing.' " She suddenly realized even though the
cake tasted very good, a physiological reaction was
missing that she expected from a piece of cake. This
awareness was her first reaction; but having gained it,
she was able to focus anew on the enjoyable taste of
the fat-free cake. It was a pleasant experience and
did not create the overwhelming compulsion to eat
more than she was used to when she ate cake. It was
a relief to know that she could enjoy the taste of previously
"forbidden" foods without the discomfort of the in-
tense craving afterward.

Everyone—even a person with normal brain chemistry—is familiar with the kind of craving triggered by taste alone. Everyone at some time has eaten one peanut and, because the nuts
tasted good, continued to eat them until all were gone. We all
understand the commercial that says, "Nobody can eat just
one." But the cravings triggered by brain chemistry imbalances and set off by trigger foods go far beyond taste. Trigger
foods seem to turn off the signal that tells some of us when
we have had enough to eat. We don't feel satisfied even when
we are physically full.

Each person must identify his or her own trigger foods, because they are not the same for everyone. Identifying what
they are requires noting our physical reaction to certain foods,
looking at ingredients, and comparing our reactions to the different foods.

Exercise

1. List your five favorite foods. Are these foods that are mostly high in fat, sugar, salt, or chocolate? Or are they combinations?

2. What are the foods that cause you to want to continue eating beyond levels usually considered normal or adequate?

3. Do these foods produce a strong pleasurable sensation or relieve feelings of discomfort while you eat them (or for a period of time after you eat them)?

4. On a scale of 0 (*no craving at all*) to 10 (*a craving too strong to resist*), rate each of the following foods according to the strength of the craving each triggers.

    Hard candy (without fat)
    A chocolate kiss
    Potato chips
    Iced white cake
    Iced chocolate cake
    Chocolate cake without icing
    Sugar-free hot chocolate
    Chocolate ice cream
    Vanilla ice cream
    Vanilla frozen yogurt
    Chocolate sugar-free frozen yogurt
    Strawberry mouse (made with cream)
    Strawberry Jello (with sugar)
    Lemonade (with sugar)
    Root beer float (with ice cream)
    Plain bread (no butter)
    Croissant (no butter)
    Glazed donut
    Jelly (alone)

Peanut butter sandwich with no jelly
Jelly sandwich with no peanut butter
Skinless chicken
Hamburger
Fried egg
Custard (with sugar)

A craving that results from eating hard candy, Jello, lemonade, jelly, or frozen yogurt indicates that sugar is a trigger. A craving triggered by potato chips, hamburgers, croissants, peanut butter, and fried foods indicates that fat is a trigger. Sugar-free and fat-free chocolate foods indicate chocolate as a trigger. Cake, icing, mousse, soft candy, ice cream, and donuts indicate that the combination of fat and sugar is the trigger, but this does not rule out the possibility that either separately may also be a problem.

The questions in the exercise above should have helped you close in a bit on the identity of your trigger foods, but you will probably need to observe further and experiment. Look at labels to see what is really in the things that you eat. For example, Jon loves tortillas and found himself eating a lot of them; he even put scrambled eggs in them for breakfast. In attempting to identify his trigger foods, he checked the ingredients in the brand of tortillas he bought. He discovered they were made with lard and contained a high percentage of fat. He then looked for, and found, a brand low in fat and made without lard.

In figuring out what your trigger foods are, consider that they are not necessarily the foods you like best (although they often are). But on eliminating the substance or substances that you've learned do create cravings, you may find that you can identify many enjoyable foods that do not trigger a craving to eat more.

Both fat and sugar are high in calories and low in nutrition, so they provide little to satisfy real (physical) hunger. In addition, fat and sugar provide very little bulk. Bulk sends a signal to the brain that we have eaten; without that signal, the brain continues to tell us to eat more. Most people find it easier to avoid eating trigger foods in the first place than to control the compulsion that, once tasted, they set up. (The easiest way to avoid eating them is to avoid buying them.)

Weight spiraling may actually increase cravings for high-fat foods. This means that each time we lose and regain weight we find it harder to resist the foods most likely to cause us to gain weight. And research is showing that *fat calories are more fattening than other calories.* This news is contrary to what we have been told for many years: that a calorie is a calorie. Fats are more easily converted into body fat than are carbohydrates. So eating 100 calories of butter is going to add more fat than eating 100 calories of oatmeal.

> **N.Y.:** I really know how to count calories. I have done it through diet after diet after diet. But I always thought that as long as I stayed within my calorie limit it didn't matter much what I ate. So I used a high percentage of my calorie allotment in my favorite foods—high-fat foods. Later I identified fat as my trigger food and began to eat much less of it, and now I not only have less trouble with cravings, I can eat more without gaining weight.

Emotional Hunger

Even if a weight problem is not initially a psychological issue, people who are overweight often sustain psychological damage from the stigma that society puts on obesity. As weight spirals up, self-esteem spirals down.

The tendency to gain weight easily usually does not develop because of some emotional problem. In fact, many people who undergo intensive psychotherapy continue to be overweight even when they've resolved psychological problems that may have contributed to their overeating.

> J.D.: I have been in some sort of psychotherapy for over twelve years and none of it has helped me lose weight. It has helped me express my feelings, but it has not solved my weight problem. It has been beneficial, though, because it has helped me recognize and handle guilt, depression, and emotional needs that have affected my life.

Physical and emotional conditions do interact and affect us. When we are overweight, we are physically uncomfortable, clothes may choke or pinch us, and movement may be more awkward. In addition, people with weight problems often have poor self-esteem, depression, and guilt; they perceive themselves as defective. Because our society places such great value on being thin, people who are not thin may very early receive the message "There is something wrong with you." Accepting that message implies something more than a sense of *having* a defect. It all but dictates that we see ourselves as *being* defective. That perception can lead to the belief that we do not have the power to bring about good things in our lives. Extra pounds can mean very heavy baggage indeed.

The pain of any social stigma can lead us to avoid social interaction, and fear of intimacy is common among people who are overweight. Loneliness and boredom create a craving for love, belonging, fun, companionship. Lack of intimacy and interaction with people create an emotional hunger that is often mistaken for physical hunger, so we interact with the refrigerator. There is probably some truth in the observation that no one feels lonely eating ice cream.

> L.J.: I would usually binge in bed while watching TV. I began to ask myself if I was really hungry or if I was lonely. One night I realized that I was terribly lonely and here I was in bed like I was having an intimate affair with food. I was physically full from bingeing and yet I was acutely aware of an empty space in the middle of my soul. It was not long after that experience that I sought help.

Emotional hungers arise when our emotional needs are not met. These needs include love, acceptance, self-esteem, challenge, expression, fun, pleasure, recognition, comfort, security, fellowship, and meaning. Because such cravings feel physical, they seem to call for physical satisfaction. We remember that when it seems no one else loves us, sugar does.

Exercise

To begin to distinguish physical hunger from emotional hunger, give yourself these tests.

1. Eat a nutritious meal, then eat absolutely nothing for six hours (unless there are medical reasons why you should not go that long without eating). How do you feel physically? What you feel are probably signs of real hunger. Your stomach probably feels empty and it may be growling. You may feel a little weak or shaky, even

a bit queasy. You may feel other physical sensations that are difficult to put into words, sensations that usually cause you to say, "I'm hungry." Make a mental note of all the sensations you have. Write down anything that will help you remember how physical hunger feels.

2. At a time when you are aware of feeling lonely, bored, anxious, or angry and you want to eat, notice how you feel. You may find that you're experiencing a general uneasiness or a vague longing for something you cannot describe. Impress upon yourself the thought that this is probably emotional hunger.

3. When you feel a desire to eat, ask yourself some questions:

   a. *How long has it been since I ate nutritious food?* (If it has been less than three hours, you are probably not physically hungry.)

   b. *What am I hungry for?* (If you want nutritious food, you are probably physically hungry. If you want junk food, especially food that helps you feel nurtured and comforted, the cause is very likely emotional hunger.)

   c. *Would I still feel physically hungry if, right now, I could have an emotional need met (for nurture, fun, mental stimulation, love, etc.)?*

Eating to relieve emotional pain works for a little while, not only because food tastes good but because it stimulates the production of brain chemicals that produce pleasure. But these feelings pass very rapidly—then the emotional hunger is intensified by feelings of guilt and remorse.

There's nothing so bad that a binge won't make it worse.

Judi Hollis[14]

Low-Calorie Diets
Increase Weight Spiraling

> *For years Sharon alternated between starving to lose*
> *weight and giving in to uncontrolled eating. Every*
> *time she lost weight, she regained it as soon as she*
> *quit dieting. When she dieted, food craving was triggered*
> *by her not eating; when she stopped dieting, food craving*
> *was triggered by her eating. "This no-win situation*
> *was so depressing to me," she said, "I came to believe*
> *there was no way out."*

This certainly seems like a catch-22 situation: We are over-weight, but when we diet we lower our metabolic rate and further deplete brain chemicals. The combination of altered brain chemistry and emotional hunger makes us crave foods that trigger a desire to overeat or binge.

> *My life consisted of brief periods of controlled eating followed*
> *by excessive well-deserved bingeing. Dieting always began*
> *with firm resolve, clenched teeth, and white knuckle*
> *abstinence. When the pain of living without food became*
> *unbearable, I was soon back with my tried-and-true comforter.*
> Judi Hollis[15]

When we know no other options to overeating and being overweight, we turn to more dieting, usually in the form of very-low-calorie diets. It seems to work, for a while. The good feelings of losing weight offset the discomfort of dieting. Then, because of a lowering of the metabolic rate, weight loss slows and may almost stop. This is when the scale shows us the error of our "weighs." By this time we are growing tired of dieting, we are sapped of energy, and appetite is increasing—we are hungry. And discouraged.

Hunger is our body's way of getting us to eat. Physical cravings for "forbidden" foods result from the body's being deprived of adequate nutrition and from brain chemistry imbalances that our stringent dieting has caused or aggravated. Emotional craving results from our overwhelming sense of being deprived of pleasure; we feel deprived because of a lack of flavor and texture satisfaction. Chronic hunger, deprivation, cravings, and preoccupation with food become stronger than the will to continue restricted eating.

Whether or not we have reached a goal weight, cravings that develop from the deprivation of restricted eating prompt us to overeat, so that we rapidly regain the weight we lost. In addition, dieting has caused us to lose touch with normal body cues that tell us to eat when we are hungry and stop eating when we are full. So, paradoxically, we may ignore true physical hunger, and we will overeat when we do eat. Both overeating and restricted eating are attempts to meet our needs that *don't* meet our needs.

Since metabolism has slowed, we regain the weight lost and proceed from that point, becoming heavier than before. Guilt and depression are the natural result. Good feelings achieved because of temporary weight loss are gone. Dieting defeats its own purpose.

By its very nature, dieting is not intended to produce permanent change. It is restricted eating for a limited period of time. It is a temporary measure. *I am on a diet* implies that *I am eating in a way that is outside my normal way—and I will return to my normal way of eating when I reach my goal.*

Is This a Hopeless Condition?

Having any or all of the conditions that may be a part of the weight spiraling syndrome does not mean there is nothing that can be done about it. A predisposition to gaining weight doesn't mean we are destined to keep gaining weight (or to keep gaining and losing). It may seem that nothing *can* work—but that's only because nothing we have done so far has worked. We have tried to fix ourselves by willpower alone, without the knowledge and skills needed to take care of ourselves properly.

We may have looked to some product or program to fix it for us. *When we lost weight, we gave the credit to that product or program. But when we gained it back, we blamed ourselves.* Having a tendency to weight spiral means we have to stop blaming ourselves and start nurturing ourselves.

When we have tried to get help in the past, our problem was usually treated either as a weight loss issue (lose weight and your life will be great) or as an emotional issue (it's not what you are eating but what is eating you). The truth of the matter is, it is usually both, and focusing exclusively on one or the other does not work.

Resolving emotional issues might stimulate the production of feel-good brain chemicals, but it will not, alone, change our metabolism, any more than losing weight will, alone, magically heal us. We do have to eat differently and exercise. But unless we also learn to live in ways that support emotional well-being, we will not continue to do the things that allow us to be physically healthy.

The weight spiraling syndrome cannot be "fixed"—attempts to do that only make it worse—but it can be managed. We can learn to eat differently without feeling deprived. We can learn to give our bodies what they need without triggering cravings and compulsions. We can give up dieting as a way to lose weight and we can give up losing weight as a life goal. We can start enhancing our lives—physically, mentally, emotionally, spiritually—rather than restricting them.

> *Sharon has given up losing and regaining weight as a*
> *way of life. She is losing weight—slowly—by eating*
> *nutritious food and walking daily. She has reduced*
> *the compulsion to overeat by eliminating foods high in*
> *fat and sugar from her food plan. Walking raises her*
> *metabolic rate and burns calories, and it increases*
> *her vitality and endurance. She has accepted the*
> *weight spiraling syndrome as a condition she will always*
> *have. She has learned to be satisfied with gradual weight*
> *loss. Best of all, she no longer feels that her weight*
> *is due to her lack of willpower. She is learning to*
> *feel good about herself as she is.*

Recovery is much more than banishing burdensome weight. *Recovery is finding what we have lost:* good feelings about ourselves, a sense of wholeness and wellness, peace with ourselves, serenity with who we are, and an ability to be in charge of our own lives. In the process of fighting against weight spiraling, we have lost, not weight, but peace of mind, self-esteem, health, and a sense of having power over our own lives.

Recovery is discovering who we are, giving up what we're not, and making from that the best self that we can be—recovering the self that has been lost along the difficult road we have traveled.

Recovery is a process of ongoing change and growth. In order to make these changes, we need to be willing to let caring for ourselves become a priority. This may be a big step, but recovery is worth the effort. *We* are worth the effort. We can do it, with the right information, some new strengths and skills, a fuller understanding of ourselves. With new hope, we can look ahead and realize that the light at the end of the tunnel isn't just another train barreling toward us.

Whether or not we lose weight, we'll experience recovery's benefits. They are not the by-products of weight loss; weight loss is a by-product of a better way of life. If we fix our sights on weight loss alone, we obscure our vision and may not recognize those other benefits, even if they're right there in front of us. Or they may shrivel in the inhospitable environment we present and not flower at all in our lives.

A commitment to recovery is a new kind of commitment. It takes a new life focus: a focus not on the scale, but on health and fulfillment.

In recovery we learn to be in charge of our own lives; we are able to live noncompulsively; we feel better about ourselves; we feel buoyed by increased energy, increased physical and emotional strength; we are healthier; and we will probably live longer and be happier.

Exercise

Reflect on what you have learned in this chapter. Then complete this sentence:

Something I am beginning to understand about my weight spiraling condition is that . . .

Chapter 3

The Regression Spiral

The process toward loss of control of eating behavior brings to mind the story of a man and a horse. And a miscue. The preacher who'd sold the horse told its new owner that the obedient creature was trained to go when he heard the words *Praise the Lord* and to stop when he heard the word *Hallelujah*. No problem, the man thought, he could remember that. He took the horse out to an open area for a ride. "Praise the Lord," he said confidently, and the horse took off. The man was enjoying the ride, sitting tall in the saddle, not really paying attention to where he was going, when he happened to look up and see that they were heading straight toward the edge of a cliff. "Whoa," the owner said. But the horse just went faster. The man, beginning to panic, thought and thought but couldn't recall what to say to stop the horse. Finally, just in the nick of time, he remembered. "Hallelujah," he yelled out and the horse came to a skidding stop at the very edge of the cliff. The man took out a handkerchief, wiped his brow, heaved a sigh of relief, and said: "Praise the Lord."

Does this sound anything like your experience with weight

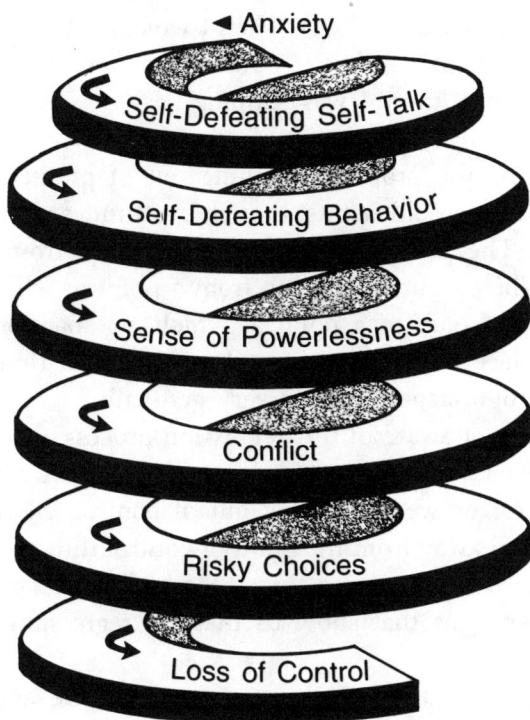

REGRESSION SPIRAL

◄ Anxiety

Self-Defeating Self-Talk

Self-Defeating Behavior

Sense of Powerlessness

Conflict

Risky Choices

Loss of Control

control: You had complete confidence that you could handle it, but before you knew what had happened, you were out of control? This is a painfully common experience for those of us who have repeatedly lost weight and regained it. Loss of control seems to happen suddenly, but in reality it doesn't.

K.M.: When I gained all that weight back it seemed that one day I was exercising and watching what I ate (I called it a diet back then). Then I woke up the next day and the weight was back. I didn't see it coming. I honestly did not know I was slipping back.

Regression is the process of sliding out of productive functioning back into old habits, thoughts, attitudes, feelings, and behaviors. The process of regression takes us from being in control to being out of control, from a point at which we are following our plan to a point at which we abandon it. This can take place over a long or a short period of time; but we do go through stages, usually very gradually.

If we are not aware of this regression process, we may have a false sense that, at any particular time, either we are in complete control or we are utterly out of control. In reality, we usually spiral away from the point of control through stages of regression. We can reverse this process if we learn to recognize danger signs that show us that the regression is occurring.

At first, indications of regression are subtle and can go unnoticed by us and by other people. As the regression becomes stronger and gathers momentum, the signs become more obvious. But the later in the process we sense it is occurring, the greater our difficulty is in doing anything about it.

While the pattern of regression varies from one person to another, there is a constancy in the process itself. Familiarity with that process allows us to recognize our own pattern. So let's look at the common stages of regression that take us from good self-care management to loss of control.

Exercise

You may already be aware of some things that cause you to slip into old habits, thoughts, feelings, and behaviors. If you do, write down what they are. As you read the description of the regression spiral, make notes of feelings and thoughts that are stimulated.

Anxiety Crisis

Regression usually begins with a stressful situation that accelerates to an anxiety crisis. Stress is a normal part of living. It motivates us to take action and to live productively. None of us would want to live totally stress free even if that were possible. But this stress of normal living does not put us in risk of regression. However, when stress becomes intense, accelerates to anxiety, and becomes a crisis—major or minor—then the possibility of regression is strong.

Stress changes body chemistry. When stress hormones are released, brain chemistry is altered. When these changes occur, we feel differently, we think differently, and we act differently. When these stress reactions are intense, we are more vulnerable emotionally and are at risk of responding to the anxiety in a self-defeating way.

The stressful situation can be physiological (pain, sickness, fatigue, hunger, improper nutrition) or situational (a stressful event or condition). How we respond to stressful situations and what creates anxiety for us depend very much on our beliefs about ourselves. The ability to cope varies not only according to our circumstances but also according to our self-perceptions. When we feel confident and sure of ourselves, we are better able to respond to stressful situations in constructive ways.

Anxiety is triggered and intensified by the shame associated with being overweight, losing and regaining weight, secret eating behaviors, and painful memories of embarrassing situations. People who have been overweight most of their lives may have come to see themselves as ugly ducklings. The inability to control our weight reinforces the belief that we are defective, especially if we have health problems as a result of our weight or we know we are increasing our risk of serious health problems. Surely, we tell ourselves, we must have serious character defects if we can't control what we eat even when we realize that our behavior threatens our health and our lives.

Being overweight frequently creates shame based on the faulty beliefs that we alone are responsible for our being overweight, that being overweight is an indication of lack of self-control, or that we are less attractive and less deserving than other people.

> **M.S.:** I remember, as a little girl, standing with my father in a grocery store when he looked at me and said, "Can't you hold that stomach in?" I can't tell you how much shame I felt. I was ashamed of who I was.

Most fundamentally, anxiety points to our beliefs about ourselves. Anxiety may be a vague unpleasantness, a whisper of danger from some cold, dark place in the mind. Whether or not the danger itself is real, our perception of it feels real—and our physical and psychological reactions to it are real. When our avoidance behaviors do not protect us from situations that cause us to face the shameful beliefs we have about ourselves, we experience anxiety.

Some anxiety comes from ongoing situations, some from isolated events. We all have things that we live with that challenge us. Or we may experience occasional or unexpected anxiety when something unusual occurs. *Any situation that puts us at risk of regression is a crisis.* Do not underestimate the power of a seemingly small incident to create anxiety.

Self-Defeating Self-Talk

Unless we manage anxiety in a constructive way, we usually begin to have self-defeating conversations with ourselves. Self-talk is what we say to ourselves in our minds (sometimes out loud). We talk to ourselves all the time; it is a normal process. The messages we give ourselves can be positive and empowering, but in the midst of high anxiety, we are at risk of this self-talk becoming self-defeating.

It is as though there are voices inside our heads that inundate us with messages we don't need to hear. Self-defeating self-talk arises out of the shameful beliefs we have about ourselves and, in turn, reinforces those beliefs. If what we say increases anxiety so that we continue regressing, it is self-defeating.

Sometimes what we say to ourselves directly reflects what we believe about ourselves: *I am a klutz. I am unlovable. I am undeserving.* When what we believe is too painful to say, we mask the belief in other words. We may say: *Nothing good ever happens to me. Nobody ever gives me a chance,* or perhaps *I don't need anyone,* when what we really believe is that we are unworthy of good things.

Bill lost thirty pounds, but deep down he believed he was not capable of maintaining his weight loss. He

*couldn't acknowledge that, so when he began to regain
weight he said to himself, "No one supports me. I
can't keep my weight off because no one gives me
any help." Bill masked his real belief about himself, but
the outcome was still self-defeating.*

Some self-talk helps us avoid painful situations. When painful situations arise, the first voice we hear is the one in our head giving us messages that enable us to avoid painful realities: *Escape; get out of this situation. Run.* However we escape, the intent is the same: to remove ourselves from a situation in which we feel inadequate or undeserving or uncomfortable.

When we're in the midst of a stressful situation, increasing anxiety feeds the self-defeating self-talk, making it louder and faster. The self-talk seems to take on a life of its own: We don't have our thoughts; our thoughts have us. Our emotions become more charged, our thoughts become more erratic, and our self-image becomes more negative. As this happens, we become less able to respond constructively to the situation; we feel like a dog chasing its tail. The more energy our self-talk has, the more stressed we feel; the more stressed we feel, the more out of control our self-talk. As the anxiety increases, the self-defeating messages may become so loud that it seems other people should be able to hear them.

Self-Defeating Behavior

As the regression continues, we find ourselves behaving as if the self-defeating messages we give ourselves are true, whether or not they are. *When we believe something is true, we act as though it is true.* Our thoughts, feelings, and actions work together in accordance with what we believe. Self-defeating self-talk becomes self-defeating behavior.

When we act as though that talk is true, we rob ourselves of positive experiences that are important for our recovery. Self-defeating messages keep us from trying new things, meeting new people, or taking the risk to get involved in enriching activities.

In a sequence in the comic strip "For Better or Worse," Elizabeth was feeling bad about herself. She went to school on the first day after summer vacation telling herself that no one liked her. Consequently, she was not friendly to anyone and did not join any of the groups. Instead, she went off by herself and said, "I knew it. No one likes me." It is true. If we tell ourselves that no one likes us, we will act as though no one does. We take no action to allow others to like us, and our belief becomes a self-fulfilling prophecy.

Some of the loudest and most insistent self-talk messages are those that tell us to escape. They lead us back into avoidance behaviors—the very lifestyle we'd been progressing away from. Let's face it, our favorite escape activity was eating, and when we head in the direction of avoidance, we're heading in the direction of unhealthy eating behaviors. Avoidance does not help us learn better ways to respond to painful situations. Escaping only allows our fears to grow so that the next time they are even stronger. The farther we run, the longer the way back.

A common faulty belief is *I must be loved by everyone all the time.* That one makes us easy prey for the self-talk message *I have to do whatever other people want me to do.* When we believe we are responsible for everyone's needs, we tell ourselves that we must sacrifice our own well-being for others. And we do just that. When we don't meet the needs of everyone, a voice in our head whispers *Try harder.* So we try harder, do more, and still say *I have to do better.* The more we do, the more others expect from us, confirming our belief that in order to meet the needs of others we have to sacrifice our own well-being.

This is sure to get us away from caring properly for ourselves. If everyone else's needs come first, we will not take the time to exercise or prepare the proper foods or go to support group meetings. And we can always justify that with the self-talk messages *I just don't have time. My job demands so much. My family needs so much. My friends expect so much.*

When we live out our self-defeating self-talk, we reinforce that reality. It is now out of our head and in the here and now, for everyone to see. It becomes a concrete manifestation of what we believe. The negative emotions that fueled our self-defeating self-talk now energize our behavior. The stronger those emotions, the stronger the self-talk statements and the corresponding behavior. There is a cumulative effect as the regression spirals. Anxiety intensifies; self-talk speeds up and becomes more self-defeating; and behavior is reinforced. The spiral gathers momentum.

Sense of Powerlessness

If we believe and act as if our self-talk is true, and other people act as though it is true, we begin to see ourselves as powerless to change it. We come to believe that we have no options, that nothing will ever change. This is the way it has always been; this is the way it will always be. This perception of powerlessness is accompanied by a sense of hopelessness and by feelings of being trapped and severely deprived.

As the regression spirals into this stage, self-talk escalates into absolutes. We begin to use all-inclusive statements, such as "I will *never*," "He always," and "*Everyone* does this," and "I'm defective and there is nothing I can *ever* do about it." These absolute and all-inclusive statements close off the possibility of positive outcomes and do not allow for the possibility of change.

This could be called the "yes-but" phase. We believe that nothing will work to make things better, no matter what we try. We say to ourselves, "Maybe I could learn to play the piano," and a voice inside says, "Yes, but you didn't stay with the violin when you tried." So we don't try the piano. Someone suggests we go to Overeaters Anonymous. And we hear, "Yes, but you don't know anyone there." So we don't go to OA. Someone says, "Would you like to talk? You seem discouraged." And we tell ourselves, "Yes, but I can handle it by myself." Every time options are offered for making things better, we give ourselves "yes-but" messages.

What is becoming apparent at this point is that even though we may have lost weight, the self is not magically different. As the excitement and sense of accomplishment of doing well for a while begins to wear off, old feelings begin to come back. If weight loss can't fix everything, we see no positive options.

> L.K.: I remember when I was the lightest I had ever been, I was feeling pretty good about myself, but I really hadn't changed. I began looking in the mirror again and feeling fat. I began observing to myself that my clothes didn't look right, that I didn't look right. I was the same as I had been two weeks before when I was feeling good about me. Now I felt cheated. Life had dealt me another blow. I began to focus on the fact that I was still overweight. It seemed that all that work had made no difference.

We feel so locked in, so trapped, that there seems to be no way out. We feel hopeless and helpless. There is no way that life can be different. We feel defeated. We have an overwhelming sense of being deprived. It's not fair. We cannot eat the way other people do. We can't get pain relief the only way that works for us. We can't do what makes us feel good. We feel deprived of acceptance and approval. And the only way to get acceptance and approval is to further deprive ourselves. The solution is no solution. We feel trapped in deprivation. Our only options are to regain weight or to feel deprived for the rest of our lives. We are going to be miserable no matter what we do. We are in pain and there is no way out.

Our feeling of deprivation reminds us of what we have lost. We no longer have our old faithful method of pain control. We'll *never* have it again. Not only have we lost the comfort and nurture of eating, we have lost a lifestyle: going out to eat to celebrate; enjoying the companionship of other people over ice cream; planning what we will eat; and looking forward to the fun of shopping for food, cooking our favorite foods, simply eating.

We are overwhelmed by the losses. Without a way to relieve the pain, we feel despair and hopelessness. What was supposed to make things better, hasn't. And we feel powerless to do anything about it.

Conflicts

The anger and frustration of feeling so defeated and deprived lead to conflict. When we are trapped in deprivation, there is a war going on between the only two options we can see: (1) being deprived of the comfort of food for the rest of our lives or (2) eating and regaining weight we have lost (and being further deprived of acceptance and approval). Either option is painful. Because of the lack of good options, we feel frustrated and oppressed.

When we feel trapped in deprivation, we spiral rapidly into conflictual living. We feel totally overwhelmed by the impossibility of our situation, by the expectations of others, by our inadequacy, by the pain of life. It is like being exhausted from swimming when we're only halfway across the river. Whether we turn back or go on, we have to keep swimming. We need an island and we can't find one.

If we have lost weight and still feel bad about ourselves, we are probably disillusioned and discouraged. If we regain weight, everyone will know we have failed. We resent the pressure and the expectations.

Because we are in conflict with ourselves, inevitably we will be in conflict with others. We feel deprived and we resent people who can eat whatever they want without gaining weight. We feel powerless to maintain self-care and we resent people who remind us to exercise. We feel trapped and we resent people who offer solutions.

We are at risk of developing conflicts with the people who are most supportive. They begin to look like jailers. We become defensive. We distance ourselves. We spiral away from people. We disconnect. Relationships weaken. As people respond in anger to our anger, relationships become conflictual. And then it becomes easier to blame others. Yet we find that the bone of contention provides little nourishment.

Our anger at being deprived comes out in irritability toward people who have nothing to do with our situation. We feel persecuted, not just because we can't eat what we want, but because our waiter ignores us and doesn't bring our water. His actions say we are not worth a glass of water. We find ourselves irritated by the person who puts us on hold when we are calling long distance, by the delivery man who keeps us waiting because he couldn't find our house. Other people say we are overreacting and we know we are; but knowing that doesn't cancel our response—and now we're also angry at those people for picking on us. We feel like a nudist crossing a barbed wire fence.

We begin to interact with the environment in a conflictual way. The world is against us, out to get us, and we are helpless to stop it. There's no hot water when we take a shower, our shoelace breaks, and we find ourselves in the slowest line at the bank when we're in a hurry. Our ballpoint pen won't write and every pencil we pick up needs sharpening. Stress colors our vision and fuels the internal conflict.

The whole regression cycles and recycles. Conflicts substantiate the self-defeating messages we give ourselves. Stress levels rise as we are caught up in the syndrome. We hold on because we really want to make it; we just don't see an option that is not painful. So we hold on through the pain. The war between our two painful options intensifies; eating for relief looks better and better. Progress is slow. Pain relief is fast. We know what is going to take our pain away. We are trying to hold on. We are gritting our teeth to keep from eating, biting the bullet instead of a Twinkie.

Risky Choices

Amid the emotional turmoil of being in continuous conflict, we begin to neglect self-care and put ourselves in diet-risky situations. We may allow ourselves to get hungry, angry, lonely, and tired—conditions that especially invite overeating. We may overload our schedule, then overload our shopping cart with convenience foods. We may buy tempting foods and put ourselves in situations in which we are unlikely to resist the temptation.

Lead me not into temptation. I can find the way myself.

Rita Mae Brown[1]

Life has become so uncomfortable that pain casts a shadow over everything and we begin using poor judgment, taking chances that jeopardize recovery. Because we are in conflict with people, we begin to spend more time alone. We might say up late watching an old movie, then sleep late the next morning and consequently skip breakfast or eat a donut. We don't have time to exercise and we don't take a break for meditation or other quiet time. We might get to work late and, because we are behind, skip lunch or eat fast food. We don't plan our grocery shopping. We don't want to bother with fixing nutritious food, so we eat whatever is convenient.

The pain is intense. We are looking for pain relief. Our self-talk spirals out of control; we feel powerless to change. We have to have something to relieve the pain. So what do we do? We begin to take chances with our self-care, experiment with old behaviors, play around with explosive situations, make choices that put us at risk of losing control. We tell ourselves that we should bake enough cookies for ten people, in case someone happens to stop by. We may also take chances unrelated to eating that can be physically or emotionally harmful.

Whatever our risky choices, we keep telling ourselves they're acceptable, because we are not out of control. We are just playing around, experimenting. We are on the edge of the cliff with one foot already over. We may take risky choices because they seem harmless. Or we may justify them because of all the stress in our lives. We are making our way back to what we know will relieve our pain.

*Carol is a pediatric nurse in an understaffed hospital.
She sometimes works through her dinner hour to be
sure that her patients get the care they need. Inter-
nally she is in conflict with the system that makes her*

choose between eating and providing quality care.
She allows herself to get angry, hungry, and tired. On
her way home she must pass a convenience store that
sells her favorite comfort food, brownies. Carol is
at high risk of stopping to buy some comfort.

When we are at this point in the regression spiral, like Carol, we are in pain. We are at risk of using food to relieve our pain. Making risky choices is playing Russian roulette with recovery.

We tell ourselves if no one knows, it doesn't count. So we start eating away from home and work. We buy one donut on the way to work, and we eat it in the car. We stop with one, but we keep thinking about it. We plan all day to buy another on the way home. We end up getting three.

There's a difference between the occasional slips we have made before and the ones we're making now: Before, because we were in a better place emotionally, we could get back in control; now, we are just next door to losing control. Our behavior, our self-talk, our feelings, and our thoughts are all supporting our slide over the edge of the cliff. We tell ourselves we are still in control because we are not bingeing and we are stopping short of what we really want. But we are angry that we have to stop short of what we need to feel better. Our emotional state increases the chance of slips escalating into relapse.

Loss of Control

At the tail end of the risky choice stage of regression, the pain is so severe that we need fast pain relief. Food works fast. It provides immediate gratification, a shortcut to feeling good. We know we can feel good right away, without doing anything else to satisfy our needs.

Once we have slipped, we may tell ourselves we've already blown it so we may as well "eat the whole thing." Soon our behavior is out of control. For a while we may tell ourselves we will start again tomorrow, but finally we say, *I give up. I quit. It's not worth the fight anymore. I can't do it, anyway.* The old identity reasserts itself by claiming, "This is who and what I am." Uninterrupted regression always ends in loss of control of eating behavior. It may happen suddenly or it may sneak up on us. Once we are there, the illusion of pain control keeps us there until we take specific action to regain control.

The shame of the failure is so painful that we need to get relief in the quickest way we know. We are back into the self-defeating cycle of eating for pain relief, feeling overwhelming remorse and shame, and eating to relieve the pain of remorse. We are again eating to relieve the pain caused by eating. Doing something to stop this cycle would mean giving up our source of comfort again. We have reached the point that the anticipation of relief from eating is dashed against the reality that the eating episode does not relieve the pain, it only makes it worse.

Usually the regression takes place over a long period of time—weeks or months. But sometimes we can run through this whole process in a matter of hours, a day, or a few days. We may encounter a stressful situation that triggers anxiety. That causes us to begin negative self-talk, which we act out as self-defeating behavior. We feel powerless to change it, and because of our frustration, we begin blaming other people. We develop conflicts and very quickly may make a risky choice to eat something that is not part of our self-care plan.

Rhonda lost sixty pounds and had maintained the loss for six months. She was faithful to her self-care plan. She bought herself two new skirts, wore them each

once, washed them, and hung them in her closet for several
weeks before wearing them again. She did not realize
they were 100 percent cotton and that they had shrunk.
One morning she put on one of the skirts, looked in the
mirror, and panicked (anxiety). The skirt looked as
if it had been sprayed on. She tried the other. Too
tight. She thought she had gained weight. She looked
at herself in the mirror and said, "I'm ugly" (self-defeating
self-talk). She wore one of her "fat" dresses and didn't
spend much time on her hair and makeup (self-
defeating behavior). All day she felt ugly and was not
her usual beautiful self. She wondered if other people
were looking at her and thinking she was ugly. She
began to say to herself, "Why try? I'm going to gain
weight no matter what I do" (more self-defeating self-talk).
She felt she would always be fat and ugly and there
was nothing she could do about it (feeling powerless).
She felt it was unfair, and became irritated with coworkers who could eat whatever they wanted without
gaining weight. She had a heated discussion with a coworker and did something she had never done before,
cried at work (conflict). When she started thinking
about what she could eat to feel better (risky choice),
she recognized that she was in trouble. She thought about
what she could do to feel better instead of eating.
When she got home she said to her husband, "I feel
ugly. I'm having an ugly day." He put his arms around
her and said, "You may be having an ugly day, but you
are not ugly. You are beautiful." Then she went to
an Overeaters Anonymous meeting. At the meeting
she began thinking clearly, realized that weight does
fluctuate sometimes even without overeating, and affirmed
herself for not using food to comfort herself. As she

*began to think more clearly, she realized that her
skirts must have shrunk. She now calls that "Rhonda's
ugly day"—to remind herself that the regression spiral can occur rapidly and also to remind herself that
she can reverse the spiral if she chooses.*

If we learn to recognize the regression spiral when it is happening, whether over a long or a short period of time, we can
learn to interrupt it and reverse it before it becomes destructive. Part Three of this book—Reversing the Spiral: Regression
Prevention will help you learn to recognize when you are
heading for trouble and to plan what action you can take to
reverse the spiral.

Exercise

Now that you have read the description of the regression spiral, write down anything that you believe contributes to your
regression that you were not aware of before.

Part Two

Choosing Recovery

Chapter 4

Hitting Bottom: Admitting What We Are Powerless Over

After the pain of hanging on for so long to dieting, loss of control of eating may at first bring relief. We no longer have to hold on by our fingernails. Letting go of the struggle feels good, and may actually be euphoric. We may even fool ourselves into believing we will not have to pay the price (especially if no one sees us eat).

But eventually—sometimes sooner, sometimes farther down the road—pain returns. For some, it comes back in the form of remorse following the first binge; for others, pain is delayed until the added weight becomes apparent. But for most people, a return to out-of-control eating eventually becomes more painful than the stress of hanging on had been.

When that happens, we realize that the "mouth-watering" anticipation, the expectation of relief, greatly surpasses the eating experience itself. The eating is not working as expected to relieve the pain. We'd talked ourselves into believing we could be judicious in rewarding ourselves for our excruciatingly good behavior. How stupid of us, we may now think; how self-deceiving.

When we realize we are out of control, but we don't know what to do about it, shameful feelings and thoughts threaten to overwhelm us. We focus entirely on the failure. We don't give ourselves any credit for maintaining weight for as long as we'd managed to do. We recognize that we can't eat our way out of despair, but we feel powerless to stop.

We may attempt to hide the reality that we are out of control, but our behavior inevitably becomes obvious to others. Try to hide a baby gorilla, and eventually it will outgrow the closet. Shame, laced with anger, causes us to push aside people who want to help. Humiliation keeps us from acknowledging that we need help. Bone-deep, we think we don't deserve help; it can hurt to know that people care. We feel threatened by their expectations for us. We are constantly dodging these expectations. We may feel like screaming, "What do you want from me? Do you want me to give up the only comfort I have? Do you want to deprive me of all pleasure?" The people who were "safe" when we were in control seem "unsafe" as we perceive them attempting to "catch" us and shame us back into losing weight.

> A.L.: When I lose weight and then lose control of my eating again, my pain starts when it becomes obvious to others that I am regaining weight. I have scripts in my head of what I believe people are thinking. It is like I have on a hearing aid that is sensitive to words related to weight, food, and eating. If someone makes a statement that contains the word *size*, that is all I hear, and I'm sure it's directed at me. If people don't say anything at all, I am sure they are thinking about how much weight I have gained. When I eat, I'm sure everyone is watching me. When a concerned friend asks me how my diabetes is, I hear an accusation: You are not watching your diet. If someone says, "You look good in that color," I'm sure she's thinking, Too bad she's so fat. I know people are

thinking that I should get back on my diet, and that I could if I had some self-discipline. I resent what I believe people are thinking, but it is really what I'm thinking of myself. It should be easy. All I have to do is just do it—I must be a slob, or I would. But only I know what it will cost me. It will mean I can no longer use eating to relieve my pain. I feel as if I'm bleeding to death and people are asking me to give blood.

Maybe the most painful thing for me when I begin to regain weight is putting away all the new clothes I bought, and having to buy more "fat" ones because I gave them all away. But going back to the bigger sizes is always very painful. I can no longer make myself believe I'm just on a plateau and that I'm going to get back on track tomorrow. Or that what I have gained is not noticeable. Going shopping for new clothes is terrible. I hate looking at myself in the mirror in the fitting room. Nothing I try on looks good. I am grieving the loss of the "thin" person who bought clothes the last time I looked in that mirror. And I am in despair because of the fear that I will never see that person again. Worst of all, when I look in that mirror and see a person who can't control her weight, I see someone who can't control anything.

When we attempt to get back on track, we usually wage a battle within us. A part of us wants to believe we can do it. Another part wants to surrender to hopelessness; it keeps us locked into the illusion that eating is relieving our pain. But even when hopelessness is ascendant, an inner wisdom is telling us that our behavior is increasing our pain rather than relieving it.

A faint but resolute voice rises from the ashes into consciousness, telling us that we deserve more than we are giving ourselves, that we *are* more than we have been acknowledging. We are worth the effort to keep trying until we find something that works for us.

This voice of hope is telling us that in order to get out of the painful place we are in, we must acknowledge our position. There is power in saying, "I'm in trouble and I know it." We cannot change until we acknowledge that something in our life is not working and has become unmanageable; that that something is important in its own right; that the problem, left unaddressed, will taint other aspects of our existence. Yes, it's painful. But there is power in acknowledging the truth.

Exercise

Write a description of the most painful experience you have had related to your weight spiraling syndrome. What was the situation? Who was involved? How did you feel? What decisions did you make as a result?

Shame Keeps Us Locked into Hopelessness

If our beliefs about being overweight are faulty, the actions we may take to lose weight will almost certainly be inappropriate. Our beliefs, and thus our actions, are based on incorrect information. And when our actions fail, we blame ourselves—and reinforce the belief that our being overweight is a character defect. Many of the beliefs most of us have had about being overweight are not true and have not helped us change our condition.

Most of us have tried many products and spent a significant amount of money because we believed something would help us that didn't. Maybe the belief was that grapefruit eats up calories. Perhaps it was that we shouldn't eat after a certain time of day. Maybe we used tablets that expand in our stomach or pills that cause us to burn calories faster. Maybe we thought diet pills could do it all for us. Maybe we believed that certain combinations of food are more nutritious or less nutritious or more fattening or less fattening than if eaten separately. Maybe we ate only certain foods on certain days or at certain times of day. While there may be some truth in some of these beliefs, we have probably spent time, energy, and money on many that were not true and did not work.

When we are not aware that repeatedly losing and gaining weight causes us to gain weight more and more easily, we may try one rapid weight loss method after another, feeling good when we lose but feeling worse and worse about ourselves when we regain.

All the ways we have tried to be thin that did not work have contributed to shameful perceptions of ourselves. Hearing how someone else lost weight and kept it off does not increase our hope; it increases our shame. If others can do it, then it must not be the product or program that is faulty, it must be us.

Many of the things we believe about ourselves come from teachers, schoolmates, neighbors, associates. Many faulty beliefs are societal messages that are generally accepted as true. We receive them from books, magazines, television, movies, radio, songs, pictures, conversations with associates and strangers.

T.E.: I feel that society should take some of the blame for how I feel about myself, because I have been hearing the same distorted messages over and over again. I know that may be a cop-out, yet I feel it's justified. My parents were kind, but there were double messages going on all the time. One minute I shouldn't eat that and the next I could. One minute, diet; the next was, "Eating this one piece won't hurt you."

Society teaches us that being overweight is a character flaw, not a physical condition. Words associated with being overweight suggest negative personality traits that go beyond physical characteristics. Many faulty beliefs that develop about being overweight are not actually spoken. Heroes and heroines are slim. Seldom are persons who are good, noble, and true portrayed as overweight. By the size of seats in movie theaters or ballparks, booths in restaurants, desks in school, society gives us the message that it is not all right to be overweight. Our shame is increased when we find it difficult or impossible to go through a turnstile, sit in a lawn chair, put on a hospital gown, fasten a seat belt, or fit in the bathroom on an airplane.

One of the most shameful moments Chet can recall was also his most disappointing. He'd gotten box seat tickets to a Kansas City Chiefs football game, the fulfillment of a lifelong dream. He loved football but had never been to a professional game. He was filled with excitement and anticipation. But when he got to the stadium, he discovered that he couldn't fit in his seat. He had to stand in the back the whole game.

S.G.: When you are overweight, you don't remember a time when you felt good about how you looked. The evidence is right in front of you; just look in the mirror. You don't like to eat in public; you feel judged. People offer you more food and look at you funny when you accept it. Or when you say no thanks. When you go in for a checkup, the doctor hands you a diet and says, "Lose weight." Fat people are thought of as funny or disgusting. When we find a dress or suit we like, we find there isn't a short in the fat sizes. People don't talk to you about it. They are embarrassed. They tell you that you have pretty eyes and don't mention the rest of you.

The first time Joyce heard the word obese *she was nine or ten. She was in a young girls' group taking a first aid course. When the word* obese *came up in the lesson, someone asked the leader what it meant. The leader said, "Ask Joyce. I'm sure she knows what it means." Then she laughed, and so did the girls who knew the word. When she got home and asked her mother what it meant, she was humiliated and hurt because others had a laugh at her expense. As an adult, she still has a hard time saying the word and avoids it as much as possible.*

Many people are affected less by what is said or done than by what is not said or done. The absence of affirmation from family, friends, and associates reinforces the belief that being overweight is a character flaw. The affirmations we get when we are losing weight turn to silence when we stop losing, and that eloquent silence lays the foundation for the belief *I would be a worthwhile person if I only lost weight.* In order to let go of the shame, we have to stop blaming ourselves for what we have not known how to change.

More than anything else, Jenny wanted to be 110 pounds. She believed that, like magic, everything in her life would be great when she got down to her ideal weight. She had lost and gained weight many times, and every- thing—good and bad—in her life revolved around her

weight. Somehow, she thought, finally getting down
to 110 would make her life so perfect that she would
never regain again. When she was in college she decided that now was the time. She had to do it. She
just knew that, if she tried hard enough, she could attain
her goal. She put everything she had into her diet and
exercised to the point of exhaustion. She lost twenty-
eight pounds in a month. But the joy of losing was
lost in the fatigue and the temper flare-ups she couldn't
seem to control. Still, she kept going. She believed her
life depended on having the self-discipline to stick with
this weight loss plan, no matter how difficult the effort.

Jenny began to notice that her skin seemed flabby even
though she weighed less. She didn't like what she saw
in the mirror any better than she'd liked the Jenny
who weighed much more. She felt very depressed.
When the depression, fatigue, and mood swings got so
severe that she was frightened, she went to see her doctor.
Her blood sugar levels were very low, and most devastating of all, she found out that her weight loss
had been primarily loss of muscle mass. Her skin was
stretched and had lost its elasticity.

Jenny had wanted so desperately to lose weight and
be beautiful, but now she felt uglier than when she'd
started. Before, at least, she'd had lovely skin. Now, her
breasts were so floppy they required reconstructive surgery.
She suffered through the trauma of two operations.
During much of that time, she was bedridden. She
regained the weight she had lost. She was filled with
shame. She had tried as hard as she knew how and had
really messed herself up. She couldn't even lose weight
right. In fact, she couldn't lose weight, period; here
it all was, back again.

Admitting Powerlessness

The first step in changing anything is acknowledging it. Acknowledging that our focus on weight is making our lives unmanageable is the beginning of the conscious awareness necessary for a manageable life. Being honest with ourselves about the extent to which weight spiraling is restricting or controlling us is an essential part of making the changes that will free us. Step One of Overeaters Anonymous states: *We admitted we were powerless over our compulsive eating and that our lives had become unmanageable.*

Exercise

List some ways the weight spiraling syndrome has made your life unmanageable. Has shame of your body kept you from participating in activities you might enjoy? Has an unfounded belief about your abilities kept you from trying? Has fear that the extent of your problem will be exposed kept you from socializing with certain people? Has your shame kept you isolated? Has compulsive eating caused you to do things that violate your value system? How has the condition affected your feelings, your attitudes, your thinking, your relationships, your behavior, your spirituality?

For some people the idea of admitting powerlessness is in itself shameful. Perhaps the idea of acceptance or surrender seems like weakness. Perhaps it seems like giving up or not trying. Not so. *Acknowledging powerlessness is not a weakness but a strength.* Acceptance of what we cannot change is not a weakness.

We may find that when we acknowledge what is most shameful for us, we will experience a freedom not possible as long as we try to hide our problem or our feelings of shame about it. Being powerless over how our bodies react to certain foods does not mean we are powerless over everything. The energy and resources we have used trying to hide painful issues can be used for productive living.

When we are able to admit our limitations, we are then able to learn to manage and restructure our lives to accommodate those limitations. Acceptance becomes strength. Some people do not recognize that acknowledging limitations is part of a healthy self-perception. They see it as negative. It can be positive. Limitations give boundaries to potential.

In working with addiction clients, we, the authors, have heard Alcoholics Anonymous criticized by people who say, "What I don't like about AA is that it teaches people to say they will always be alcoholics even if they are not drinking." They perceive this tenet as negative thinking and not compatible with having an image of self as healthy and well. But actually the acceptance of this limitation (being unable to drink) allows people with alcoholism to stop fighting against what they cannot change and to focus on what they can change.

Because of our physical makeup, there may be foods we cannot eat without triggering a craving for more. We can fight against this truth, or we can accept it and put our energy into living fully in spite of this limitation. How we live with our limitations determines whether they are facts or problems. We enjoy a healthy balance between recognizing our potential and recognizing our limitations by *knowing when to pull our heads in and when to stick our necks out.*

P.K.: I always wore dark clothes because I was told they would make me look slimmer. I didn't want to call attention to myself, so I didn't do anything special with my hair or makeup. As I accepted the fact that I would probably never have a perfect figure and became aware that there was nothing shameful about that, I made some major changes in my appearance. I started wearing bright colors that I look really good in. I got my hair styled and learned some new makeup techniques. I am having a wonderful time. I feel bright and colorful and people say I look great.

Shame causes us to live defensively—to protect ourselves from being embarrassed, feeling foolish, or letting others know how painful our lives are. The great waste in using avoidance behaviors to protect ourselves from shame lies in the time, energy, and talent misdirected; strengths, talents, and gifts used for survival are *not* being used for creative and productive living. Recovery means replacing our defensive way of life with a lifestyle that can liberate us from the bondage of our shame.

E.P.: When I believed I overate because I was weak and undisciplined, I never ate large amounts or ate junk food in front of other people. But I hid Ding Dongs under my bed, ate Snowballs alone in the car, and locked myself in the bathroom to eat a half gallon of ice cream. When I ordered carryout fast food I always said it was two orders and told them to put it in two sacks so they would not think I was going to eat it all myself. This sort of behavior worked pretty well to hide what I thought was true about me—that I had no self-restraint. But I will never forget how mortified I was when my sister found the Ding Dongs under my bed.

Now that I am recovering and am no longer hiding Ding Dongs, I realize how much time and energy I spent figuring out where and when I could eat without anyone seeing me. I now spend that energy making jewelry, playing golf, and taking yoga classes. I also have more time and motivation . . . for planning healthy meals in creative ways.

It is important for us to recognize that in acknowledging powerlessness over some things *we are not saying we are powerless over everything.* We are saying that there are issues that we, by our strength alone, are powerless to change. They may seem enormous, even overwhelming, without the defenses we have used in the past to protect against them. We acknowledge that we, by ourselves, do not have the strength or resources to handle them. We stop putting all our efforts and energy into what we cannot do anything about.

Once upon a time, the animals decided they should do something meaningful to meet the problems of the new world. So they organized a school. They adopted an activity curriculum of running, climbing, swimming, and flying. To make it easier to administer the curriculum, all the animals took all the subjects.

The duck was excellent in swimming; in fact, better than his instructor. But he made only passing grades in flying, and was very poor in running. Since he was slow in running, he had to drop swimming and stay after school to practice running. This caused his web feet to be badly worn, so that he was only average in swimming.

The rabbit started at the top of his class in running, but developed a nervous twitch in his leg muscles because of so much make-up work in swimming.

The squirrel was excellent in climbing, but he encountered constant frustration in flying class because his teacher made him start from the ground up instead of from the treetop down. He developed "charlie horses" from overexertion, and so only got a C in climbing and a D in running.

The eagle was a problem child and was severely disciplined for being a non-conformist. In climbing classes he beat all the others to the top of the tree, but insisted on using his own way to get there.[1]

The Serenity Prayer offers words of wisdom for people with the weight spiraling syndrome: *God grant me serenity to accept the things I cannot change, courage to change the things I can, and wisdom to know the difference.* When we recognize what we do not have the power to change, we can stop trying to change what we are powerless over and put our efforts into making the most of what we do have the power to do something about.

Exercise

Make three columns on a page of your notebook. Label one "Things I Can Change," another "Things I Cannot Change," and the third "I Don't Know." Think of things in your life that you wish were different and put them in the appropriate column. From time to time as you look at the list try to move what you can from "I Don't Know" to one of the other columns.

Forgiving Ourselves

In the process of identifying what is true and what is not, we might uncover some things that are shameful for us, that really are based on fact. Maybe there are some behaviors that we legitimately regret, like the times we ate in secret and felt deceptive and dishonest. It is time to forgive ourselves.

C.J.: Even though I had learned not to blame myself for having a weight problem, I needed to forgive myself for some of the things I had done because of it. I did things I told myself I would not do. I was ashamed of sneaking food and hiding food, buying junk food with money that needed to be used for something else, eating all of something I had cooked for my family, stealing my children's Halloween candy, getting angry because someone ate something I planned on eating, lying through my teeth about what I ate or didn't eat. One time I baked brownies and gave everyone in the family one for lunch. Then after they left, I ate the rest. In order to hide it, I baked another batch and out of that one I ate the amount that the family had eaten for lunch. It looked as if I hadn't eaten any, but I had eaten a whole batch. Because I valued honesty, I always felt ashamed of such behavior. I needed to forgive myself for the things I had done that violated my own value system. Working the Twelve Steps of Overeaters Anonymous helped me wipe the slate clean. Letting go of that shame has helped me change my behavior. I still do things that I am ashamed of once in a while, but I try to learn from my mistakes and forgive myself.

It is freeing to look at ourselves and recognize who we really are, being fully human and having limitations. We can consciously choose to let the shame go and forgive ourselves. We can free ourselves of what has clouded our vision of our beauty and worth. We no longer see ourselves as defective or defeated. And in the place of shame, we can allow in pride, self-esteem, and a belief in ourselves as beautiful and good.

Exercise

As you think about the ways you have blamed and shamed yourself for your weight problems, do you feel ready to forgive yourself? If not, write about anything that is standing in your way.

Chapter 5

What Is Recovery and How Do We Get Started?

M ost of us can lose weight by ourselves, but for recovery we need help. We can white-knuckle weight loss because we know it will end. We can endure, we can hang on—for a period of time. To live in serenity and comfort while managing the weight spiraling syndrome—not a problem we solve, but a condition we live with—we need a source of strength greater than ours alone. We cannot just endure, because what we are doing is not temporary. We need more, we want more, than the endless pattern of dieting and overeating. We need help from outside ourselves to begin a better way of life. It is not that we need something or someone to do it *for* us. We need support for what we need to do.

A Power Greater Than Ourselves

Acceptance helps us recognize that we need help to learn a new way of living. We recognize that our inability to solve all our problems alone, without help, does not mean they cannot be solved. We know from experience that by willpower and our own efforts we are powerless to change the endless pattern of losing and gaining weight.

Step Two of Overeaters Anonymous says: *Came to believe that a power greater than ourselves could restore us to sanity.* With this step we are acknowledging that we are not God, and we don't have to be. There is a power outside us that can help us do what we have been unable to do by our own efforts alone. Developing faith in a power outside ourselves is the birth of hope.

You may wonder about the phrase "restore us to sanity" in this step. This certainly does not mean that we are actually insane. But the shame of being overweight, of not being able to maintain weight loss, of binge eating, of feeling worthless and defective, may have locked us into a way of thinking about ourselves that feels a little like insanity. With this step we develop the faith to become open and receptive to a power that can help us begin to transcend the limitations of our own ability, to think clearly and rid ourselves of the shame that has enmeshed us in ineffective behaviors.

This step does not define "a power greater than ourselves." That is up to us. Some of us call this power God. Some of us accept this power into our lives as love or as a creative force. Others accept this power as a group of people (such as Overeaters Anonymous) to turn to for help. Regardless of our personal beliefs, what matters is that we become willing to accept help outside ourselves. In this book this source of help will be called a higher power; you can translate the term as whatever best suits your concept of a power greater than yourself—whether for you that means God or Love or Inspiration or Essence or Grace or . . . just Help.

This power does not work separate and apart from us but empowers us to do what we have been unable to do alone. Through insight, courage, knowledge, and hope, we are empowered beyond our own efforts, enabled to walk through the door into empowerment and a manageable life.

Exercise

Complete each of the following statements three ways:
  For me, "higher power" means . . .
  Turning to a power greater than myself means . . .

Accepting Help from a Higher Power

Some of us already have a relationship with a higher power, but we may feel undeserving, reluctant to turn to that power for help with our overeating; we believe we should be able to take care of such a mundane problem ourselves. Because some of us accept the blame that society has put upon us, we may secretly believe that our higher power blames us, too. Some of us may have asked for help, but when the pattern of losing and gaining continued, we gave our higher power the credit for helping us lose and blamed ourselves for regaining. When we truly come to believe that weight spiraling is not a will-power issue, we know we do not have to "deserve" help. But we do have to accept it.

> Before I could come to terms with my higher power I had
> to renounce my tendency to play God. I had to give that role
> back to a higher power.
>   Robert Hemfelt and Richard Fowler
>   *Serenity: A Companion for Twelve Step Recovery*[1]

Step Three of Overeaters Anonymous says: *Made a decision to turn our will and our lives over to the care of God as we understood him.* There is relief in knowing that we can now let that power work in our lives. We can turn over the struggle, the guilt, and the shame. Turning to another power for help does not remove these struggles, it gives us help in facing them. Recovery is full of change and risk—and growth. We struggle as we achieve spiritual growth; it is a process of facing our fears and our shame and accepting the help we need to overcome them and move on.

The paradox of this step is that through surrendering, we can gain power. As we let go of those issues we have been powerless to change, we find a source of help that empowers us. This paradox brings to mind a story about monkeys in India and a device for their capture: a small box chained to a tree. The box contains a nut. There is an opening in the box, and it is large enough for a monkey to put in his hand but too small for him to take it out while holding on to the nut. He must let go to get free. The monkey holds on to the nut; he will not let go, and is captured. Letting go of trying to do everything by ourselves releases us. We are free to utilize additional powers, within ourselves and outside ourselves.

This higher power is not a force that recovers *for* us. It is not magic. It is a power that works *with* us, enabling us to use our own strength to make better choices. We are not weak. We have developed and utilized our strength in the past as we have dieted and lost weight and learned to survive stigma and discrimination. We do not leave these strengths behind us. We take them with us into recovery and use them *with* the strength we receive from opening up to a higher power, meeting new people, and getting to know ourselves better.

Our personal strengths are the sails of the ship, a higher power the wind that moves us.

Exercise

Think about the strengths you have developed over the years as a result of the struggle with your weight. List these strengths and start to think about ways you can use them in recovery.

When we come to believe that there is more power available than we have utilized in the past, hope is born. And with hope comes trust. We begin to trust a power that we can rely on in recovery. As we do, the road to recovery becomes solid enough to travel securely (even if we must pay some tolls along the way).

A higher power relationship is vital to our balanced recovery, providing a road map to new meaning and purpose. Allowing a higher power to help us removes us from the center of our universe. Rather than being a loss, this can be expanding. We become part of something that gives our lives greater depth and purpose, provides comfort and security, and satisfies a hunger that food cannot.

> *Could it be we each have a special, inner hunger which all the nutritious food and human companionship in the world will not satisfy? Could it be that my spiritual self is a child hungry for the love and support of a Higher Power?*
>
> 　　　　　　　　　　　　　*Listen to the Hunger*[2]

There is within all of us a yearning for something beyond the self. We want meaning and purpose that transcend our own personal world and that, even in transcendence, work a connectedness with something or someone beyond ourselves. Finding this connectedness helps us live fulfilling and satisfying lives. Not having it leaves an emptiness, a hunger. We may try to fill the emptiness with food, but it needs more than food to satisfy.

Our source of ultimate power is also a source of nurturing. As we sense that we are not alone in our struggle, we increase our receptivity to companionship with a higher power and allow that power to further influence our life choices.

When I am out of touch with God, I am spiritually hungry.
There is a gaping emptiness at the center of my being. I try
to fill the emptiness with food, but there is never enough.
Finally, the pain of bingeing leads me back to God, and
I realize my hunger was not for food but for a spiritual
connection. Listen to the Hunger[3]

Accepting Help from Other People

We all need help from others. We need to turn toward the help we've been turning away from. This step may seem humiliating, but once taken, it can bring relief. There are people who want to help us and who know how. Help may be found in support systems we have used in the past as well as sources new to us, whether they are Overeaters Anonymous, a therapy group, a church group, or other sources of support. These groups are far more than organizations; they are *people*, supportive friends who share our struggle and empower us to help others as well.

Recovery is not accomplished in the vacuum of "self." Opening up to others is a risky step, because others may tell us what we are afraid to hear. But we are already becoming painfully aware of what we most fear hearing—that our way of dealing with pain must change. Turn to people who support your decision to make a commitment to recovery, people who will acknowledge your pain but support you in taking positive steps. We don't need people to pretend we are doing all right when we are not, but we do need people who will accept us and support us even when we are not doing as well as we would like.

> C.L.: As I recover, I am learning not to beat myself up so much if I don't follow my program. I take a look at what happened, figure it out, and go on from there. I'm learning through my self-help group to keep reaching out and to be as active as I can. Being around nonjudgmental people who are not going to give me negative feedback is helping me a lot.

There is power in community. We can do many things in cooperation with others that we cannot do alone. Sharing our pain, our hopes, our disappointments, and our efforts to keep trying can turn failure into a step in our success. Supportive people, when given the opportunity, can reflect our strengths back to us and give us renewed energy for going on. They can also provide a more objective and positive perception of life, one that we may be hard-pressed to find by ourselves. It is from supportive people that hope is rekindled and fanned into a flame.

As we allow people to help us regain hope, we are able to begin helping others find the hope they have lost. As wounded warriors, we can utilize our diminishing pain and onetime hopelessness to help others through their despair. This is the gift that keeps on giving.

Exercise

Complete this sentence five ways:

A source of help I believe I can use is . . .

Choose one of these sources and identify the first step you will need to take to get the help you need.

Living in the Present

Only when we are able to accept the ongoing nature of the weight spiraling syndrome are we freed to live in the present. This sounds contradictory, but when weight loss is the goal, we can't focus on today. Everything is *when* . . . We are waiting *until* . . . Everything is looking toward our goal, getting there. But when we recognize that it is not a "get there" thing, we are freed to live fully in the present, one day at a time.

Exercise

Make a list of things you tell yourself you will do when you are the size you have always wanted to be (or a list of things you have done only when you were that size). As you read your list, ask yourself if there is any reason why you can't begin doing those things right now.

Recovery is not a destination, it is a journey. The journey is made up of todays. These moments. And we don't have to wait *until*. We don't have to hold on *until*. We are able to live fully with an emphasis on *now*.

D.K.: My life used to be filled with dreams of what I would do when I was skinny. My dream list was really a list of what I couldn't do at the time. I couldn't swim because people would see me in a bathing suit. I couldn't take a college course because I couldn't sit in a desk with an arm on it. I couldn't ask someone for a date because I might get rejected. I couldn't sing in the choir because of shortness of breath. I didn't ride horses, go on amusement park rides, or play tennis. When I changed my focus from weight loss to recovery, that all changed, too. I joined the choir and started taking tennis lessons (from someone who has allowed me to build up gradually and progress slowly). I even decided there was no reason why I couldn't swim (although I will admit that I wore my robe right to the water's edge and jumped quickly into the pool). My greatest recovery discovery has been realizing that the most I can ever attain is living fully right now. If I do that, my "laters" will be taken care of. As I have changed my focus to the present, I have found it easier to lose weight. In fact, when I am living fully in the present it seems to me that instead of losing weight, it loses me. It has happened more as a by-product of my new life than the result of concentrated effort. I am pretty close to the weight I have always dreamed of being, but I'm glad I didn't wait until now to begin living as I have always wanted to.

Anytime we are focused on what we are aiming for, an event in the future, we are focused outside "now" and outside ourselves. We abdicate responsibility; we give it to what is going to happen. We believe that when certain things occur we will be all right. We are dependent on things around us changing before we can change; external change must precede change in ourselves. We are not all right now, but we will be—at that moment when *something* happens to release us from the discomfort of the present.

The catch is that the magic moment never arrives. If it does, it is very short-lived and then we are looking ahead to another moment, one that really will make things right for us.

Rather, our attitude should be that the only time we can change anything is right now. We are not really living at all if we are always preparing for the future. If we are looking to a time when we become a certain size, our weight goal becomes a *wait* goal. We wait until the good things happen; in the meantime, we endure. But we cannot make a better future by giving up our todays.

When recovery is our goal, we experience it *now*. It is in process. When we no longer focus on the destination, we can enjoy the journey. All we have in life and all we will ever have is right now. In recovery we make friends with ourselves and accept ourselves as we are today.

Accepting Ourselves

When the focus is no longer on what we are going to be sometime in the future, we can accept ourselves as we are today. We don't have to wait until we attain our goal in order to feel worthwhile. We accept ourselves as we are at this point in our journey. We are in recovery. That doesn't mean we have it made—we are not perfect—but we accept ourselves no matter where we are in the progressive process. We have elected progress as our goal, not perfection.

We don't have to fix ourselves before we are worthwhile. Accepting ourselves as we are frees us from the waiting game. If we must make ourselves perfect—which we are powerless to do—before we are worthwhile, we will always be waiting.

Exercise

First list what you lovingly accept about yourself right now. Then list what you are working on changing about yourself. In response to your second list, say to yourself twice a day for a week: *As I make changes in myself, I am in the process of learning to accept all that I am.*

When being thin is a condition for accepting ourselves, we measure our value by how we restrict ourselves. And that is where the focus of our lives has been—on restricting ourselves. We can't enrich or expand our lives when all our energy is focused on trying to fix something that we are powerless to change. When weight loss alone is our goal, we are always waiting to feel good about ourselves. When recovery is our goal, we are already there.

B.P.: My self-esteem is at an all-time high. My weight has dropped down to my high school level because I no longer feel I have to stuff my mouth to feel good. I am more interested in feeling good emotionally. I take long walks and I meditate. I am in touch with my higher power. I am learning that my worth isn't related to my size. I don't blame myself anymore for my weight spiraling syndrome, and I turn to other people for support. For me, good self-esteem is the key to weight loss and to feeling good.

Power to Change

Acceptance of what we are powerless over helps us become aware of what we do have the power to change. Admitting that we are powerless to control weight spiraling by dieting allows us to learn to manage it by living differently. This new awareness gives us the courage to move into a new way of life, a life no longer defined by what we are not doing but by what we are adding to our lives to enhance them.

Recovery requires change; change requires courage. Change is a risk because we don't know how it will turn out. Anxiety with what is unfamiliar is normal; recovery requires the courage to risk change. Facing the challenge of change is necessary to get to the point that the new way of life is comfortable, then familiar, then joyful. Even the smallest change can produce new positive feelings and thoughts that increase our courage for the next step.

With a new sense of power in our lives, we become aware of new options for well-being and the ability to choose those options. New choices we make in recovery give us positive outcomes that strengthen us for further change. We become willing to let go of old behaviors, ones used as a protection from pain, and find new security in a healthier way of living.

Acceptance that our lives have become unmanageable is the very beginning of freedom. Acceptance allows us to move forward rather than focusing on unresolvable issues and failure. It allows us to let go of the past and move into present experiences that, with help, we can control. Moving from powerlessness and failure to power and success creates new energy—energy that excites further cycling of hope, progress, and energy.

We can be freed from the hopelessness and despair that come from failing over and over again. We can begin to see recovery as a journey consisting of many lifestyle changes rather than as the event of being cured. We can begin to experience *I can*, rather than *I can't*.

Exercise

Complete this sentence five ways:

When I reflect on my ability to recover, I feel . . .

Chapter 6

Self-Care to Support Recovery

"Remember, this is not a weight loss plan," Sara's doctor told her as she reread a copy of the agreement they had just made. "This is a plan for taking care of yourself. If you follow it, you will lose weight, but that's a side effect. This is a plan for caring for yourself in a way that will allow you to be healthy and to feel good and to keep off the weight you lose. We will revise it as you progress."

Sara and Dr. Grant had agreed on a nutrition plan that she felt she could live with comfortably. They had discussed exercise, and since Sara had always had difficulty sticking with exercise, they agreed to begin simply. At first Sara would look for ways she could be more active while keeping her regular routine. She would walk down the stairs at work instead of taking the elevator. While waiting for her ride home, she would stroll back and forth. While watching television, she would get up and move around during commercials. "I can do that," she had said, feeling relieved that he was not asking her to agree to jog three miles a day.

The plan for the coming week called for Sara to go

to an Overeaters Anonymous meeting and for her to see a movie with a friend. Feeling confident that she could follow the agreed upon plan, Sara signed both copies. She took one and Dr. Grant kept one. Because the plan was reasonable, she found it easy to stick with it throughout the following week.

When she went back to see Dr. Grant, he was pleased that she had followed the plan and they discussed how it could be expanded. Sara had lost weight by following the nutrition plan and finding ways to be more active. She had gone to an Overeaters Anonymous meeting and enjoyed it. She was eager to expand her plan to include a daily walk and regular attendance at Overeaters Anonymous. She and Dr. Grant discussed other ways to have fun, and she agreed to try some of them.

"Dr. Grant," she said, "this contract I have with you is helping me stay on track by making it very clear what my boundaries are. Because it is so specific, I know when I'm doing what I need to do to feel good, and when I'm not. In the past, I have said I was going to lose weight and I did. But it was easy to drift away from what I needed to do because I never identified exactly what I was going to do other than eat less. Having a self-care plan makes it easier for me to stay aware of what I am doing. I can expand it as I go, to support recovery."

Self-care is what we *do for ourselves* to support recovery. A self-care plan for supporting recovery differs from a weight loss plan or even a weight management plan. It is a plan for enhancing and enriching our lives, rather than for restricting them. It is a plan for caring for ourselves physically, mentally, emotionally, socially, and spiritually. A self-care plan is a way to nurture and care for ourselves in new ways so that the old way—overeating—is not necessary.

Just as with any other chronic condition, there are changes we must make when we recognize and accept the permanent nature of the weight spiraling syndrome. We identify specifically what our plan needs to include in order to help us stay healthy and well and to prevent the weight loss/gain cycle.

Good self-care helps us raise metabolic rate so we can eat more without gaining weight; it enables us to alter brain chemistry so that we feel good without overeating; and it allows us to keep weight stable or weight loss steady. But self-care goes beyond physical care of ourselves. It includes ways to meet emotional and spiritual needs and encourages lifelong personal growth.

A self-care plan is a personalized plan based on our needs and lifestyle. First we identify what we are already doing on an ongoing basis to care for ourselves. Some of us have plans that we started as part of a weight loss or maintenance program.

Exercise

Title a section of your self-application notebook "My Self-Care Plan." On the first page, make a list of everything you are presently doing to lose weight or to maintain weight loss. Evaluate these activities and ask yourself these questions: What activities are working for me? What might need to change to switch the focus from weight loss to living a healthy and full life?

A self-care plan must include what we will add to our lives as well as what we will give up. If it is only a plan for "doing without," it will not work permanently. So the first thing to ask ourselves is whether the plan is enriching or restricting. In recovery the focus is no longer on what we are losing, but on what we are gaining.

No one else can say specifically what should be in your plan; that is up to you. Keep in mind that a plan for weight loss is not synonymous with a plan for recovery. Here are some guidelines for formulating a personal self-care plan to enhance recovery.

Overeaters Anonymous

Many of us have spent most of our lives struggling by ourselves to lose weight or to control our eating. Managing a weight spiraling condition is not easy under any circumstances, but trying to do it alone is far more difficult. We increase the chances of staying with self-care when we include other people who are strongly supportive of our efforts.

Overeaters Anonymous (OA) is such a group. In it we meet people who understand our struggles because they have had the same struggles. They support our efforts, and they are available when we need them.

Learn from the mistakes of others. You can never live long enough to make them all yourself.   Unknown

Through OA we can always have the phone number of someone who understands and will help when needed. Its meetings draw people who are interested in socializing and having fun without overeating. Let's face it, we live in a society that overeats for fun. We need a place to go where we can find interesting people who do not have to eat to have a good time.

OA offers a spiritual program for recovery. It is based on the understanding that we have a condition we are powerless to fix, that we need help in the form of a higher power and other people in order to live serenely and courageously with this condition.

OA helps us keep in touch with life issues. It is not something to do while losing weight. It is not a program to help us lose; it is a program to help us gain—gain more from life. It is patterned after Alcoholics Anonymous and uses the same twelve steps for living. These steps have helped thousands of people learn to live with conditions that cannot be cured, *but can be managed.*

Some of us find it difficult to meet and interact with new people. But supportive and nonjudgmental people do exist, and can help. If OA is not an option, consider forming a support group with other people who are concerned about their health and are open-minded about weight management—people who are seeking a lifestyle that is supportive of self-care.

Exercise

In the Self-Care Plan section of your notebook, write down plans you are ready to make for becoming involved in a support group. If you have never gone to OA, you might make a plan to go three times during the next three weeks to check it out. It is usually good to go to at least three meetings, to be sure you understand what it is really all about. If you have already gone to OA or another support group and you've decided to make it a regular part of your self-care plan, write down what group you will join and how often you will attend meetings.

Nutrition Plan

A nutrition plan is a plan for what foods we will eat, how much, and how often. It is a plan for eating in a way that allows us to be healthy and in control of eating behavior, but is not so restrictive that we cannot maintain it. Some people wonder why they need a nutrition plan as part of their self-care. They say, "I just won't binge or overeat anymore." The main lesson most of us have learned from our history of weight spiraling is that saying we won't binge doesn't mean we won't. We have said that many times but have done it anyway. Just not bingeing anymore puts the focus on what we are *not* going to do. A nutrition plan puts the focus on what we *are* going to do.

Besides, we don't have a way to know when we are on or off track unless we set some boundaries for our eating. *We don't know when we are in trouble unless we have a way to know when we are doing well.* How will you know if you are on the train to Chicago unless you know which train goes there?

How much we eat depends on our individual rate of metabolism, whether or not we want to lose weight, and how physically active we are. We must determine how much of what kinds of food it takes for us to be healthy while losing weight or maintaining our current weight. What we eat can include a wide variety of foods but should be balanced among all the food groups—protein, carbohydrates, fats, dairy products, fruits, and vegetables—and plenty of water. The food pyramid recommended by the U.S. Department of Agriculture suggests that we eat, daily, nine to eleven servings of grains (bread, cereal, rice, pasta); three to five servings of vegetables; two to three servings of fruit; two to three servings of dairy products (milk, yogurt, cheese); and two to three servings of protein foods (meat, poultry, fish, dry beans, eggs, nuts). In addition,

FOOD GUIDE PYRAMID

A GUIDE TO DAILY FOOD CHOICES

The Pyramid is an outline of what to eat each day. It's not a rigid prescription, but a general guide that lets you choose a healthful diet that's right for you. The Pyramid calls for eating a variety of foods to get the nutrients you need and at the same time the right amount of calories to maintain a healthy weight.

KEY
□ Fat (naturally occurring and added)
◩ Sugars (added)
These symbols show that fat and added sugars come mostly from fats, oils, and sweets, but can be part of or added to foods from the other food groups as well.

Fats, Oils, & Sweets
USE SPARINGLY

Milk, Yogurt, & Cheese Group
2-3 SERVINGS

Meat, Poultry, Fish, Dry Beans, Eggs, & Nuts Group
2-3 SERVINGS

Vegetable Group
3-5 SERVINGS

Fruit Group
2-4 SERVINGS

Bread, Cereal, Rice, & Pasta Group
6-11 SERVINGS

SOURCE: U.S. Department of Agriculture/U.S. Department of Health and Human Services

The **Food Guide Pyramid** emphasizes foods from the five food groups shown in the three lower sections of the Pyramid.

Each of these food groups provides some, but not all, of the nutrients you need. Foods in one group can't replace those in another. No one food group is more important than another—for good health, you need them all.

the plan advises that fats, oils, and sweets be included sparingly.

Exercise

Write down everything you eat for a week and compare it to the food pyramid to see if you are eating a balanced diet.

All of the food groups have a role in keeping the body functioning well. Protein provides the body with the material it needs to replace worn tissue, fight infection, manufacture hormones and enzymes, and digest food. It is also a source of energy. Protein is made up of amino acids; they are the building blocks even of brain chemicals, so an inadequate supply can affect mood and thinking. The body stores very little protein, so we should eat it every day—but we should remember, too, that the body needs less protein per day than most people eat.

Carbohydrates are the body's major energy source and help it use other nutrients. There are simple carbohydrates (sugars) and complex carbohydrates (starches, grains, fruits, and vegetables). Complex carbohydrates are better for you than simple carbohydrates, because sugar calories are empty; sugars supply the calories without the vitamins and minerals. It is nice to know that most carbohydrates are fat free.

Fat provides the most concentrated source of energy, supplies essential fatty acids, and enables the body to absorb certain vitamins. While it is important to get an adequate supply of dietary fat, we can usually get as much as we need incidentally, by eating other foods, without adding butter or oils to our diet. Only about 3 percent of total calorie intake needs to be dietary fat.

Vitamins enable the body to use the protein, carbohydrates, and fat that fuel and maintain the body. We need a variety of foods, particularly fruits and vegetables, to provide the body with essential vitamins. Vitamin B_{12} (without which we develop pernicious anemia) is available only in animal foods. However, many packaged foods, such as breakfast cereals, are fortified with this vitamin.

Minerals are necessary for building healthy bones and teeth, for carrying oxygen to body cells, and for maintaining muscle tone. They also help vitamins work efficiently. Calcium, necessary for building and maintaining bones and teeth, is found primarily in dairy products. Because such foods are characteristically high in fat, we should take special care to get adequate calcium as we reduce fat intake. We can eat low-fat dairy products (for example, yogurt, skim milk) or get calcium from such green leafy vegetables as broccoli and collard greens.

Water helps regulate body temperature, aids in digestion and in elimination of waste, and is essential to the survival of all cells. We need six to eight glasses of water a day. Fiber has no nutritive value, but it performs a useful role in digestion. Fiber contributes to good health and provides a feeling of satisfaction, so we eat less overall. High-fiber foods require more chewing, causing us to eat slower, and slow eaters usually eat less. *The Tufts University Guide to Total Nutrition*, by Stanley Gershoff with Catherine Whitney,[1] is a good source of additional nutritional information.

How often we eat can vary, but it is important that we not get hungry. We should eat smaller amounts more often, when the alternative is that we get hungry and overeat. Some of us have been told, while on a low-calorie diet, that hunger is our friend. But prolonged hunger is not. Hunger is nature's way of telling us we need to eat, and if we don't listen, hunger becomes our enemy. It leads to craving and to overeating and bingeing.

Sara used to go all day without eating, thinking she was cutting calories. But by dinnertime she would grab the fastest and easiest foods she could find, because she was too hungry to take time to cook. Usually the most convenient foods are not the most nutritious or the most satisfying. Once she started eating she found it difficult to stop. She ended up eating more than if she had eaten breakfast and lunch. Now that her self-care plan includes eating regular meals, she no

longer skips meals and has more energy all day long.
She now realizes she was depriving her body of the fuel
it needed for her busy life.

To avoid hunger, eat several times during the day, dividing the allotted amount of food into three moderate meals and three nutritious snacks. This practice is usually more satisfying than eating three large meals. Research indicates that we burn more calories this way, because eating gets our metabolism going. A nutritious breakfast provides the initial energy we need; it sets us up to function well throughout the day.

R.G.: At one time when people told me I needed to eat breakfast I always said, "I eat breakfast. I just don't eat it until noon." I didn't eat in the morning because I wasn't hungry until I ate. Eating immediately triggered cravings. Now I have discovered that it is not the eating itself that caused the craving but eating certain foods. If I eat fresh fruit and whole-grain cereal with skim milk, I'm all right. It is only when I eat foods with fat in them that the cravings start. By eating a nutritious breakfast and a small midmorning snack, I have more energy and eat less lunch.

Choose nutritionally dense foods. Foods that are high in fiber, low in fat and sugar, and high in vitamins and minerals are more satisfying and prevent hunger. They also make us healthier, and when we feel better we can be more active and less tempted to binge. Adding complex carbohydrates (whole grains, beans, peas) to our nutrition plan is a very good way to make eating more satisfying and nutritionally sound. Complex carbohydrates satisfy our taste buds and fulfill nutritional needs as well. Some nutritionally dense foods are whole-grain bread, pasta, and cereals; beans, peas, and lentils; fruit; egg whites; buffalo meat, poultry (no skin), and fish; broccoli, cauliflower, potatoes, and spinach; feta cheese, farmer's cheese, cottage cheese, yogurt, and low-fat milk.

A nutrition plan should be individualized. If you don't already have one, you may want to talk to a nutritionist (your doctor can recommend one), who will help you devise a plan for supporting your normal activity while losing weight or maintaining your present weight. An exchange plan, a point system plan, or a fat gram system are helpful ways of balancing nutritional intake while allowing you to choose how you want to "spend" your allotment of calories each day.

An exchange plan takes the number of calories right for you in a day's time and divides them appropriately between the necessary food groups. You may have a certain number of exchanges of protein, a certain number of carbohydrate exchanges, so many fat exchanges, so many dairy product exchanges, and so many fruits and vegetables.

A point system plan allots a total number of points per day and tells you how many points certain foods count. You choose how you will "spend" your points, keeping in mind that you need a certain amount from each food group. A point is roughly equal to seventy-five calories. We, the authors of this book, prefer the point system because it offers flexibility and provides an easy way to keep track of what is eaten during the day. (However, people who have previously used the exchange system sometimes find points confusing.) If you choose the point system, there is a great little book, called *Points in Your Favor*, that can be ordered from META (see Resources). The book explains the system and provides suggestions and recipes for using it.

The fat gram system is a plan for keeping track only of the

amount of fat eaten. It is based on new information available about fat: that fat is really more fattening than other nutrients.

> *The fat in your diet determines your amount of body*
> *fat . . . the key to a permanent low amount of body fat is*
> *not cutting calories or "dieting." It's a permanent low-fat*
> *diet.* Martin Katahn[2]

By limiting fat intake, most people can eat a reasonable amount of fruits, vegetables, grains, and legumes without keeping track of them and still not gain weight. If you believe this approach may be valid for you and you want to try it, you can find helpful information in *The T-Factor Diet*, by Martin Katahn and *Controlling Your Fat Tooth*, by Joseph C. Piscatella.[3] The latter recommends a personal fat budget to calculate daily allotment and keep track of fat intake.

Another reason for reducing consumption of fat is that it seems to be the primary trigger food for most people. If lowering the percentage of fat in your diet reduces cravings and allows you to eat more without gaining weight, then it is an option worth considering.

L.V.: I have stopped counting calories and it is so liberating. I just count fat grams. I allow myself thirty-five grams of fat a day. I am very firm about staying within that limit because that allows me to pretty well eat my fill of nutritionally dense food. I eat a lot of fruit, beans, potatoes, and whole-grain bread. I try to eat foods from every food group every day. I eat three meals and three snacks, and I don't get hungry. Limiting my fat intake has allowed me to enjoy other aspects of my recovery more fully because I'm not so involved in figuring out how much of everything I can eat.

A combination of calorie points and fat points may be your best option, especially if you want to lose weight. *Points in Your Favor*, mentioned above, lists fat points as well as calorie points. Whatever the method of counting, nutritional balance remains very important. The body must have vitamins, minerals, proteins, carbohydrates, and fats for health and energy. Fad diets that do not provide all these in adequate amounts can be harmful to your health. Reducing fat (but not eliminating it, because fat enables the body to use vitamins and minerals) and increasing complex carbohydrates and high-fiber foods are good rules of thumb for a person trying to prevent weight spiraling.

Exercise

1. List some nutritionally dense whole-grain foods you enjoy.
2. List some legumes (beans, peas, etc.) that you enjoy.
3. List some low-fat protein foods you enjoy.
4. List some vegetables you enjoy.
5. List some fruits you enjoy.
6. List some low-fat milk products you enjoy.

Work out a nutrition plan that includes many of the foods you have listed. You may want to ask a nutritionist to help you. Write your nutrition plan in the Self-Care Plan section of your notebook. Include how often you will eat as well as what and how much you will eat.

Avoiding Trigger Foods

Some of us find a nutrition plan easier to follow if we eliminate trigger foods as nearly as possible. We may need to experiment a bit to identify what those foods are. Avoiding trigger foods as much as possible is the surest way to avoid bingeing. The most common trigger foods are high in fat. They may also be high in sugar or salt, because those substances enhance the flavor of fat. The body doesn't need a lot of them anyway, so minimizing them will not harm us. Foods high in sugar and fat are high in calories, too, so restricting them allows us to eat larger quantities of healthful foods. Most of us are like Bryl, who says, "I have never left a fast-food place satisfied." The high-fat content of food available there sets up a compulsion for him to eat more. He handles that danger by avoiding those "fat" food restaurants.

People for whom sugar alone is a trigger food may be able to replace sugar with artificial sweeteners. However, if fat is the trigger and sugar only a taste enhancer, switching to an artificial sweetener will not solve the problem because sweeteners also enhance the flavor of fat.

You might want to check out your body's reaction to fructose. It is what makes fruit taste sweet. If it does not create a craving, it may be a good substitute for table sugar. And the good news about it is that some studies show it actually reduces appetite and is more satisfying than either regular sugar or artificial sweeteners. Fructose is sold in health food stores and used just like regular sugar. Use a little less, as it is somewhat sweeter.

Some foods are triggers for emotional reasons, triggers by association. Are there certain foods that you associate with pleasurable experiences, with nurturing, comfort, or fun? Maybe your mother said, "Oh, are you hurt? Here, have a cookie." Maybe your grandmother cooked certain dishes just for you, making you feel special. Maybe you have fond childhood memories of peanut butter and jelly sandwiches for Saturday lunch. Whatever foods create a craving should be avoided, whether the craving is triggered by a physiological reaction or by association.

There is a wide variety of opinion about the extent to which we should avoid trigger foods. Some people say trigger foods are like alcohol for an alcoholic and should be eliminated entirely, but that is unrealistic and dangerous. We must have fat and carbohydrates to live. So we must each decide where the line is between enough and too much.

Other people say that the sense of deprivation that comes from identifying "forbidden" foods—foods we can never eat—creates stronger cravings than eating the foods in moderation. They say there are no "good" or "bad" foods. But let's be honest, some foods are better for us than others. Some foods have almost no nutritional value, yet are high in calories and high in "craving potential." If you don't want to call them "bad," that's all right, but they're certainly not as good for you as fresh fruit. And they are very difficult to eat in moderation.

There is no simple answer to this, and certainly not one that applies to everyone. But it is important to figure out what triggers us to eat more or to binge, so we can avoid those foods to whatever extent is best for us.

I can resist everything except temptation.

Oscar Wilde
Lady Windermere's Fan

If you believe that by permanently depriving yourself of certain foods you risk bingeing on them to relieve the pain of feeling deprived, include them in your nutrition plan in a controlled way. Some people allow a "treat" periodically as part of their nutrition plan to relieve the feeling of an unrelenting deprivation. In order to eat the treat safely, they follow a control plan for managing the craving that is triggered.

Sara occasionally gets a small ice cream cone, away from home, then takes a walk in the park. When the ice cream is gone, more is not readily available, and the exercise helps to relieve the craving. For Sara, this is much better than eating a bowl of ice cream at home from a large container in the freezer. Ice cream in the freezer continues to call to her until she goes and gets more—and more and more.

Remember that eating trigger foods, even in moderation with a control plan, is risky and should be done very carefully. Eating foods that satisfy without triggering craving is the best way to avoid overeating. Such "safe" foods are nutritionally dense (high in nutrition but low in calories), usually low in fat, and high in carbohydrates: potatoes, fruits, beans and peas, whole-grain products. The news about these foods is good, and it's getting better all the time.

Exercise

Make a list of what you now believe to be your trigger foods. Beside each, list an item you can substitute to make it easier to eliminate that trigger food from your food plan. For example, if strawberry ice cream is a trigger food, perhaps you could substitute fresh strawberries.

Physical Activity Plan

Exercise burns calories, raises metabolic rate, alters brain chemistry, reduces appetite, offsets craving, helps us relax, and provides fun for a new lifestyle. Many overweight people associate exercise with drudgery or pain; all they exercise is caution. They enjoy long walks only when these walks are taken by people who nag them about their eating.

Actually, physical activity can be fun, stimulating, and relaxing. A good exercise plan can add pleasure instead of pain to life. The trick is finding a physical activity program that is right for you, something you enjoy doing.

> *My idea of exercise had been walking to get the mail when*
> *I could not talk anyone else into doing it. That had to change.*
> *Walking became and continues to be one of the gifts I give*
> *to myself.*   Larrene Hagaman[4]

Moving encourages moving. The more we move, the better we feel and the more energy we have. Exercise helps us feel good physically, emotionally, and spiritually. It provides a safety value for stress, helps with weight management, lowers blood sugar, strengthens the heart, increases energy, and improves sleep. We feel enlivened when we move. Movement allows us to feel our muscles work, our heart beat, and the blood flow through our body, creating energy and a feeling of well-being.

Regular exercise plays a key role in reducing craving for dietary fat. Research indicates that exercise produces endorphins (the brain's natural pain relievers), which not only help us feel good but actually neutralize brain chemicals that otherwise would increase our craving for food.

> *. . . we have seen that exercise-induced endorphins can help*
> *people who eat too much fat. . . . The relaxing, de-stressing*

*impact of increased endorphins seems to give people better
control over food choices.*   Dr. Judith Stern[5]

According to the National Center for Health Statistics, frequent exercisers have higher levels of endorphins and demonstrate more positive moods and less anxiety than those who exercise little or not at all. In the book *Controlling Your Fat Tooth*, Joseph Piscatella has this to say:

Acting as natural painkillers, endorphins generate a happy, self-satisfied attitude and are associated with feelings of increased self-esteem and control. People who exercise regularly tend to have a higher level of endorphins than those who exercise little. . . .[6]

Regular exercise in which we use the whole body and keep moving at a steady pace—dancing, jogging, walking, swimming, bicycling—is aerobic and not only relieves stress and gives us a lift, but burns fat. It is a good idea to have a variety of activities from which to choose so that an exercise plan is not dependent on partners or on the weather.

Before beginning an exercise program, you'd be wise to get an okay from your doctor. Start slowly (if necessary, with as little as five minutes of easy movement three days a week) and build up very gradually to twenty-five to forty-five minutes of aerobic exercise a day. Talk to an exercise physiologist about an individualized plan for gradually reaching your goal. Ask your doctor to recommend one. It's all right to give yourself a day off, perhaps once a week, but try not to let three successive days pass without exercising.

In order to prevent lowering our metabolic rate, we must *never* cut calories very much without also exercising. Remember that very-low-calorie dieting causes us to lose muscle. By losing muscle, we reduce the body's ability to burn fat. Exercise creates muscle, and the more muscle we have, the faster we burn fat; the fitter we are, the faster we burn. As a bonus, the body continues to burn calories for up to twelve hours after exercise.

When we are involved in exercise that we dislike, we will probably not keep doing it. Boredom is the main reason for discontinuing physical activity; we start slow and taper off. We continue exercise that's well suited to our personality and our body because we enjoy it.

> C.G.: It is important for me to take time out to be recharged. I think of my exercise time as an essential and special time-out for reenergizing myself.

The secret is finding an exercise program that is right for us. What is right for one person is not necessarily right for another. It is important to David to walk outside every day. He enjoys the time alone. He enjoys the fresh air and nature. He likes to be alone to pray and think and plan his day. It is a special time he gives himself. Merlene, on the other hand, doesn't stick with exercise if she has to do it outside. She doesn't enjoy walking if it is too hot or too cold or too wet. A treadmill works better for her, because she can walk in comfort regardless of the weather. As she exercises, she watches television or talks to someone or listens to music. The time she gives herself is special to her needs and refreshing to her spirit, even though it is very different from David's.

Many people, like David, enjoy walking alone and using the time for meditation and reflection. They relax from the stress of the day or find inner peace and calm for the day ahead. This can be a very special time to gain emotional as well as physical strength.

The treadmill works for Merlene, but many treadmills and exercise bikes sit in a corner unused after the first week they are brought home. Irene finds an exercise bike extremely boring and much prefers biking outside or walking on an outdoor track with a friend. She enjoys being outside, but for her, company is the element most important to her pleasure in exercising. Irene admits quite readily that it's companionship that has kept her physically active for five years. When the weather is bad, she and her friend walk on an indoor track or at a shopping mall.

It took Sara quite a while to find a type of exercise that seemed right for her. Anything that required her to leave the house was difficult to fit into her busy schedule. An exercise video turned out to be the perfect solution. Because she had never had much physical activity, it was difficult at first. She could not even make it through the warm-up. But she stayed with it, working up to fifteen minutes, twenty minutes, thirty minutes, forty minutes. She could do it early in the morning, before other activities would interfere. She got immediate results. She lost weight without further reducing calories. She felt better. Her blood sugar came into normal range. Her appetite decreased. The immediate rewards encouraged her to stay with the exercise; then she realized she enjoyed it. Most of all, she is proud of herself. For the first time in her life, she has stayed with an exercise program for more than a few days.

What one person can do easily might be painful for another. Go at your own pace. Physical activity doesn't have to hurt to be worthwhile.

B.S.P.: When I started walking, I had to take it very slowly. At times, I could only walk around the block. My husband would make fun of me. I had to stand up for myself and say, "Look, it may not hurt you, but I have to set limits for myself. I am not going to be in pain, or else I will give up." I had support from my doctor. He said only I could determine what hurt and what did not. I didn't have to compete with anyone. I have now worked up to being able to walk three miles in forty-five minutes or less, and that's hills and all. It took a while, but I can do it. I also know that if for some reason I can't keep up that pace for one day, that's okay, too. When I start getting rigid and don't see choices, I get discouraged and give up. It is important for me to know there are always other choices and other ways of doing things.

Perhaps you would enjoy an exercise class but think you must wait until you are less self-conscious about your size. There are exercise classes for people with weight problems; you might feel comfortable in one of those. A local hospital or health club may be able to help you locate such a class.

Even if you just do not enjoy exercise, with a little imagination you will be able to find ways to make physical activity more enjoyable. Myrna has made a tape of her favorite music to listen to when she walks alone. It is very upbeat music with an inspiring message. She sings right along with the tape and has a marvelous time.

In several of his books Martin Katahn talks about his experience with tennis. When he decided to do something about his weight, he took tennis lessons; he became very good. His love for tennis and the thrill he experiences in doing something so well spill over in all of his writing. If things like walking or biking seem boring to you, try something different, perhaps tai chi or square dancing. Take lessons; learn how to do a physical activity well. Learn to play tennis or golf; take horseback riding, yoga, or dancing lessons.

> *To be alive is to be moving. The unmoving water becomes the stagnant pool. The moving body freely channels the energy of life. Moving encourages movement. The more you move, the better you move. Energy creates energy—in a continuous, circling process—in a constant dance. . . . Exercise makes us feel good—not just physically, but emotionally and spiritually. . . . As if the physical advantages of exercise were not enough, its connection to the ways we think and feel about ourselves is remarkable. The moving body is the body releasing stress, letting go of pent up emotions and unblocking channels for energy.*
>
> Regina Sara Ryan and John Travis
> *The Wellness Workbook*[7]

Exercise

Complete each of these sentences three ways:

A type of exercise I might enjoy is . . .

Someone I enjoy exercising with is . . .

Something I could do to increase the enjoyment of exercise is . . .

Look over your answers, and in the Self-Care Plan section of your notebook write down an exercise plan that you think is realistic for you. Include what you will do, how often, and with whom.

Altering Brain Chemistry

Many activities besides physical exercise, alter brain chemistry in a way that feels good, reduces stress, provides satisfaction, and relieves craving. Laughing, playing, crying, talking to a friend, praying, meditating, holding a baby, singing, riding a roller coaster, painting a picture, having a stimulating discussion, making love, doing something for someone else, fishing, sailing, going to a movie: All are healthy ways to give our bodies and our spirits a lift. Enjoy life, choose activities that are mood enchancing. Bill B. makes the point very well in the book *Compulsive Overeater*:

> I started making a fantasy list of all the things in the world I would like to do now or ever thought I would like to do. . . . I looked over my list and realized that I hadn't done many of those things. I had chosen to eat. . . . I picked out six that were possible or that I had not tried before. I made up my mind I was going to do all of them. I was going to live, be happy. . . . I made a concerted effort to give myself happiness, to enjoy life. Whenever I say, "Oh, I don't want to do that" or "It's too much trouble" or "I'm afraid to do that," I have one foot in the door to going right back where I came from—just feeling bad instead of living life and enjoying it. . . . Don't sabotage yourself by figuring out ways not to enjoy life.[8]

Exercise

List ten things you would like to do before you die. See if you can find two that are possible to begin doing now.

Life should be fun and fun a priority, not something we do when and if we have time. If self-care is not enjoyable, we will stop doing it. It should be something we do *for* ourselves, not *to* ourselves. We can become so serious about eating right and getting regular exercise that we never allow ourselves to have fun. Life without fun is like a long dental appointment.

Playing is just as important as any other part of self-care. Without it we are not likely to stick with the rest. Without it life becomes boring, and we are at high risk of going back to what we know will help us feel good—eating. Pamper yourself. Daily. Play is not a bonus for working hard, keeping our noses to the grindstone, or fulfilling all our "should's." It is a necessary and important part of life. Having fun is a human need, and many people who have used eating as a way to feel good have not learned how to have fun without food. Recovery is enhanced if we learn.

We can learn to have fun, just as we can learn to eat right or to exercise. Have fun with children or grandchildren, with a spouse, or with friends. Find people who know how to have a good time. Get involved with people who are interesting and stimulating, people you feel good being with, people who reflect back your worth.

Exercise

Make a list of activities that are fun for you. Think of some things to put on your list that you haven't done for a long time or maybe have never done at all. Consider climbing a mountain, making sand castles, playing kick ball, building a snowman, playing badminton, skipping rope, going roller skating, playing hide-and-seek, walking in the rain, making some pottery. Make copies of the list and put them in places

where you will see them often—in your purse, in your desk
drawer, on the refrigerator, in the bathroom.

It is important that we find satisfaction in activities we do
well, maybe sports, painting, playing the piano. Discover or
rediscover something special about yourself. Develop some
skills you didn't know you had or have forgotten you had.
Perhaps you have a knack for doing something you haven't
paid much attention to.

A.F.: I have recently taken up sculpting. I really love it.
This may be the most satisfying thing I have done in my
whole life. Right now I am sculpting an elk. Sometimes
I take him home from class just so I can look at him and
touch him. Sculpting is so satisfying to me that I don't
even think of eating.

We can learn to have fun at work or at the park or in the
garden. Fun is its own reward. Fun feels good, and it enables
us to feel good about ourselves. Change your schedule periodically, and go—to a movie, the health club, the library. Go for
a walk on your lunch hour. Read a funny book. Take horseback riding lessons. Join a softball or bowling league. Take up
golf. Discover a new avocation. (Conceivably, it may become
your vocation, a word that means "calling." Do you know
what you are called to do?) Learn a new hobby or craft. Find
ways to move that are fun. Spend time with animals. Get involved with the environment. Volunteer to work (or play)
with children. Someone has said that children are proof that
God loves us and wants us to be happy. We can learn from
them a lot about enjoying life.

Exercise

From the lists you have made of activities you want to do before you die and activities that are fun for you, select one, or several, that will be part of your Self-Care Plan. Write down what you will do, how often, and with whom.

Find activities and people that elicit your laughter. Laughing is a marvelous mood enhancer. Try it. It provides a surge of feel-good brain chemicals and leaves a feeling of well-being. It is life's shock absorber. Laughter heals, reduces stress, builds and maintains relationships, prolongs life, relieves anger, facilitates learning, boosts performance, and enhances creativity. Look for things all around you to laugh about. We, the authors, keep a notebook of funny things children in our family have said. Here are some favorites:

My teeth are shivering.
God made me an eating person.
You plug it in and I'll plug it out.
Why are you sleeping with your breakfast? (to someone eating in bed)
I need a couple of water.
A ghost is hollow on the inside and doesn't have any shell on the outside.
Don't call Mom the old lady. She's no lady.
Sometimes I snore when I laugh.
Trix are for folks, too. You can have some; you're a folk.

Laughing increases heart rate, stimulates circulation, cleans and clears the eyes, and strengthens the immune system—all in addition to producing a surge of endorphins. It allows us to take ourselves lightly while taking other things seriously. Laughter is internal jogging, and we don't have to get dressed to do it.

> *There ain't much fun in medicine, but there's a heck of a lot of medicine in fun.*   Josh Billings[9]

Another way to increase the production of feel-good brain chemicals is to use deep relaxation, meditation, or prayer. Many recovering people set aside a time for themselves each day, an uninterrupted period of about twenty minutes, to do whatever they want: rest, relax, pray, read, contemplate. Time alone every day can truly enhance our lives. We all need some time to call our own.

> *How beautiful it is to do nothing and rest afterward.*
>   Spanish Proverb

It may seem that your life is so busy you can't afford to take that private time, but your being busy makes it even more necessary to you. Such brief retreats can make active time even more productive. Find a place of solitude (away from the TV and the telephone), a place of serenity where you can get quiet and relax deeply. Create a sanctuary within yourself.

Exercise

Do you want to include a quiet time in your Self-Care Plan? Write down the time and place you can best create that special sanctuary. List at least two activities for your quiet time that would enrich your life.

Another way to alter brain chemistry that might be helpful for you is to take a vitamin and amino acid supplement. As we have said before, good nutrition is important in balancing brain chemistry. Adequate supplies of amino acids, the building blocks of brain chemicals, are essential for restoration of the balance of these chemicals.

A neuroscientist, Kenneth Blum, has developed a vitamin–amino acid compound that seems to help reduce craving in people who have a history of overeating and bingeing. It has been formulated to affect the production of brain chemicals most needed by people who experience food craving. In one two-year study, 248 people who had lost weight were divided into two groups, one taking the amino acid compound and the other not. While both groups, as a whole, regained some weight, the group taking the amino acids regained only a quarter as much as the other group. The more successful group reported a decrease in food craving and binge eating with few reported side effects.

> **PhenCal 106 is available without prescription, but it would be a good idea to talk with your doctor before taking it. For more information, call 1-888-PHENCAL.**

Taking an amino acid compound has been found to be safe and effective, but it is not a magic cure. It is not a substitute for fun, balanced eating, meditation, exercise, or creativity as a way to alter brain chemistry. A life full of activities that fulfill physical and emotional needs is the only long-term answer.

Satisfying Emotional Hunger

Recovery is enhanced when we learn to distinguish physical hunger from emotional hunger. Unless we learn to tell the difference, we are apt to use food to satisfy emotional hunger. If the emotional fuel tank is empty, we cannot fill it with sugar.

S.T.: Most of the time I overeat for emotional reasons. I just moved into a new apartment and I don't know anyone around me yet. When I am getting ready to put something in my mouth, I ask myself if I am really hungry or if I am lonely. Most of the time I realize I am lonely. Usually when I eat because I am lonely, I am heavy on sugar, as if to say, "Why can't I have something sweet in my life?" When I don't feel good about me I eat to fill up the emptiness.

What emotional need is triggering our hunger? As we get to know ourselves better, we learn to recognize emotional hunger and figure out what we are hungry for. Then we can learn to prevent that emotional hunger by living a full life that meets our needs, instead of settling for a quick food fix.

When we become aware that our emotional needs are not being met, often we need to be with other people—to talk, to listen, to laugh, or just to be together.

Exercise

Complete the following sentence at least seven ways:
Something I can do, other than eating, to satisfy emotional hunger is . . .
Review your responses to this sentence stem. In the Self-Care Plan section of your notebook, write down some activities you will begin doing to satisfy your emotional hunger without resorting to eating.

Sponsors, Partners, and Friends

We need other people in order to break out of old ways and learn new behaviors, to help us see ourselves differently, and to stimulate us to think in new ways. In the past we may have substituted food for healthy relationships. Many of us ate to satisfy the emotional hunger for love and belonging, for social fun, and for the stimulation that comes from interacting with other people. When we are no longer vainly using food to fill those needs, we can address them appropriately—directly. We need other people. We must give ourselves permission to ask for and accept help.

> *You don't need help fallin' down, but a hand up sure is welcome.*
> Ken Alstad[10]

Recovery is not balanced if it always focuses on ourselves. Mutuality—giving and receiving in relationships—provides that balance. Many people find it helpful to select, or accept, one particular person to be of special help in recovery. This person may be a recovery partner, an OA sponsor, or a long-time friend. A recovery partner is someone also recovering from weight spiraling, someone who gives us support and also gets supports from us. Our special helper may be someone to exercise with, someone to go out to eat with, someone to confide in and to listen to.

According to standard practice of OA, a member with a great deal of experience with the program makes himself or herself available to a new OA member. The sponsor provides support, answers questions, discusses various aspects of the program, assists the new member in identifying meetings that will best meet his or her needs, and guides the person to books and other materials that will further explain the program of OA. Members are free to interpret the principles of OA for themselves and to develop their own programs based on these principles. A sponsor is a supportive friend who will provide help as it is needed and requested.

Lonesome creates diseases that friendship cures.

Ken Alstad[11]

We may find supportive people also in a therapy group, at church, or among friends. What is most important is that we know or find people with whom we can be open and honest and with whom we can share our feelings, our pain, and our victories. Building healthy relationships is a vital part of healthy living and an important aspect of recovery. We do not get vitality in recovery without sharing it. Healthy relationships are *mutually* supportive.

> **For information on agencies that, in their treatment programs, utilize many of the principles in this book, contact Lisa Havens, (616) 271-5577, or Stephen Emerick, (937) 879-4324.**

Professional Help

Also available to us are people who are professionally trained to help with various aspects of living that are part of recovery. Some of us can benefit from getting assistance from a counselor, a treatment program, a physician, or a dietitian. Many of us need help from professionals in more than one of these areas.

Wisdom dictates that we select professional help that recognizes a weight problem as a condition having both physical and emotional symptoms. Avoid those who treat it as a personality defect, irresponsible behavior, or something that can be easily remedied "with a little willpower." Professionals who understand can provide reliable guidance for recovery.

Agencies that, in their treatment programs, utilize many of the principles in this book include CenterPoint in Kansas City, Spring Haven in Augusta, Kansas, NeuRecover in Wichita, LMH Inc. in Tipton, Indiana, and Cornerstone in Tuston, California (for addresses, see Resources at the end of the book). These are not weight loss programs but sources of professional help for weight spiraling. For information on seminars and retreats, contact META, our (the authors') organization (also listed in Resources).

Exercise

Ask other recovering people for the names of a nutritionist, a physician, and a counselor who understand the weight spiraling syndrome. Write their phone numbers where you will have them when you need them.

Weight Loss Programs

If you need to lose weight, you may benefit from following a plan that is part of a commercial weight loss program. Just be very careful in selecting one and in utilizing the plan. Beware of programs that promise rapid weight loss, *especially if the calorie allotment is very low.* Beware of those that promise a "magic" cure. Weight loss promises that are too good to be true are usually too good to be true. Part of recovery is giving up looking for magical cures, fad diets, and rapid weight loss methods.

We should avoid weight loss programs that furnish all the food so we aren't in charge of our own nutrition choices. Whatever weight loss program we choose, we should remember that our goal—a well-balanced life—is different. By their very definition, all weight loss programs have weight loss as their primary goal. That doesn't mean that we can't use them, especially if they are sensible and flexible and allow us to make our own food selections. We can use what is helpful for weight loss but shouldn't forget that our plan is to do more than that; it is to continue with balanced self-care to support full recovery.

Education

It is important that we continue to learn more about healthy ways to maintain recovery and to live well. In the past when we regained weight, that unhappy result was usually due not to lack of willpower (as we thought) but to lack of coping skills. When we had not learned ways of feeling good other than eating and never learned to raise metabolic rate, then we really did not have enough information to enable us to maintain weight loss. A lot of promising research is going on in relation to overeating, metabolic rate, and brain chemistry. Good information is good news: The more of it we have, the easier our recovery is. Such information has been coming thick and fast in the 1990s and has shown no signs of petering out; quite the contrary is true. The press is blossoming with useful and empathic features, columns, editorials, and up-to-the-minute news about weight spiraling and the misconceptions that surround it.

Exercise

Look at the self-application exercises you have completed in this chapter. Decide what self-care activities you are ready to do now, and list them under the heading "My Self-Care

Plan." State what you will do, how often, with whom. Talk to a friend, a counselor, a nutritionist, an OA sponsor, or a family member who will support you in good self-care. Ask that person to witness as you sign your Self-Care Plan. Consider this plan a contract, one made with yourself and with your witness. Ask that person to review your Self-Care Plan with you once a month.

One Day at a Time

When we are not already in recovery, some or all of self-care planning can sound scary and overwhelming. Some of it may feel like a great loss, because it means giving up behaviors that have provided comfort or relief from pain. Remember, however, that some of what we are giving up has, in the past, actually created our pain. So even as we are giving up a source of pain relief, we may also be giving up the source of the pain itself.

A.L.: When I began recovery I was overwhelmed by all that was required. My whole life had to change and it seemed impossible. But I have taken it one day at a time. Now a year later I realize that not only have I made these changes but they are a normal part of my life. I eat sensibly (no bingeing) and exercise three times a week. I attend twelve-step meetings that help me feel safe. Although I am not always satisfied with my body, I do love it. I accept who I am, a child of God. My self-worth is not measured by a number on a scale today.

Exercise

Complete the following sentence five ways:

As I think about my self-care plan, I am becoming aware . . .

Chapter 7

Keeping Self-Care
a Priority

*Rich was explaining his newfound lease on life to Leo.
"I have lost ten pounds and I never felt better," he
said. He went on to describe his total commitment
to his new way of life. This time he knew he had his
weight problem whipped. Because he felt and looked so
good, he felt he could continue for the rest of his life
to eat those foods that would contribute to his controlling his weight. The exercise was not bad, the meditation
was refreshing, the OA meetings were meaningful. For
a while Rich did not mind taking time out for them.
But as the weeks went by, his attitude changed. He
recalls, "It seemed that all of a sudden I was bored with
eating beans, exercising every day, and attending OA
meetings. I felt deprived of my freedom to do anything I wanted when I wanted. Those new activities
that I had 'tagged' onto my life were now weighing me
down. I quit exercising, attending OA, meditating; and
I started fast-food hopping."*

*Rich's self-care never varied much. The foods in
his nutrition plan were good for him and he liked them.
But he ate cereal and grapefruit for breakfast every day,*

tuna fish and veggies for lunch, beans and rice for
dinner. For his daily exercise he used a stationary
exercise bike. In order to attend three OA meetings
a week, he often turned down invitations to do something
fun; and he began to resent "having" to go to the meetings.
When Rich decided to reestablish a self-care plan,
he realized that he needed to go about it differently.
And he did. He looked carefully at what had changed
that caused him to think of his self-care plan as a burden
instead of an opportunity, as a straitjacket instead
of wings.

M any times, we make honest commitments to continuing self-care that we do not keep. We let the plan fall away from us, because of unrealistic expectations for ourselves, lack of understanding about our needs, or lack of information about what works. The most common reason for discontinuing good self-care is that it becomes something we do *to* ourselves rather than *for* ourselves.

Exercise
Complete this sentence five ways:
 In the past I have discontinued my self-care when . . .

Self-care is a special way to nourish ourselves not only physically but mentally, emotionally, socially, and spiritually. It can be fun, interesting, and challenging. It is not a plan for restricting ourselves. Remember, our self-care is designed for recovery, not for weight loss. We maintain this care not just to make things better in the future but to make life better today.

We will not continue self-care just because we "should." We will not continue it if we think of it the way Scotty thinks of oatmeal. He and Amanda did not want to eat their oatmeal even though their dad was insisting it was "the right thing to do." Amanda was putting hers on the table and playing with it. "That's it," her dad said, lifting her away from the table. "You can just starve." Looking up from his oatmeal, Scotty inquired, "Can I starve, too, Daddy?"

When the cure is worse than the condition, most of us will chose the condition. We do not continue self-care because it is "the right thing to do." We continue it because it is a treat (not a treatment). That is not to say there is never any discomfort connected with it. There may be times when we choose not to do or eat something because we want to nurture ourselves with health rather than with immediate pain relief or pleasure. Part of recovery is learning to see things differently. It is putting on a new pair of glasses through which we see what self-care offers us rather than just what it costs us. These recovery glasses bring into our awareness choices we did not realize we had before. We see options for living *well* that we could not see when nurturing meant immediate pain relief.

Care of Self as a Priority

Many times we break honest commitments to self-care because it is too far down on our list of priorities. We think we have to take care of everyone else first, so we don't have time to take care of ourselves. Some of us have demanding jobs. The needs of family are important. The needs of friends are important. But we are important, too. Health is important. If we want to make worthwhile contributions at work, at home, or in the community, we must have health and energy.

Most of us don't make care of ourselves a priority because we don't make ourselves a priority. For ongoing recovery we need to give ourselves permission to take good care of ourselves—with just as much consideration as we give our children, others we love, or our jobs. We are worth it.

> **I.D.:** My daughter has cystic fibrosis and needs lots of special care. Sometimes I think I don't have time to fix myself the right food or to get in my physical activity. But I realized a long time ago that my health is important, too. If I don't take care of myself, I won't have the health and energy to take care of my daughter. In order to stay on a program of health I have to consider my needs. It's been too easy for me to think of everyone else but myself.

In *The Wellness Workbook*, Regina Sara Ryan and John Travis note that "few of us would approach the servicing of our automobiles with as little care and attention as we give to our bodies."[1] That's all too true. Most of us care for our cars, our pets, and our lawns better than we care for our bodies. Some people can get by with that, but those of us with the weight spiraling syndrome can't. We have a serious, potentially life-threatening condition. Our bodies require special care and we'd better put ourselves high on our list of priorities.

Sometimes, because other activities temporarily take priority, we truly don't have time to cook special meals for ourselves. This puts us at risk of eating junk food or boring food. Plan ahead for those times by freezing individual helpings of nutritious and appetizing food to heat up when you are in a hurry. Some fast-food restaurants now offer items that are not high in fat (be sure to check fat content for yourself).

Exercise

Pick up nutritional information from several fast-food restaurants. Compare menu items so when you do need to get fast food, you will know where to go and what to order.

You can also get exercise without setting aside special time. Walk to the post office or to the bank; it may take no more time than getting the car out of the garage and stopping to get gas. Walk up stairs instead of waiting for an elevator. Walk around the airport while waiting for a plane. Take a walk with your children or your spouse instead of sitting down to talk with them.

We are worth good self-care, and the quality of our lives depends on it. Besides, if you think you can't make time now to take care of yourself, how are you going to have time to be sick?

It is Not All or Nothing

If we have an absolute self-care regimen that we believe we must follow exactly the same way all the time, we feel we have failed when we vary from it. We think that if we are not perfect, we are terrible. If the regimen fails for some reason, everything falls apart. We commit to going to the health club four days a week and it closes a week for repairs. Then what do we do?

> **M.D.:** Once I lost sixty pounds and never "cheated." I exercised and never ate anything I shouldn't. I was on a roll. I was perfect. And I kept that up for quite a while. Then I got pregnant and my doctor told me I should eat

more. It was very difficult for me to eat that extra bread and extra fruit. It was like I set this regimen in my mind and that was the only way I could do it.

Being flexible is one of the best forms of self-care insurance we can have. Life is not paint-by-number. If we are so rigid that we cannot adapt to a variety of situations, such as going out to eat or having a special meal, maintaining self-care will be difficult if not impossible. Flexibility allows us the freedom to adapt self-care to our lifestyles. It allows us to adjust eating so that if we want a little something extra for lunch, we can eat a little less for dinner.

Physical activity is important, but life demands that we adapt to some situations as they come along. Options and alternatives for physical activity allow us to modify our plans in accordance with the weather, illness, or other special circumstances—including opportunities for pleasure.

R.S.: Walking is important. But it does not take precedence over meeting my child's teacher.

A good nutrition plan does not mean the elimination of everything we have ever liked to eat. Our nutrition plan should be flexible enough to include some of the things we especially enjoy, or at least some good substitutes for those things. The more choices and alternatives we have to draw from, the better most of us do in maintaining good self-care.

In order to make his nutrition plan less boring, Rich decided to try some new ways to prepare food. He shopped around for cookbooks that had recipes that were creative and imaginative as well as low calorie.

*He got an international cookbook that had recipes
from the Middle East, the Orient, and Latin America.
And he found some recipe books with interesting ways
to fix tofu, miso, and sprouted seeds (all low in fat
and highly nutritious).*

*He discovered that with some adjustment in preparation,
he could eat some favorite foods he had thought were
off-limits forever. He found he could occasionally have
his favorite breakfast of biscuits and gravy—if he
made whole-wheat biscuits and low-fat skim milk gravy.
He realized that even though some of his favorite foods
were not as nutritious as grapefruit and yogurt, he'd
be better off modifying their preparation and eating
them from time to time than he would be if he told himself
he could never have them again and felt deprived by
his grim stoicism. He was able to eat French toast
by using egg substitute, cooking the bread in a Teflon
skillet sprayed with cooking oil, and eating it with a
sugar-free fruit spread and no butter.*

*Rich also started making a fruit dip out of plain
yogurt flavored with dry, sugar-free pudding mix. He
thought that one up himself. When he started sharing
some of his food preparation ideas with some of his recovering friends, they began experimenting and sharing ideas with him.*

A self-care plan is intended to be a guide, not a straitjacket. It is intended to free us, not restrict us. We can use it as an aid to our continuing in recovery or as a justification for moving away from recovery.

Exercise

Review your Self-Care Plan for flexibility. For each activity you have listed, ask yourself if there is a way it could be made more flexible and still maintain the structure you need to continue with good self-care. Write down the possibilities you might want to incorporate or give more thought to.

Avoiding Boredom and Deprivation

Thinking we can never eat a certain food again can cause feelings of deprivation and self-pity; we see only what we *can't* eat. That way lies danger, so we should look to broadening the boundaries of what we *can* eat. Most of us eat the same foods over and over again, but variety keeps us from being bored.

We need to get out our recovery glasses to see what we can have. We need to wear them to the grocery store. What's new and different? What have we overlooked? If we really look, we may see something new and exciting almost every time we go. All kinds of new fruits and vegetables are available: ugli fruit, star fruit, broccoflower, cactus pears, whiterose potatoes, tomatillos. Have you tried jicama? It is low calorie and very good.

Exercise

Next time you go to the grocery store, see how many fresh produce items there are that you have never eaten. Each time you shop look for one new product to try.

How about some old familiar products that could be fixed a new way? You may agree with the person who said that cu-

cumbers should be well sliced, dressed properly, and thrown out. But what about sweet potato, eggplant, squash? If your local grocer doesn't offer enough options, go to a farmer's market. Almost everything there is good and nutritious. More important, it is fresh and may have more flavor than the same products in the grocery store.

Back at the grocery store, look at the many new fat-free products. Many are nutritious as well as appetizing. Look at some creative cookbooks. Try new recipes. Try new food combinations. Modify recipes to provide more nutrition and less sugar and fat.

Exercise

Try some of these suggestions for reducing fat in recipes:

Substitute apple sauce for oil.

Substitute egg whites for whole eggs.

Use low-fat cheese and fat-free mayonnaise.

Do you miss butter? Make a substitute by blending cottage cheese with Butter Buds.

Do you miss ice cream? Frozen yogurt is very good even when it is fat free and sugar free.

You don't know a substitute for potato chips or french fries? How about the natural taste of a potato?

Remember, a good plan for eating right ensures that we do not feel deprived in following it. People who believe that they must eat cottage cheese every day for the rest of their lives become bored and abandon their entire plan.

I do not like broccoli, and I haven't liked it since I was a
little kid and my mother made me eat it. And I'm President

of the United States, and I'm not going to eat any more
broccoli.   George Bush

Life may be too short to stuff mushrooms, but some time
should be given to make mealtime special. We need to sit
down when we eat, to know we did eat. Chew food well and
enjoy the taste. Do not deprive yourself of flavorful foods;
they are not necessarily high in calories. Too much bland food
can drive anyone to a hot fudge sundae. Get out the china;
make meals more attractive even when you're eating alone.
Even grapefruit and lettuce are more appealing on china than
on paper plates.

I never eat when I can dine.   Maurice Chevalier

Maybe you're tired of chicken and don't like fish. Try buffalo. It is as low in fat as chicken and fish and tastes like beef.
It makes better chili and spaghetti sauce than ground turkey,
and if not overcooked (that dries out the meat) buffalo burgers, roasts, and ribs are delicious. For more information,
write to the National Buffalo Association, 4 East Main Street,
P.O. Box 580, Fort Pierre, SD 57532.

Exercise
Try buffalo meatloaf or buffalo burgers:
- 2 pounds ground buffalo
- 1 envelope onion soup mix
- 2 egg whites
- 1½ cups crushed crackers
- ¾ cup water
- ¼ cup powdered milk

Mix ingredients, form into a loaf and bake at 350°F for approximately thirty minutes or form into patties and cook as burgers.

Make it fun to plan interesting, healthy menus. Through creativity, we can enjoy what we eat: We focus on what we can have, and we keep expanding that list of can-have foods.

Neither does exercise have to be boring. If you get bored easily, you can do something different (or the same thing differently) every day. You can experiment with a variety of physical activities until you find something that you really enjoy. Nothing will keep you exercising better than doing something you look forward to.

Rich was certainly bored with that exercise bike. He tried a number of physical activities, looking for something he really liked to do. He found it in swimming. He'd always thought he wasn't a natural swimmer and didn't enjoy the water, but one day he realized that self-consciousness about his weight may have been his real problem. He decided to give swimming another try, now that he felt better about how he looked. As he practiced, he got better fairly rapidly. As his skill increased, he enjoyed his exercise more and more. Now he does lap swimming regularly and loves every minute of it.

Self-Protective Behavior

Our physical condition calls for us to take special care of ourselves. This care includes protecting ourselves as much as possible from anything that puts recovery in jeopardy. Self-protective behavior is characterized by firmness—in accepting our own needs and in not allowing other people or situations to push us into reactions that are not in our best interest. We are responsible for protecting ourselves from anything that threatens our health and well-being. This might mean changing a situation, avoiding certain situations, changing our reactions to certain situations, or learning to interrupt some situations before they get out of control.

Some of the positive actions we need to take in order to care for ourselves may not be comfortable for some other people. We need to acknowledge to ourselves, and will sometimes need to point out to others, that we don't have to do everything everyone expects of us. This doesn't mean we shouldn't do *anything* others expect of us; it means we have both the right to question how our actions will affect our recovery and the responsibility to nurture our own health.

Others may not always accept the changes that our new perspective may work in us. If we expect this resistance and have a plan to deal with it, we will be more successful in our response.

Exercise

How often do you say yes when you really want to say no? List some instances that come readily to mind. Pick one that especially disturbed you. What was the result of saying yes when you wanted to say no? If you could do the encounter over, how might you handle the situation for a better outcome?

When someone asks for your help, ask yourself whether you have the time to spare and whether your recovery might be jeopardized by something in the nature of the effort you've been asked to make. If you weigh the situation and it seems right, say yes. If not, say no. You don't have to make excuses, just tell the truth. "I don't have the time. I would have to skip Johnny's baseball game or forgo self-care activities that I mustn't skip." There is no need to feel guilty; you are taking care of yourself. This stance may be new to you and you may feel uncomfortable for a while, but as we practice these things we become more confident in our ability to use self-protective behavior. Of course, we're not suggesting that the need for self-care be used as an excuse to be self-centered or irresponsible. Over time we learn to balance self-care activities with other life activities.

For a while you may find it difficult to refuse when someone offers you something to eat that is not part of your nutrition plan. We naturally feel uncomfortable refusing the offer of food, especially when someone we know has made it. Eating has a strong role in our society. It is tied to a myriad of social events, formal and informal, and to expressions of friendship or goodwill. When we refuse food, we feel as though we are rejecting the person offering it. When we develop a strong understanding that we're doing no such thing, we can more easily communicate to others that our choice has nothing to do with anyone but ourselves. It may be helpful to think of a humorous response you can use to prevent a tense situation when you refuse a cookie or a piece of pie. Try saying, "No, thanks. I'm allergic to that. It makes me break out in fat."

Exercise

Think of some responses you will be comfortable using when friends encourage you to eat what you choose not to. For example, "Thanks, but I've had my quota of that for today." Write down your responses and practice them before you

need them. Think of possible arguments people may give
you, such as "One won't hurt," and practice repeating your
sentence, "Thanks, but I've had my quota of that."

Evaluate your social circle. Do your friends reinforce your
old lifestyle or support your recovery? Perhaps you can enlist
the help of people you care about. Explain how important
your recovery is to you and tell them it would be easier to
maintain if you knew you had their support. You might be
surprised how often you can turn sabotage (which is usually
unwitting) into support.

There will always be people who do not understand your
situation, who do not understand that you are dealing with a
physical condition, who do not understand how complex recovery can be. They think you should "just push away from
the table." You don't have to buy into the mistaken beliefs of
other people. You may want to take the time to explain the
facts to some of them, but you also may have to accept the ig-
norance of some who are not open to understanding.

Detaching emotionally from people who do not understand
and whom we cannot change will help us feel more comfortable in our decision to take care of ourselves. We can learn to
detach from them rather than "eat at" them—and at ourselves, in our frustration. Look around you. Who are "safe"
people and who are "high risk"? Who will support your recovery and who will not? It is up to us to set our boundaries.
Kate has a way of setting boundaries with high-risk people
when they phone. She tells them that she has something she
needs to do shortly and can talk only a few minutes. When
the conversation becomes uncomfortable and risky, Kate immediately says she has to go.

When we do not feel good about ourselves, we find particular difficulty in setting boundaries and letting people know what those boundaries are. Most people do not maintain good self-care without learning to feel good about themselves— strengthening self-esteem. As part of self-care, we need to undertake regular activities that help us do that.

This feeling of being valuable is a cornerstone of self-discipline because when one considers oneself valuable one will take care of oneself in all ways that are necessary. M. Scott Peck[2]

Life Balance

When we focus as much on not eating as, once, we focused on overeating, we are still fixated on food; our lives are still out of balance. Life should be focused on living. A very pronounced emphasis on any aspect of self-care can create deficits elsewhere: We have physical, psychological, social, and spiritual needs. We need to spend time nourishing our bodies, taking care of our family, being a friend, furthering our careers, developing our talents, and giving and receiving spiritual nourishment. Food is but one important part of our balanced diet for a healthful, useful, and joyous life.

The excitement of recovery may cause us to be unrealistic about our limitations, about the time that we have to reinforce the good things that are happening. We are right to feel enthusiastic about recovery, but we're not right to be unrealistic. There are only twenty-four hours in a day, and we must choose how we use them. We burn out when we try to do too much too fast; recovery is a lifetime commitment. We don't have to do it all at once. In fact, no one can. We must give ourselves time and room to grow, one day at a time.

We should build self-care around our individual lifestyles,

around job, family, and other activities. To do otherwise may be to feel burdened and deprived by the self-care regimen and less likely to stay with it. Self-care is not static; it changes as we learn more about ourselves and our needs and as we grow in recovery. We should do ourselves the kindness of remembering that few things are started and perfected at the same time.

Recovery has more to do with the quality of life than with not overeating. It is not just a matter of what we *stop* doing. It is more a matter of what we *start* doing. Gradually, one day at a time, we reorient the focus of life from eating to full and enriched living. Recovery is more comfortable when we fill life so full that food is just not that important anymore.

> *This is it! It's my life. Whatever it takes, I want to spend the rest of it thinking about something other than food.*
>
> Judi Hollis[3]

Recovery is always expanding. As we learn recovery skills, of course, it is normal to focus more on selection and preparation of food, arranging physical activities, going to support group meetings. We must learn to eat differently, change metabolic rate, gradually increase physical activity. But as recovery expands and we incorporate these changes they become a natural part of life. We are then able to concentrate on other aspects of living a full and satisfying life.

The two of us, David and Merlene, were camping in the mountains. There was a hiking path that led several miles up to the top of a nearby mountain. I, Merlene, wanted to make the climb but didn't know if I had the stamina. So I told myself I didn't have to go all the way to the top. I would just go as far as I could and turn around. I looked up to the first plateau and decided to go that far. When I got that far I realized I could go a little farther. My attention was on the distance, but I kept climbing, one plateau at a time, until I got to the top. I was elated when I was able to look out from the mountain I had just climbed. The next day I decided to do it again. But this time I knew I could make it to the top, so I was not concerned about the distance or the difficulty of the climb. I looked at the beauty of the mountains, the flowers, the birds, and the sky. My focus was no longer on the difficulty of the climb but on the rewards of the experience.

Like mountain climbing, self-care changes may be difficult. But they're not impossible. Sometimes recovery may be a little like getting into a swimming pool in May: Jump in and it warms up. There is a price to pay for recovery, but there are also rewards. Remember that pain is not always bad, and we do not always add to our health by avoiding it. Sometimes we achieve a goal only through some struggle and pain. When we believe that pain is to be avoided at all cost, we deprive ourselves of some of the more fulfilling experiences of life.

Acknowledge the pain and sadness of the changes required to support recovery. Know that it takes courage to make these changes. It is all right to grieve your losses, and to say "This is awful" when it is. At the same time, allow yourself to enjoy the benefits of what you are doing.

The process of recovery can be its own reward as we become better and better able to be in control of our own lives. But there are also the rewards of a healthier body and an enriched life. Recovery can be joyful—not free of pain and sorrow, but full of excitement, purpose, and meaning.

Exercise

Complete the following sentence as many ways as you want to:

 I'm discovering . . .

Part Three

Reversing the Spiral: Regression Prevention

Chapter 8

Regression Prevention and Interruption

Clara remembered distinctly the moment she made a firm decision to make no further attempts to lose weight. She was taking all the too-small clothes out of her closet and putting the larger sizes back in. What was the point? She had done this so many times. It was no way to live. She told herself she was not capable of maintaining weight loss so she might as well give up trying. She would just learn to accept herself as a large person and never again face the disappointment of failing.

That moment came two years ago, and now her doctor was telling her that she had Type II diabetes: She had to lose weight. If she lost weight, he said, she could control her diabetes without medication; if she didn't, she was facing some serious health problems.

Not even her doctor's dire prediction motivated Clara to begin a new weight loss program. But when the prediction began to come true, she was frightened. She was developing a number of complications because of her diabetes and realized that she must find the courage to lose weight. Knowing there was no point in repeating

PROGRESSION SPIRAL

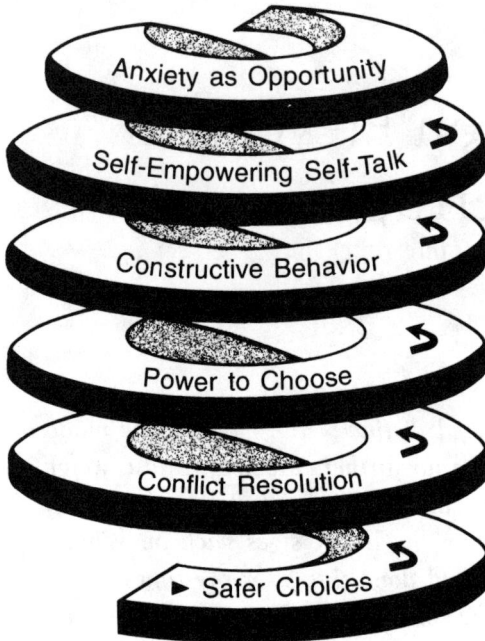

Anxiety as Opportunity

Self-Empowering Self-Talk

Constructive Behavior

Power to Choose

Conflict Resolution

► Safer Choices

what she had done in the past, she went to a counselor who helped her change her focus from weight
loss alone to a new lifestyle.

The counselor also introduced her to the principles
of regression prevention. By looking at what had happened to her in the past, Clara was able to see the
spiral of regression that had taken her from the point
at which she was following her self-care plan to the point
at which she had given it up. She realized that in
the past, once she had begun to slip, she had let go
and allowed the slip to become a rapid slide into relapse.

She made a commitment to her counselor to take certain actions to prevent further regression when she recognized she was in trouble.

Clara has had her ups and downs, but when she begins to regress she recognizes it and takes some action to interrupt the process. She knows she does not have to spiral all the way to the bottom before she can do something to interrupt what is happening. Recently she told her counselor that, even though she sometimes gets off track temporarily, for the first time in her life she is able to regain recovery before putting back all the weight she has lost. She is delighted that she is able to stop the destructive process of regression before she is back where she started. As her doctor predicted, she can control her diabetes without medication— and she feels better than she has for years.

A commitment to recovery does not mean that we will not struggle anymore or that we will not regress from our commitment. Recovery is a process of growth, not an occurrence that, once accomplished, changes us for all time. We continue to have unresolved issues, areas of shame, and unexpected rough spots—some related to recovery, some not.

People in recovery relapse from to time. *Relapse* is loss of control of eating behaviors and self-care that follows a commitment to recovery and an indeterminate period of maintenance. A relapse does not usually occur all at once; it happens over time, as we gradually give up trying.

Regression is moving away from recovery and good self-care into relapse. Often we do not recognize this regression until we are in complete loss of control. Regression can be so gradual and so subtle that when we look back on it we wonder: How did we get into regression? How do we stop it?

Exercise

Complete this sentence five ways:
  When I relapse I feel . . .

No matter how much we would like to believe otherwise, we never "have it made." Sometimes we think that because we are doing well, we'll always do well; that because we now know what to do, we will always do it. Old behaviors don't just go away, simply because we know what to do.

> A.L.: At first, I could eat yogurt and whole wheat muffins and grapefruit and feel perfectly satisfied. I lost weight and didn't feel hungry. It seemed to work so well and I felt so good that I thought I would always be able to eat that way. When people from my support group told me I needed more variety, I told them I didn't see why. I had lost my compulsion to overeat. I thought I had it made. But when I did get burned out on those foods and started slipping back into old ways of eating, I regressed rapidly. It took me a long time to realize that doing well doesn't mean I have it made forever.

For ongoing recovery from a weight problem, we need two plans operating in our lives. One is a *self-care* plan and the other is a *regression prevention* plan. A self-care plan identifies what we will do regularly to stay well and healthy. A good self-care plan addresses the needs of the whole person: the physical, emotional, social, and spiritual requirements. It helps us change our metabolic rate and brain chemistry in ways other than by eating. It helps us satisfy emotional hunger so we don't literally feed it. And it helps us live a balanced life so both social and spiritual needs are met.

We need to have a healthy self-care plan, but if we don't know what to do to keep from losing control when we get off the plan or vary from it, then it probably won't work permanently. Good self-care lowers the risk of regression but does not guarantee prevention. A plan for regression prevention helps us identify when we are getting off track, then helps us get back on. Self-care plans are plans for what we will do regularly. Regression prevention plans are contingency plans—"what if" plans: They tell us what to do when we recognize we are slipping away from good self-care. Let's use an analogy to make the distinction between a self-care plan and a regression prevention plan.

If I want my car to get me to work every day, I need a plan to keep my car in good shape. So I regularly check the oil, keep gas in the car, have periodic tune-ups, do regular maintenance. Time passes without incident, affirming the soundness of my day-to-day plan. I have reason to be pleased. But I've kept in mind that I may go out some morning and find that my car won't start; then I'd have to do something different from (or in addition to) my usual routine. I've already joined a Road Club for that purpose. If I call them, they will send someone out to get my car started.

When I become aware that my car maintenance plan does not guarantee my getting to work every day, I need to look at why my car didn't start and revise my plan. But to be sure I do get to work, I need a maintenance plan for my car *and* a contingency plan in case I meet with a problem.

If our goal is to live a healthy and productive life, we need a self-care plan for regular maintenance and a regression prevention plan for what to do when we have trouble anyway. Together, a good self-care plan and a regression prevention plan ensure a healthy recovery.

Preventing and Coping With Slips

We can slip from a self-care plan at any time. A slip—a temporary lapse from fully following our plan—is usually one instance of unplanned eating in which we eat more than expected, or eat something outside our limits without a plan to compensate for it. Part of good recovery is avoiding slips in the first place. But keep in mind that *a slip is not relapse*; it is not loss of control. And it does not mean we are in regression. How we react to the slip determines whether it will be a temporary setback or part of a continuing regression that can lead to total abandonment of self-care.

A slip is risky, because it sets up the possibility of our rapidly spiraling out of control, but it need not lead to further regression. The more powerful the regression spiral, however, the more difficult it is to keep a slip from leading to loss of control. Regression prevention skills not only help prevent slips, but they lower the risk of a slip becoming part of a slide.

AVOIDING SLIPS

According to the research of G. Alan Marlatt and Judith R. Gordon, there are two types of circumstances in which a slip is especially likely to occur.[1] In one of the two, we are experiencing such feelings as boredom, depression, and loneliness. In the other, we want to celebrate or to make a certain time special, perhaps in going out to eat or in sharing a holiday. Plans for handling these situations can prevent a slip from occurring.

> I.D.: My daughter is often hospitalized. When she's in pain, I am in pain. To make her stay easier, I used to buy her candy. Recently I realized that I was buying my own pain relief. In such a situation buying certain treats is risky and can lead to a slip and a fast regression. Since

recognizing that, I have started taking her a flower a day. She enjoys that as much as the candy. And so do I.

Exercise

Label one section of your notebook the "Regression Prevention" section. On one page make three columns. In one column list high-risk emotions for you (boredom, depression, loneliness). In another column list circumstances under which these emotions are likely to occur. In the last column identify ways to cope with or reduce the risk of experiencing a slip at those times. On the next page make two columns. In one, list high-risk occasions (times you celebrate or have a good time). In the other column, describe what you can do to cope with and lower the risk of having a slip at those times.

Sometimes we feel strong physical cravings to eat something not on our plan, something we know has a strong possibility of leading us into relapse. At those times we need to take immediate positive action until the craving passes. Here are some suggestions: Go for a walk, play a game, call a friend, go to a movie, drink a couple of glasses of water, take a nap, eat something nourishing. We need to think of other ways of braking the craving impulse and removing ourselves from the eating cues around us. Relaxation exercises may help to release stress, alter brain chemistry, and in general allow us to feel better.

Exercise

Complete the following sentence seven ways:
  When I experience a craving to binge or eat a trigger food,
    I can relieve the craving by . . .

A SLIP IS NOT A SLIDE

If a slip does occur, it can be a minor digression from self-care or part of an escalation into old behaviors. It can remain just a slip if immediate action is taken to regain control. Many of us tend to give up self-care altogether when a slip occurs. When we believe that maintaining self-care is all-or-nothing, we are apt to slide rapidly from one small lapse into relapse. If our goal is progress, not perfection, then we can look at a slip as a minor detour and get right back on track. There are ways to handle slips so they do not become slides.

A plan for getting right back on track can provide effective damage control. The slip can remain just that when we take fast action to regain control. Our immediate-action plan for accommodating a lapse might be to subtract the appropriate number of calories from our meal plan, or we might prefer to increase our exercise. A flexible self-care plan can help prevent our spiraling away from self-care. We allow ourselves some variation, so we do not have to feel that we have failed if we digress.

Let's say you eat a handful of cookies and that violates your self-care plan. What are your options?

1. You can tell yourself you have already blown it so you might as well eat the whole bag.
2. You can fast the next day.
3. You can start over next week.
4. You can do additional exercise as soon as possible.
5. You can cut your calorie intake somewhat until you have compensated for the extra calories.
6. You can say, "Well, I slipped," and immediately take action to keep yourself from eating more of the cookies (such as giving them to your children to take next door to share with their friends).

What you choose has a lot to do with whether or not your slip becomes a slide into relapse. If you choose option 1, you put yourself at high risk of rapid regression into relapse. If you choose 2, you also endanger your recovery, because you set yourself up to binge. If you choose 3, you will probably continue to overeat "until next week" and next week will never come.

If you choose 4 or 5, or a combination of the two, you can compensate for the slip and go right on with no serious damage. Although 6 does not give you a way to compensate for the extra calories, it is better than 1, 2, and 3.

Even if you do nothing to compensate, you can prevent regression by recognizing right away that you slipped and by taking action to get back on track. You do *not* let the slip serve as an excuse to continue overeating, or as an excuse to do the same thing again in a few days, or as an excuse to say, "What's the use?"

J.D.: A slip used to be the worst thing that could happen to me. I would tell myself I couldn't do anything right. I don't do that to myself anymore. I just say, "I made a mistake. What am I going to learn from it, and what am I going to do that's different next time?" One of the best things I have done for myself in the last two years is to not get down on myself if I do mess up. And I do mess up sometimes.

Many of us believe that if we don't have willpower all the time, we don't have it at all. Our recovery goes better when we realize that recovery is a process; that within any process, we will do better at some times than at others. We can get off track, but there is always a way back.

A word of caution here: Allowing ourselves too much flexibility eliminates the structure and boundaries that give us a sense that we are on track. As we cut corners more and more, we become unrealistic about the importance of self-care, until it is something we do only when it is convenient—and finally not at all.

> *One thing that used to get Clara in trouble was saving up her food points during the day so she could eat more in the evening. She could endure being deprived all day because she could reward herself later, but in following that course she was setting herself up to binge. She stopped paying attention to balanced eating and was using her calorie points for things like pie and extra butter on her rolls. Pretty soon she wasn't staying within her allotted points because she was setting off cravings for more pie and more rolls and more butter. Her hunger was never satisfied, because she was spending her points on high-calorie, high-fat foods and not getting enough nutritious, satisfying foods. This was a risky situation, one she could have prevented. She ultimately realized that and reversed the spiral. She set definite boundaries for her use of calorie points so she would recognize a slip when she made it.*

Often a number of slips occur before we are out of control. And sometimes we can get by with a few slips. Or the first time we say we can have "just one," maybe we do; but maybe instead, we decide that since we stopped with one before, we can have two. As more and more slips occur, we may not get right back—and then we begin to view a slip not as a minor departure from our plan but as a failure that proves we cannot maintain. So we give up.

Exercise

Complete the following sentence seven ways:
    When I have a slip, instead of giving up I can . . .

We are more likely to make good choices in regard to a slip when we are in a healthy frame of mind and we are thinking clearly. The farther we have regressed, the less likely we are to prevent a slip or to stop a slide once a slip has occurred. We are far less likely to make good choices about much of anything when we are feeling bad about ourselves, feeling sorry for ourselves, feeling angry toward others and life, feeling trapped and deprived, giving ourselves self-defeating messages, or putting ourselves in situations that place us at high risk of regressing.

Interrupting Regression

Regression is a process of sliding out of productive functioning and back into old habits, thoughts, attitudes, feelings, and behaviors. It takes us from a point of being in control to a point of being out of control. That loss of control does not happen suddenly. We don't just wake up one morning and find ourselves no longer in control of our eating and self-care plan, no longer in recovery. The regression spiral takes us gradually from the point at which we are following our plan to the point at which we abandon it. This process can happen over a long or a short period of time, but usually we go through certain stages. There are indications that this regression is occurring, but we may be unaware of them. We can learn to prevent or reverse the regression spiral once we've learned to recognize its signs.

Having some pain and difficulty in recovery does not necessarily mean we are regressing. But if we are not paying attention to our recovery and are gradually slipping away from it, we are in regression. At first, the indications are subtle and can go unnoticed. As the regression becomes stronger and gathers momentum, it becomes more obvious. But the later in the process we become aware that it is occurring, the more difficulty we encounter in trying to do anything about it.

In Chapter Three we looked at a generalized pattern of regression, but the process differs for everyone. Regression prevention lies in identifying what our own regression spiral is like, then planning to keep from getting caught up in its coils. Like caution lights that come on in a car as a warning that the motor is hot, the fuel is low, or the emergency brake is on, we show indications when recovery is in trouble. The sooner we observe the warnings and do something about them, the less likely we are to develop serious problems.

As we become more familiar with our own particular regression pattern and learn to recognize when we are experiencing it, developing safeguards against regression and taking action to stop it becomes easier.[2]

Because of the nature of relapse and regression, we need to set up a plan ahead of time to protect us when we are not thinking clearly. Ulysses, the mythic hero, believed that hearing the sirens' song would drive him mad. He had his crew bind him to the mast of the ship before they sailed past the irresistible sirens and told his men to ignore his requests for release. He took action when he was thinking clearly to protect himself when he knew he'd not be thinking clearly—and he enlisted the help of other people to do it.

Exercise

Review the typical regression spiral described in Chapter Three. Does this sound like what happens to you as you spiral away from taking good care of yourself? Write the story of your regression. What happens as you move gradually from good self-care to the point at which you are no longer in control of your eating behavior? Try writing the story in the third person; that may help you be more objective. Write as though you were describing a close friend, someone you really care about.

In the following six chapters we will ask you to look at what might cause you to regress from taking good care of yourself and to lose control of your recovery. We will look at each stage of the regression spiral and discuss how many of us feel, think, and act when we are at that point in regression. We will ask you to think about how *you* feel, think, and act at that point, so you will be able to recognize each of the stages as you may reach them in an actual regression. We will provide some suggestions for ways you can interrupt each stage; we will ask you to make some plans for actions you can take to reverse the regression spiral at any given stage.

If we learn to recognize when we are in trouble and do something about it, we have not failed. But the earlier we recognize regression, the easier it is for us to do something about it. How do we know when we are in trouble? Sometimes we don't. Sometimes the thoughts and feelings that accompany regression are subconscious and we're really not aware we are regressing. But even if we are not consciously aware of what "it" is, most of us have some inner knowledge, however un-defined, of what will cause us problems in recovery.

One morning I, Merlene, couldn't find my glasses. The last time I remembered seeing them was the night before when I checked to see if they were in my jacket pocket in the car. Now they were no longer there. I searched everywhere, to no avail. Finally I said to myself, "There is a part of my mind that knows where my glasses are. I just need to get in touch with the part of my mind that knows." I then went on about my morning activities. While I was brushing my teeth, suddenly, like a bolt from the blue, I almost heard the words "Your glasses are in the trash." Feeling a little foolish because I had no idea why they would be there, I went to the kitchen and looked in the trash can. Sure enough, there they were. I still don't know how they got there, but my subconscious mind knew where they were.

Regression prevention helps us get in touch with the part of our minds that already knows what could lead to relapse. We can identify potential problems by remembering what has caused us to regress in the past and imagining what might lead to regression in the future.[3] We do give signals to our-selves and others that we are in trouble. If we can figure out what those are before they occur, we are more likely to bring them into conscious awareness so we can recognize them when they first occur.

LOOKING HONESTLY AT OURSELVES

Identifying what leads to regression requires looking honestly at ourselves and the characteristics we have that can cause us problems in recovery. We can't succeed unless we know why we fail. Steps Four, Five, Six, and Seven of Overeaters Anon-ymous encourage us to identify our "character defects," to admit that we have them, and to become willing to let go of them. We become better able and willing to look at ourselves as we are and to acknowledge the things about us that can interfere with full recovery. This sincere effort is necessary to preventing regression. If we are unwilling to look at ourselves and the characteristics we have that lead us away from recovery, we continue to be in denial of those things that can get us in trouble.

> *The truth will make you free—but first it will make you damn*
> *mad.*   M. Scott Peck[4]

Inability to look at ourselves as we are supports the belief that we should be perfect. When the shame of being imperfect keeps us from accepting our humanness, we cannot learn from our mistakes. Preventing regression requires learning from our mistakes so we can stop repeating them over and over again. Making the changes that will prevent regression is hard if we are afraid to acknowledge our imperfections. (How can we correct them if we don't have any?)

Self-awareness opens the door to healing. When we are too ashamed of ourselves to look honestly inside, we have no way to heal our shame. Looking honestly at ourselves is scary and can be painful. But doing it will help us develop the skill to look at the truth without running to our source of escape, food.

Fear of looking honestly at ourselves also keeps us from recognizing our strengths and our potential. People with a history of weight problems tend to look at their negative qualities and overlook the positive. Looking squarely but fairly at ourselves, we'll find assets we can use to diminish our liabilities. In order to prevent regression, we must learn to use our strengths to support recovery.

AN ACTION PLAN TO INTERRUPT REGRESSION

When we are able to recognize that our recovery is in trouble, we can take action to do something about it. We are more apt to take action if we know ahead of time what we are going to do. A regression prevention plan is simply a plan to interrupt regression when we become aware that it is occurring.[5]

A regression prevention plan is not a substitute for a good self-care plan. Nor is it a substitute for other sources of help—a doctor, a counselor, OA, a therapy group. Regression prevention plans help us stick with our self-care plan once it is established. Sometimes when we recognize that we are regressing, we need to change our self-care plan. Other times, we just need to get back to doing what has worked for us in the past.

There is no point at which we cannot interrupt the regression spiral if we learn to recognize that it is occurring and if we have strategies for stopping it. Regression prevention is not a magic answer. In conjunction with other sources of help, regression prevention can be a tool for staying in control, for centering our lives on healthful living rather than on food. Regression prevention helps us live in safety instead of living on the edge.

Exercise

Complete the following sentence seven ways:

As I think about what I have read up to this point, I am becoming aware . . .

Chapter 9

Safer Choices

Don stood in front of the snack bar in the movie theater, smelling the buttered popcorn and looking at the nachos and cheese. He was in turmoil. It had been all he could do to show up at work that day. The last few weeks had been difficult, with new job training in addition to keeping up with his regular but escalating work load. In the past he had been able to use food as a release when he felt overwhelmed and tense. Now he felt torn between wanting to maintain his recovery program and bingeing for relief. As he felt the tenseness in his chest and stomach, familiar thoughts of his favorite trigger foods returned. Images of past stress-related situations, when he ate nachos and cheese, filled his mind, urging him to eat to soothe his frayed nerves.

He had come to the movie right after work, thinking that a temporary escape would help him relax. But once inside the theater, he thought only about the nachos and cheese, so readily available. He had a choice to make. If he stayed, he would soon be bingeing. In a moment of strong resolve, he turned his back on the nachos and

cheese—and the movie. He went to a phone and
called a bowling buddy. "Sam, I really need to bowl
tonight. How soon could you meet me at the alley?"

There may come a time when the most important thing we have to do is find some safe pain relief. When the pain of being deprived, of being in conflict, of feeling powerless to change anything is so severe that it is affecting our judgment, we begin making risky choices—choices that can put recovery in jeopardy.

When we begin making risky choices, we are usually looking for pain relief and are likely to put ourselves into situations that place us at high risk of resorting to old feel-good behaviors. When our lives are out of harmony, our daily structure is at risk of breaking down. A risky choice is usually a frantic attempt to meet our needs that doesn't meet them. We need to find some safe pain relief.

It is important that we recognize *before* we are making them how risky some choices are. The moment the choice confronts us is the moment we are least apt to recognize the risk involved. When we are on the edge of the cliff, it is very difficult to move back away from it without a clear understanding of the danger we are in. When recovery is fragile, we need to take immediate action to find safe ways to feel better.

Nurturing Ourselves in Risky Ways

When we are looking for something or someone to relieve our pain, we are at risk of getting back into the old cycle of eating to relieve the pain that eating creates. We justify our risky choices by telling ourselves we are taking care of ourselves, nurturing ourselves. After all, we think, no one else will do it for us—and we deserve a break.

J.H.: I had lost seventy pounds using a commercial weight loss program. The excitement of losing the weight had kept me going for a long time. But after a while that wasn't enough to offset the sense of deprivation that was overwhelming me. The realization that losing more weight and keeping it off meant no ice cream, no fried chicken, and no brownies was more than I could accept. So I started having one day a week I called my cheating day, when I ate everything in sight. At first, it was the rest of the day of my weigh-in. I lost as little time as possible, after stepping off that scale, to begin my eating. Then I made it a twenty-four-hour period after weighing in. Then I extended it to include the following day. As my weight loss slowed, my pain increased—and so did the number of days I "cheated."

Consider these common risky choices: Allowing ourselves to get hungry. Allowing ourselves to get tired. Volunteering to bake cakes for a bake sale. Skipping support group meetings. Skipping exercise because it is raining. Thinking and talking about the pleasure of eating out of control. Spending more time with the people we used to binge with, hoping to get talked into a binge. Going to (for us) risky places, being with (for us) risky people. Cooking more food than we need. Going to fast-food restaurants or restaurants that serve our favorite binge food. Waiting for someone in front of the donut shop.

Sometimes when Ruth is making risky choices, she goes to the grocery store for entertainment. Obviously, this can be extremely risky if she is hungry at the time; it is *always* risky to go to the grocery store hungry. When we do that, everything in the store looks good, especially the "forbidden" food that we have not had for a long time. So we end up buying some of them, telling ourselves we are not going to eat them. We will just keep them to serve quickly if someone comes unexpectedly.

> **K.H.**: When I am in the risky choice stage of the regression, I buy a gallon of ice cream and have one dish. I put the rest in the freezer. But it calls my name. The first day, I can usually manage to resist. But the next day, all I can think about is the ice cream in the freezer. It keeps calling my name until I finally eat the whole gallon. I feel guilty and make an absolute commitment to keep ice cream out of the freezer. A few days later I might bake a cake for the family. I tell myself that I won't have any, but it looks so good. I have one piece. The leftover cake sits in the kitchen and I manage not to cut myself a whole slice. But I keep cutting off little slivers and putting them into my mouth and telling myself that each one will be the last. I can eat a whole cake this way.

Using Substitute Excessive Behaviors

Sylvia has found a substitute for overeating. She shops. She has more clothes than will fit in her closet, not to mention scarves, jewelry, and shoes. She has small kitchen appliances and utensils she has not taken out of the box and pictures she does not have a place to hang. She also has credit cards charged to the limit and bills she cannot pay. Well, she tells herself, it's better than binge eating.

> *When Bill lost weight, he got the confidence to ask out*
> *a woman he had been attracted to for some time.*
> *Having her accept and respond to him in a positive*
> *way was so exhilarating that he began asking out other*
> *women. He soon found himself involved with a number*

of women at the same time, giving each of them the impression he was more serious than he was. He quickly lost interest in all of them and moved on to others. When someone confronted him about the disrespectful way he treated these women, he said, "Well, it's better than sitting home alone and eating."

We may fail to recognize that we are making risky choices because what we choose does relieve our pain. If, like Bill, we tell ourselves the activity is better than overeating, we may in some cases be right. But some of the pain-relieving behaviors that we may substitute for overeating can be just as injurious as overeating itself. These behaviors can also be used compulsively to fill the emptiness. Excessive working, obsessive relationships, compulsive shopping, or excessive use of alcohol, nicotine, or caffeine are ways to relieve our pain that can get out of hand if they are used as substitutes for eating. They can also lead back to overeating.

B.P.: When I am making risky choices, I sometimes smoke to suppress my appetite. But when I smoke too much I get a headache and then tell myself I should eat to feel better.

If eating has been used to fill the need for love and nurturing, we may be at risk of forming relationships that are obsessive and compulsive. Sexual behavior can become excessive, too, if it is used to satisfy physical needs that are isolated from spiritual and emotional needs.

Involvement in OA, religion, or a self-awareness program can become obsessive if it is used to escape reality and causes us to neglect the nuts and bolts of everyday living. A given behavior can be used compulsively, or it can be a positive outlet.

It is not so much what we do as how we do it. Positive use does not result in long-term pain or create new problems.

Exercise

List some behaviors that for you could become excessive. Describe ways you can prevent them from getting out of hand.

Justification Messages

Recognizing that we are making risky choices can be difficult because of the things we tell ourselves: *I will eat just one. I will put them in the freezer for company. This is for the kids. It was on sale. I deserve it. I can go there, I just won't eat anything. No one understands my needs. I'll just have a taste. I'll start again tomorrow. No one will know. I'll eat it to get it out of the house.* Some of the choices we make are dangerous when we're in this frame of mind. But we do them, telling ourselves there is no problem. We really want to believe that if we deserve it, it's not fattening; or that if no one sees us eat it, it doesn't count.

Exercise

Write down some of the justifications you give yourself for your risky choices. Then write some messages you can use to refute those justification messages the next time you hear yourself saying them. For example, if your justification is "I will eat just one," you might remind yourself that eating just one can trigger a craving stronger than the one you felt when you were doing without.

Suggestions for Making Safer Choices

Even at the point that we are playing Russian roulette with food, we can reverse the regression—provided we don't give ourselves the message that we have already blown it. The only way to interrupt the regression at this point is to make a conscious decision to do something different. We must acknowledge that we have made some poor choices, but at the same time remind ourselves that we are not yet out of control, and we can make some safer choices for relieving the pain while also reversing the spiral.

BE ESPECIALLY GOOD TO YOURSELF

When we are making risky choices, we are right about one thing: We need immediate relief. This is no time to increase the pain by feeling guilty, by telling ourselves that we can never make it. It is not a time to further deprive ourselves of ways to feel good or set ourselves up for further "failure." *This is not the time for self-punishment.* That will just increase the pain and lead us to eat for pain relief. White knuckles and teeth grinding won't work to change behavior at this point. It is time to remind ourselves of the good choices we have made in the past, to focus on what we have done, not what we have undone.

This is a time to be very, very good to ourselves, to change our brain chemistry, to nurture ourselves in safe ways. It may be necessary to take extraordinary measures to find ways to feel good other than by eating. It is important to acknowledge that we are in trouble and to give ourselves permission to put our own needs first.

It is all right to tell other people you are going through a bad time and you need special consideration. We all need to give ourselves permission to do things that help us feel good.

Putting ourselves first at this time is not selfish. We have to take care of ourselves in order to prevent rapid escalation into out-of-control behavior. Our going back to old behaviors is not going to help anyone. We'll find it easier to care for others when we are in control of our own lives.

When we are making risky choices, we need to know and use ways to pamper ourselves so that we don't feel deprived. We should do things that feel good and allow ourselves the enjoyment of them: be with people we like, buy satin sheets, send ourselves flowers. We must learn to nourish ourselves in ways that do not include eating. *When you need safe pain relief, give yourself special self-care.*

Exercise

Here is an interesting thought to ponder: How would your life be different if you treated yourself like someone you care about? Think about that, and write down what you would do on a daily basis if you treated yourself as you treat your best friend, your lover, or your children.

TAKE IT EASY

Perhaps the most important thing to remember when we are feeling very stressed and our lives are sliding out of control is to take it easy, let up on ourselves, be flexible. Try more than one way to relieve pain without eating. Take one day at a time (or one hour). Don't worry about tomorrow. Do one thing at a time. Pace yourself.

Sometimes when we are tired of the struggle, what we really need is rest. If possible, take a nap. Sleep late. Hire a baby-sitter and go out. Stay home instead of going out. Say no to another obligation. Give yourself time off when you need it. Take a vacation in which you stay busy and do not focus on food. If you can't arrange for a regular vacation, take a mini-vacation. Take a day off or go away for a weekend. Make it a special time to do things you really enjoy.

Most of us have been conditioned to feel guilty for taking time for ourselves. We give ourselves such messages as *I am wasting time. I am being selfish. I should be doing something more productive.*

If you need permission to be good to yourself, then here is permission. Recondition yourself with the message that you have a responsibility to be good to yourself.

Give yourself permission to let go of some "have to's" and replace them with "choose to's." If we are going to give to others and fulfill all of our responsibilities, we must be functioning well; and when we are making risky choices, that means reversing the spiral by giving ourselves a break.

When you make a mistake, don't tell yourself you are stupid. You just made a poor choice. Say supportive things to yourself. Self-reinforcement helps us ride out periods like this. Praising ourselves is a reinforcer that is always available. When you are struggling, remind yourself that it will pass. Give yourself encouraging and supportive messages: *Okay, take it easy. You can handle this.*

Exercise

Make a list of "praise" messages for what you *are* doing. Here are some examples:

I'm a great mother.

My exercise program is working very well.

I am excited about eating healthy things.

I'm great at getting myself out of bad moods.

I love doing nice things for myself and others.

I'm a good boss.

I'm a supportive friend.

Keep the list handy and give yourself some of these messages when you need encouragement. A way to make this exercise fun is to see how outrageously you can praise yourself. Exaggerate. Indulge in fanciful self-praise.

I am absolutely the best cook in the world. I am the greatest lover on the planet.

Allow yourself to laugh at your outrageous self-praise, but also allow yourself to acknowledge the truth in these exaggerated messages.

POSTPONE MAJOR DECISIONS

It is best not to make unnecessary major changes when in the risky-choice state of regression. Put all major decisions on hold, if possible. First of all, remember that in this state we do not always think clearly and might not make the best decisions. Second, the pressure of making the decision will add to anxiety. We need to put our focus on taking care of ourselves first, just as if we had the flu. Then, when we are better able to cope, we can tackle the things we have put aside.

LAUGH AND PLAY

When we are making risky choices, we need to change our brain chemistry fast. Laughter is more than the sound you hear when you chase your hat down the street. Laughing and having fun change brain chemistry, creating a feeling of well-being. Play is a necessary part of life and one too often neglected. It may be that you have associated a good time only with eating. Making safer choices includes finding alternative ways to stimulate production of the brain's natural feel-good chemicals. Play and fun are relaxing, healing, stimulating, and

freeing. After we laugh we feel better, think better, and function better.

> *No matter what our heartache may be, when we laugh we*
> *have forgotten about it for just a few seconds.* Red Skelton

Fun, humor, and laughter not only help us feel better but
also promote healing. Norman Cousins, in his book *Anatomy
of an Illness*,[1] relates his experience of using laughter to overcome a chronic health condition that doctors had diagnosed
as fatal. Research today indicates that laughter is directly related to overcoming serious illness by helping the body provide its own medication. When you find yourself overcome by
the restrictions of your life and you feel your power slipping
away, expand your limits with fun and play.

> *Laughter is medicine to weary bones.* Carl Sandburg

Put some spontaneity and some zaniness in your life. Make
yourself up like a clown. Get silly with someone you love. Put
on your favorite music, sing, dance around the room. See
what you can think of that is a little absurd and a lot of fun.
Find people you can have fun with, people who can let go and
try new things.

Act silly with a child. Instead of wondering whether you've
lost your mind, the child will squeal with delight. We can
learn a lot from children about enjoying life. They can teach
us things we have forgotten about being aware, spontaneous,
and open. We can reclaim these traits—we were not truly
adult in putting them behind us—by living with a "childlike"
eagerness to experience all that life has to offer.

You don't have to be a child or be with a child to do that.

When did we get too old or too serious to play? When did we stop laughing at ridiculous things? Someone has said that we don't stop playing because we grow old; we grow old because we stop playing. Life does not have to be dull and boring. Don't let society's messages to "act your age" or "grow up" or "stop being foolish" deprive you of the richness of life that play offers. Lighten up and laugh. It can only do you good.

Exercise

Watch children play. Notice ways they behave that most adults have forgotten. In what ways could you emulate them? What stands in your way? Make a list of ways you can play and select one to do each day for a week.

USE ALL YOUR SENSES

We are aware of the pleasant sense of taste, but what about sight, hearing, touch, and smell? Pleasing our senses is a pleasant way to relax, so we can enjoy the simple things in life.

There are beautiful things to see: a rainbow, the sunrise, a child's smile, paintings, clouds, mountains. We pass by most of them without being aware.

Exercise

For one day, pretend you are going to lose your sight the next day. Look at everything as you would if this were the last time you would see it. At the end of the day, describe some of the things you saw. Write down your reactions and feelings about this experience.

What we hear can also be relaxing: quiet music, the ocean breaking on the shore, rain falling, birds singing. There are many pleasant sounds around us that we may not hear because we are so preoccupied we fail to notice them. Worse yet, noise pollution—from appliances, sirens, traffic, machinery—makes it more and more difficult for most of us to hear pleasant sounds. We need to offset noises that irritate us or that literally jar us. Carpeting and drapes can absorb noise, as can rubber pads under kitchen appliances. At times, leave the television and radio turned off. Create a pleasant environment with music and with recordings of enjoyable sounds, such as those of the ocean or a waterfall.

Exercise

Get up early one morning and take time to listen. What do you hear that is ordinarily drowned out by traffic, voices, and machines? What do you hear that is ordinarily drowned out by the conversations in your head and by your preoccupation with other life activities? Write about your experience.

Touching is not just pleasurable; it is a human need. As we have tended to become isolated as a society—distanced as families and neighbors, whether because of the increased use of technology, the impersonal workplace, or our fear of crime and abuse—physical contact has suffered. The skin needs nurturing. When this need is not satisfied, we have a hunger for touch that we commonly attempt to satisfy by eating.

Skin is the body's largest organ and often the most neglected. Be good to your skin by wearing soft clothing made of natural fabrics that breathe. Protect it from sun damage. Use moisturizers to protect it from dryness. Touching is a great source of pleasure. Blood pressure can be lowered by petting a furry animal. A hug can be very therapeutic. "Healing touch" is not just a phrase; it is an experience.

Exercise

Here are some suggestions for creative massage, taken from *The Wellness Workbook* by Regina Sara Ryan and John W. Travis.[2]

1. Roll a tennis ball under your hand as you apply pressure. Roll it over your feet, your partner's back, any muscular part of the body.

2. Remove your shoes and socks. Sit down and roll the bottom of your foot over a golf ball. Or fill a basin with marbles and rub your feet over them.

3. Massage with a dry brush or a loofa sponge. Make sure the bristles of the brush are not too firm. Use circular motions. Start with the feet and move up. (Avoid the face.)

4. Experiment with textures. Take a piece of fur, a silk scarf, a flannel shirt, a terry cloth towel, a bunch of fluffy cotton and gently massage yourself with each or exchange massages with your partner.

The sense of smell reminds us of pleasant memories. We can relive an enjoyable moment by reexperiencing the smell associated with it. We can also enjoy pleasant smells for their own sake. Part of what we think of as the sense of taste is actually the sense of smell. Think about that when you are hungering for something that tastes good. Remind yourself that it is actually your sense of smell that is hungry. Then satisfy that sense with the smell of fresh sheets, roses, the air after a rain, trees, pine needles, leather, freshly cut grass, eucalyptus.

To awaken all your senses, try filling the bathtub with bubble bath, spraying perfume in the air, putting on quiet music, turning off the lights, and lighting a candle or two before sliding into the bathtub to soak.

ENJOY WATER

There is a natural healing power to water. We use it for hydration, cleansing, nutrition, relaxation, and recreation. It stimulates, warms, cools, soothes, and fulfills the need for touch.

Showering does more than cleanse. Use it to experience the healing power of water. Try standing under a shower and enjoying the feel of the water on your skin. To awaken your senses and increase circulation, alternate hot and cold water. Try a shower massager, or shower at night with only a night light and imagine that you are standing in a waterfall.

Like a shower, a bath can be used for more than cleansing. In the bath, water can touch you all over, can embrace you. It can soothe and relax you through its buoyancy, warmth, and gentleness. A hot tub provides much the same luxurious pleasure. In addition, its whirlpool jets can relieve an aching, sore body as well as soothe and relax muscles.

Swimming is one of few activities by which we can get complete exercise and a sensuous experience at the same time. Lap swimming can be meditative as well. If you wear goggles and earplugs, the sound of water gurgling as you swim contributes to the relaxation. Because the water supports every part of the body, this form of exercise can seem effortless. The water supports as it caresses.

It is not necessary to know how to swim to enjoy a dip in a pool. You can do water exercise or just splash and have fun. The weightless feeling is very pleasurable when you can let go and just be. Enjoy the buoyancy of the water by submerging yourself and floating to the top.

Try water aerobics or water calisthenics. Exercises that are strenuous and painful out of water may be quite enjoyable in water. There is less impact on joints because the water helps support the body. Or try waterwalking, which is often used as physical therapy for people whose injuries prevent them from walking on land. It is gentler and you get the same benefit with less effort.

There is nothing quite as luxurious as surrendering to the water by floating on your back, arms to your sides, eyes closed, the water supporting you. (If you are overweight you have an advantage because the more body fat you have, the more easily you float.) Relax and feel the water surround you.

How long has it been since you had a water fight or played in a sprinkler? We, the authors, have a video of our grandson as a baby playing—with total abandon—in a lawn sprinkler. You don't have to be a baby to do that.

FIND WHAT IS RIGHT FOR YOU

What is best for you when you need safe pain relief is not the same as for someone else. You must decide what will provide the relief you need and help you get back on track when you are making risky choices. Here are some suggestions to choose from.

Meditate. Go away for a sensuous weekend with your lover. Take a nap. Sleep late. Hug someone. Hold a baby. Play with a child. Paint a picture. Color in a children's coloring book. Make a hat. Play hopscotch. Blow bubbles. Go to the zoo. Go to the museum. Take a walk in a beautiful place. Take a long, warm, soaking bath. Take a bubble bath. Think of the funniest thing you have ever heard. Laugh. Think of the funniest thing you have ever done. Laugh. Write a love letter. Play the piano. Yell as loud as you can. Sing as lustily as you can. Order something from a mail-order catalog. Run barefoot in the mud. Walk barefoot in the grass. Walk in the rain. Have a snowball fight. Do the Twelfth Step of OA. Hold a puppy. Kiss a potbellied pig. Make a list of what you like about yourself. Look at photo albums. Watch home videos. Don't answer the phone. Go to a movie with a friend. Go to a movie alone. Hire someone to clean your house. Send someone a greeting card for no reason. Send yourself a greeting card for no reason. Make yourself a greeting card. Surprise the person behind you by paying their fare at toll booth. Watch a sad movie and allow yourself to cry. Take a walk on your lunch hour. Talk to a friend. Read the comics. Read a funny book. Sit by a waterfall. Send yourself flowers. Join a bell choir. Dye your hair. Get a massage. Say no to something you would normally do. Say yes to something you would not normally do. Knead bread. Play with clay. Join a support group. Put away all your clocks and watches for a day. Locate a friend you have lost touch with. Get a facial. Play in that lawn sprinkler. Finger paint. Walk in gently falling snow. Hug a tree. Kiss a flower. Jump rope and say a child's rhyme. Roller skate. Swing. Watch "Sesame Street." Plant flowers. Answer the door in a disguise. Have an unbirthday party. Make a collage of funny pictures. Make a collage of sentimental pictures. Read a *Cathy* book. Read a *Calvin* book. Wear a fuzzy robe and bunny slippers. Ride a roller coaster. Get a pet and encourage it to pet you back. Spend a night on a houseboat and sleep under the stars. Go camping. Join a drama club. Make a fire in the fireplace. Smell lilacs. Fly a miniature plane. Rearrange the furniture. Go wading in a creek. Catch a frog. Fill your house with balloons. Have coffee on the patio at dawn. Fly a kite. Take a class in macrame. Learn to use a computer. Go trick or treating. Redecorate your bedroom. Hold a fish. Take a walk under the stars. Watch fireflies. Get a foot massage. Soak your feet in warm water. Rub warm oil on your feet. Sit in a cathedral or synagogue and meditate. Read poetry. Write poetry. Refinish a table. Go to the opera. Go to a fashion show. Wear earplugs. Play soft music. Learn to chant. Sit by the ocean. Play a tape of a waterfall or the ocean. Pray. Read the Serenity Prayer. Write a prayer. Go on a spiritual retreat. Write down your dreams. Write a children's story. Visit a sick friend. Visit an elderly friend. Write a letter to a shut-in. Get acquainted with your neighbor. Volunteer at a hospital, nursing home, or homeless shelter. Take a gift to a shut-in. Collect money for the American Cancer Society. Watch the sun rise. Watch the sun set. Listen to the silence. Go sailing. Go down a water slide. Go to a baseball game. Ride a roller coaster. Go surfing. Watch a Marx Brothers video. Ride a jet ski. Make a model airplane. Catch a butterfly.

Exercise

Using the list above for ideas, and thinking of other possibilities that are right for you, make a list of activities that will decrease your risk of overeating rather than increasing it. Put a copy on your refrigerator.

LEARN SOMETHING NEW

Tears gathered in Bonnie's eyes as she looked at Joyce, who sat across the table from her. "What's the use of going on with this?" she asked, but it wasn't really a question. "The doctor says complications from my diabetes will shorten my life if I don't take care of myself. But I don't care if I die young. What do I have to

live for, anyway?" Bonnie wasn't considering suicide,
but facing life without eating for comfort didn't make
living for thirty-five more years seem very desirable.
It had been a miserable day at work. She'd had a dis-
agreement with her boss and there had been tension between
her and a coworker. She had been thinking about
going to the All-You-Can-Eat Food Barn for lunch—
and about what she would have there—when Joyce called:
"I've been thinking about you and wondered if you would
like to have lunch with me." Unable to think of a
reason not to go, Bonnie had said all right. But Joyce
was a friend from OA, so Bonnie knew they wouldn't
go to the All-You-Can-Eat Food Barn.

As they finished eating, Bonnie was unable to hold
back the tears and the anguish she was feeling. Taking her hand, Joyce asked a question that got Bonnie's
attention: "Is there anything you would like to do that
would light up your life?"

Putting food from her mind, Bonnie pondered the
question. After a while she answered, "Yes, I have always
wanted to learn to use a computer."

"Why not start today?" was Joyce's immediate response. Bonnie couldn't think of any reason why not.
So after work they met at the computer store, where
Bonnie purchased some basic computer equipment. (She
realized she could pay for it with money she would
save from her food budget by eliminating binge
items.)

That was five years ago. Getting a computer opened
up a whole new world for Bonnie. She not only has
learned to operate one, she has learned some pro-
gramming skills, uses a computer at work, and has developed a hobby that is both fun and challenging.

Is there something new you want to try? Something you have never done before? Be creative. Try painting, writing, dancing, working on the car, crocheting, playing an instrument. Who knows what skills you may develop or what door to creativity you may open.

C.D.: At one point I was feeling very discouraged. I wasn't back into old eating behaviors, but I knew I was close. I spent a lot of time alone. I was alienated from my family and I didn't have the energy to call a friend. One evening the thought came to me: *I don't have to feel this way. I can choose. I can do something different.* The first thing I did was go to my doctor to make sure there was nothing physically wrong that was draining me of energy. He said I was all right but suggested I take an amino acid/vitamin supplement. I did that and felt some immediate relief. Then I asked myself what else I could do. I decided to sign up for a sculpture class. What a difference that has made. It has really worked for me. The amino acid supplements have helped me, too. But the sculpturing has taught me something important about myself: I have creative energy and I need to keep something creative going in my life. When I do, I don't need to eat to feel satisfied.

KEEP A JOURNAL

A journal can be used as a tool for looking inside ourselves and expressing our feelings. Write down feelings, things about daily life, hopes and dreams. This is an outlet when we are angry, worried, or sad; a way to look at our fears, a place to be totally honest with ourselves. Consider your journal your private property so you can say anything you want. Keeping a journal gets feelings out in a way that harms no one.

One night I awoke with a hot iron poker in my middle. I made my way to my little meditation corner, pulled out my journal, got a box of tissues, and submerged into my pain. Tears flowed along with the words I wrote. I waded through self-pity, anger, hatred, hurt, pessimism, despair, grief, failure, fear, and resentment. Many of these feelings had been buried for years. At one point I wrote: "This is what lack of discipline, lack of dependence on God, lack of faith and hope feel like. Right now at 3:00 A.M. on July 2, 1989, I choose the opposite. Self-pity goes nowhere but down. I can be miserable and drag the rest of my family down into the pit of despair with me. I have that power . . . or I can choose to let go and accept God's light of peace and hope, and venture into the unknown. I can be pessimistic, sour, angry; or I can be optimistic, joyful, excited. I can hate or I can love . . . love hurts; but it also heals, and healing is what I need. Eating out of control will only add to my self-hatred. I have work to do, important work." Larrene Hagaman[3]

If you have never kept a journal and don't know how to start, you can experiment with this basic structure. Write at least one sentence about each of four areas. Describe how your body feels, what your physical sensations are. Describe the thoughts you have had during the day, messages you have given yourself, or insights you have had. Describe your feelings, positive or negative, and how your feelings have changed throughout the day. Describe your spiritual state, whether you feel open or closed spiritually, and how that state is changing.

MOURN YOUR LOSSES

Part of adjusting to the reality of having the weight spiraling syndrome is acknowledging that there are losses connected with our situation and allowing ourselves to mourn. Our feelings of deprivation as we cope with our weight spiraling problem are real; there *are* things we are deprived of. Mourning is part of adapting to loss. The process allows us to accept what we can't change and frees us to focus on what we can do something about.

It is sometimes helpful to think of grieving as something we do rather than something that happens to us or that we passively experience. Then we need not think of ourselves as victims; we are participants in a normal experience that builds courage and facilitates serenity. In the book *Grief Counseling and Grief Therapy: A Handbook for the Mental Health Practitioner*,[4] the author, William Warden, sets forth the "tasks" of mourning as follows: (1) *accepting the reality of the loss*, (2) *experiencing the pain of loss*, (3) *adjusting to life without what we have lost*, and (4) *withdrawing emotional energy and reinvesting in something new*. We will describe each task with our own comments, applied to the losses experienced by those recovering from the weight spiraling syndrome. The tasks are intended to be done as we are ready, not all at once or within a specified length of time.

Task One: Accepting the Reality of the Loss

Until we count our losses, we can't fully understand why we are in so much pain. But first, we must give up the pretense that loss doesn't hurt. Accepting the reality of our loss is part of the new life we have chosen. We are betting that the new life is better than what we are giving up. In order to accept the truth of that, we must acknowledge what we are giving up. Some of the more apparent losses connected with recovery are the things we can no longer eat, the places where we will no longer be comfortable, the comfort derived from eating certain foods, the rituals we'd established around eating those foods. It is all right to talk about the losses, to say "There are some losses here for me and it hurts to give them up."

Exercise

Any change brings some loss. List the changes you are experiencing or believe you will experience as a result of beginning recovery. What are the losses that accompany each of these changes?

Task Two: Experiencing the Pain of the Loss.

There is no way around, over, or under the pain. We have to walk through it. Instead of looking for ways to make the pain go away, we need to acknowledge that we have lost our pain controller (eating) and allow ourselves to experience the pain. Our society teaches us to see pain as proof that there is a problem and therefore something to get rid of. Often, though, pain is not a sign of a problem but a normal part of life.

In order to accomplish this task of the mourning process, we have to let the pain be there. We may think that if we don't do something to make it go away, it will always be there, but that is not true. *Much of pain is resistance.* When we stop resisting and let it happen, we are able to move through it.

Exercise

As you listed the losses connected with recovery, did you notice any signs of sadness? A lump in your throat? Tears? Heaviness in your chest? What loss hurts most to give up? Write a letter to that loss. Thank it for what it has done for you and say why it hurts to give it up. Tell it you don't need it anymore and say goodbye.

Task Three: Adjusting to Life
Without What We Have Lost.

For us, developing skills to live without the thing we have lost means adjusting to our self-care plan, learning to read labels when we shop, learning how to determine what we can order in restaurants, learning to make meal plans, developing our exercise program. This gets easier as we do it, but it takes time. It takes energy and effort to make the adjustment, and for a while it is the focus of much of our activity and our thought. We need to pace ourselves in order to deal with the particulars of reordering our perspective, our life. We need to be good to ourselves and remember to take one day at a time.

Exercise

Divide a page of your notebook into three columns. Label one "Small Suffering," the next "Moderate Suffering," and the third "Big Suffering." Under each heading list adjustments you are making, according to the level of pain connected with them. Then list actions appropriate for each level that will ease your stress and make adjustment easier.

Task Four: Withdraw
Emotional Energy and Reinvest in Something New.

This is the time to detach from what we have lost and attach to something new. Reinvesting isn't about preventing ourselves from going back to our old behaviors, it is about becoming fully involved in new ones. It is about finding a joyful way to live in the present. Now is a time for turning our experience into an opportunity that will stretch us. This reorienting of our lives is an important part of the mourning process and of our recovery. Until we have done this, we have not really given up our loss and will find ourselves still wanting it back.

Exercise

What new activity would you like to become involved in? List a new goal for yourself that will stretch you and enrich your life. Dream a little. See yourself as you would like to be six months from now. What are you doing? Remember, this is a goal for yourself, not for someone else. What is one step you can take right away toward reaching your goal? When you have taken that step, look at your goal again and figure out what step to take next; repeat that procedure until you have accomplished your goal.

Acceptance comes from completing the tasks of mourning. Completion takes time. Time heals, but healing is not just something we wait out. We participate in the process as we complete the tasks.

SEEK SPIRITUAL NURSING

Sometimes when we feel out of harmony with life what we need most is a spiritual lift. Try daily prayer and meditation, perhaps a quiet time each morning when you read something that you feel you might find spiritually uplifting. Have you ever been on a spiritual retreat? Try it. What is spiritually uplifting for you? It doesn't have to be "quiet time." Listen for what *your* spirit tells you.

C.J.: When I was at the lowest point in my recovery, I felt spiritually empty. A friend suggested that I spend more time in prayer and meditation, but that was the last thing I wanted to do. She said, "When you feel least like praying, that is the time when you need it most." That got my attention. I thought, if that is true, I really need it now. She was going on a spiritual retreat and suggested that I go along, so I did. We went to a beautiful retreat center in a quiet and lovely place. I had time to be alone, to enjoy nature, to read inspiring material, to think, and to make contact with my higher power. I came back spiritually renewed and feeling in touch with a spiritual source of power that I had not had available to me before.

When we recognize that we are making risky choices and want to interrupt that regressive process, we are better able to do it if we have made plans for this possibility before it happens. We are not thinking clearly when we're in so much pain; we might not be able to figure out what needs to be done. By devising and writing down plans while we're on track, we are more apt to use them when we need them. What will you do for safe pain relief when you recognize that you are making choices that put you on the edge of the cliff?

Exercise

Label a page in your notebook "My Plans for Making Safer Choices" and complete these sentences:

Three risky choices I make when I need pain relief are . . .

Some safer choices for pain relief that I would enjoy are . . .

People who will help me choose safe pain relief when I am making risky choices are . . .

Chapter 10

Resolving Conflict

*As Celia pondered her reflection in the full-length mirror,
she became more and more upset with what she saw.
Why were the last ten pounds coming off so slowly?
She would never lose them. She felt so "stuck." She couldn't
believe that when she weighed in at her weight loss meeting
last night she had lost only a quarter of a pound.
She remembered how everyone cheered for Steve when
he announced he had lost five pounds. Men lose easier,
Celia thought, and that's not fair.*

*Already feeling overwhelmed by the unfairness of
her lot in life, Celia walked into the kitchen, to see
Tim sitting there drinking coffee and eating a donut.
She couldn't believe how much she begrudged him that
donut. "Why do you eat donuts when you know I
can't?" she asked accusingly, picking up the bagel
with low-fat cream cheese that he had readied for her.
As she walked out the door she heard Tim say, "Well,
thank you, too." Resentment kept her from responding.*

*The drive to the office was irritating. It seemed that
everyone on the road had it in for her. No one would*

*let her merge as she moved onto the freeway. She
seemed to hit every red light, and then she thought
she would never find a parking place. She ignored
her secretary as she entered the office, leaving looks of
irritation in her wake.*

    *Even the office coffee tasted terrible. "Whoever
made this coffee never drinks it!" she muttered. As
Celia adjusted her face before her first meeting of the
day, she was alarmed at what she saw. She was scowling.
Her face was frozen in stress and pain. As she thought
back on her morning, she was unable to understand
why she had carried that resentment with her. Why do
I do this to myself and the people around me? she wondered.
I really am happy with the changes I'm making in
my life. Or am I? I don't understand what I am feeling.*

Conflict is the natural outcome of our feeling disillusioned
and discouraged. The embers of internal conflict—shame
and poor self-image—fan the fires of conflict in general. Overwhelmed by our inability to do anything positive about our
condition, we extend the conflict into the external arena. At
least the external conflict makes some sense to us and the external stress feels like justification of our internal stress. It is
natural to be angry when we feel powerless to change anything. We are angry because life isn't fair, and we take it out
on ourselves and others. We are in conflict with ourselves,
others, and the world.

Conflict with Ourselves

When we are in conflict with ourselves, one part of us wants
to recover even as another part wants relief from recovery.

One part believes we are capable of recovery, another believes we can't do it. One minute we feel hopeful, the next we are convinced there is no hope. One part of us is proud of how well we have done, another is terrified we can't keep doing it. The battle goes on.

In spite of the self-defeating messages we give ourselves, there is a little voice of courage inside that will not quit, that keeps us hanging on despite the pain. This part of us knows that we don't lack willpower, that we do care about our health, that we really want something better, that we are worth it. Regression is not what we want. We are in this place of despair not because we want to be, but because we don't know how not to be. This little voice reminds us that our pain is there because we do care, because we don't want to give up, because we do have willpower. Then the voice of pain speaks to us and tells us nothing is worth this, reminds us that pain relief is just a bite away.

Exercise

When you are feeling powerless to change your life, what are the conflicts you are at risk of having with yourself? Complete this sentence five ways:

When I am in conflict with myself, the voice of despair says . . . while the voice of hope says . . .

Conflict with Others

Feeling defeated and overwhelmed produces anger and frustration. It is normal to look for something or someone outside ourselves to blame. We naturally, but unconsciously, seek out justifiable external reasons for our internal conflict. Absolute self-talk escalates into blaming self-talk. No one *ever*. They *don't.* He *never.* She *always.* They *never give me the support I need.* They *are always looking for my faults.* They *always look for what I do wrong.* They *never give me credit for what I do right.* *No one* understands.

Conflicts naturally occur with those people, situations, and things that we blame. We may get irritable with our children and frustrated with coworkers, and we may snap at a spouse. Our defense system is looking diligently for a scapegoat, a target. Heredity has done this to us. Other people are at fault. Our parents are to blame. Society is responsible. The anger inside causes us to develop conflicts outside.

Exercise

When you are feeling powerless to change your life, what are the conflicts you are at risk of having with others? Complete each of these sentences five ways:

A person with whom I am at risk of having conflict is . . .

Conflicts I am at risk of having with them are . . .

Conflict with the Environment

It is normal to be angry when we feel deprived, overwhelmed, and trapped. We are in conflict with ourselves and others. We feel out of harmony with everything, inanimate objects as well as people and pets. We are out of step with the world. Sometimes when we are in this state, we feel like the person who gave this account, which actually appeared in a company accident report:

When I got to the building I found that the hurricane had knocked off some bricks around the top. So I rigged up a beam with a pulley at the top of the building and hoisted up a couple of barrels full of bricks. When I had fixed the damaged area, there were a lot of bricks left over. Then I went to the bottom and began releasing the line. Unfortunately, the barrel of bricks was much heavier than I was—and before I knew what was happening the barrel started coming down, jerking me up.

I decided to hang on since I was too far off the ground by then to jump, and halfway up I met the barrel of bricks coming down fast. I received a hard blow on my shoulder. I then continued to the top, banging my head against the beam and getting my fingers pinched and jammed in the pulley. When the barrel hit the ground hard, it burst its bottom, allowing the bricks to spill out.

I was now heavier than the barrel. So I started down again at high speed. Halfway down I met the barrel coming up fast and received severe injuries to my shins. When I hit the ground, I landed on the pile of spilled bricks, getting several painful cuts and deep bruises. At this point I must have lost my presence of mind, because I let go of my grip on the line. The barrel came down fast—giving me another blow on my head and putting me in the hospital. I respectfully request sick leave.

Isn't it amazing how everything seems to go wrong for us, one brick after another? In our particular topsy-turvy state, we're easily angered by life in general. When we are feeling like this, our conflicts are usually not focused directly on what is really frustrating us. We feel a victim of everything. Our self-talk is angry and blaming. *I'm fat and I'm damn mad about it. Nothing will ever change and it's not fair. No matter how hard I try, nothing works out.* Our self-talk is so loud in our head that we think other people should be able to hear it, and we are angry because they ignore it and don't seem to care. They may even make light of it. We don't ask for what we need; we think others should know. And we are angry because they don't. When we're in this state, no wonder we have a hard time finding an appropriate reaction to our own anger and frustration.

Exercise

When you are feeling powerless to change your situation, with what do you wage war? Complete the following sentence seven ways:

When I am in conflict, I wage war with . . .

Suggestions for Resolving Conflicts

At this stage in the regression we are locked into self-focus. We can't see anything except our own pain. Getting out of conflictual living requires a change of focus. Anger and conflict call for *reconciliation*—restoring harmony by making peace with ourselves, others, and the world. Here are some guidelines for restoring peace and harmony.

GET AWAY FROM WHAT IS CREATING THE CONFLICT

When we feel bound up in conflict, finding peace and harmony doesn't seem like an option. The first thing to do is back off. In order to think clearly enough to identify what is really going on, it is usually helpful to separate ourselves totally from a situation creating conflict, to take a break and get away to clear our thoughts. This may mean going away for the weekend; or it may mean retreating into the bathroom, shutting the door, and being alone for a few minutes. We need to be quiet, to allow a settling down of whatever conflict threatens to overwhelm us.

Exercise

List some ways you can remove yourself when conflict is interfering with your ability to think clearly.

REFOCUS

Anger itself is not necessarily bad. But anger alone is not going to make anything better. How we react when we are angry determines whether the anger becomes helpful or harmful. Sometimes an active response is appropriate. It may be necessary to enable us to protect ourselves or someone else. Our anger can motivate us to take action; it can motivate us to make needed changes.

> *Without our anger we would indeed be continually stepped*
> *on, until we were totally squashed and exterminated.*
>
> M. Scott Peck[1]

Unresolved anger keeps us living in conflict. Recognize and listen to the anger. See what it is pointing to, see what it tells you. Then take appropriate action. Very often what we think is the problem is not really the problem. Step out of the situation. *Make a distinction between what is irritating you and what you are really angry about.* Are you really angry about the waiter failing to bring your water? Or is it because life is not fair? With whom are you angry? Fate? Your parents? God? People who don't have to be careful about what they eat? People who bug you about what you eat and whether you have exercised? Yourself, for all the times you have lost weight and then regained it so you have to do it again?

Once we are able to recognize what our conflict is really

about, what do we do about it? How do we bring peace and harmony back into our lives? How do we reconcile with the waiter, the people who bug us, ourselves, God, the dog, and the coffee pot?

When we are able to take our focus off ourselves and our pain, life sometimes looks very different. Our recognizing the importance of self-care need not lock us into a focus on self. Long-term self-focus keeps us locked in conflict.

Getting out of ourselves and trying to look at a situation from another's viewpoint can reveal a very different picture. The fact that the waiter didn't bring the water probably has nothing at all to do with us. Perhaps he is overworked or in a personal crisis. Perhaps he needs a kind word from someone as much as or more than we do.

The two of us, Merlene and David, had been out shopping and were late having lunch. I, David, was getting quite hungry. (I get irritable when I am hungry.) We decided to stop at a local shop for sustenance. The thought of their excellent oatmeal muffins and cold milk was running through my brain as I entered the store. (You need to know that there are some foods I believe I cannot eat without milk—cookies, peanut butter and jelly sandwiches. And muffins.) I ordered the muffin, but my anticipation was cut short when the woman said they were out of milk. Out of milk! How in the world could anybody who sells muffins be out of milk? "Then," I said huffily, "I won't get anything." Grunting and snarling, I started to leave, when I realized that Merlene was ordering a muffin. The woman seemed embarrassed and said something about not having milk because they were going out of business. I didn't think even that was an acceptable excuse for being out of milk. I just mumbled something and continued my sulking. But as I stood back and waited for Merlene, I was able to detach somewhat from my disappointment. I noticed the rather

*anxious look of the woman, and I asked her when they were clos-
ing down. The next thing I knew, I was talking with her about her
fears of getting another job and became more concerned with her
struggle than about my petty irritation over milk. As my focus
changed from myself to her, it occurred to me that I could easily
take some muffins home, where I had milk. By the time we left,
we were all chatting and feeling some kinship that never would
have developed had I not been able to step out of my self-focus.*

When we can refocus and look beyond ourselves, we may find
ourselves so caught up in concerns outside our own that the
things that have been irritating us become much less significant. As we refocus, many situations may look different. We
may realize that the people who bug us about our self-care
love us and want very much for us to be healthy and well. To
the extent that we can adopt another point of view, we become more open to enlightenment, and we may see a picture
of ourselves that is very different from the one that's been
lodged in our own mind's eye.

As we refocus, we may become aware that we need to take
steps to reconcile with someone. Do we need to say I'm sorry?
Do we need to make amends to someone? Do we need to
make peace with ourselves? Do we need to forgive ourselves?
Do we need to reconcile ourselves with our environment? Do
we need to laugh at ourselves?

Exercise

Close your eyes and visualize a peaceful scene, such as a
green meadow with a clear stream running through. Put
yourself in this scene and feel the peacefulness. Now imagine you are joined in this peaceful place by someone with
whom you have recently had an unpleasant encounter. (The

encounter may have taken place only in your own mind.)
Tell this person how you felt during the encounter, and listen as he or she tells you his or her perspective of the same
experience. For example, Tim might tell Celia that he had
fixed that bagel for her because he knew she was running
late and because he knew how important breakfast was for
her self-care. He might add how discounted he felt when her
only words to him were words of criticism. After you listen
to what the person who has joined you has to say, tell him
or her anything you would like as words of reconciliation.

RECONCILE WITH OTHERS

Reconciliation doesn't mean erasing differences. It means making peace with them. It means valuing and respecting differences. Harmony not only allows for differences; it requires
them. When an orchestra plays in harmony, its musicians don't
all play the same note at the same time. Rather, they act in-
terdependently and individually to produce music in which
variety and contrast are blended into a harmonious whole.
Likewise, as individuals we vary in our thinking, our skills and
abilities, our points of view, and our values, and harmonious
living requires that we respect and accept those differences.

When we differ it is usually not that one of us is right and
the other wrong. In most cases, our contentions arise from
our different perspectives and neither viewpoint is entirely
"right" or "wrong." Reconciliation requires a refocusing in order to see what the other sees. Sharing differing, even oppos-
ing, insights helps us grow. We cannot be reconciled until we
can communicate, share, and listen. Otherwise, we become so
convinced that our own individual opinions are infallible that
we refuse to participate in mutually supportive relationships.

Someone once said, *"Those who think they know it all upset
those of us who do."* It is normal and can be very good to make

value judgments about what is right or wrong or what is better than something else; we have to do that to survive. The problem arises when we believe we are capable of certifying absolute truth. *Conflict occurs when we stop looking for the truth and start guarding it.*

Reconciliation may mean recognizing that we have been hurt by another's behavior and taking appropriate action to negotiate, forgive, or detach. *Negotiating* means working with another to resolve the conflict. *Forgiving* allows us to leave the conflict behind us. That means forgiving ourselves as well as others. *Detaching*—perhaps permanently—from a situation or relationship that we cannot change allows us to focus on our own behavior and what we can change in ourselves. Reconciliation may require that we look at how we have hurt someone and that we make amends for the hurt.

Negotiating

Winning every argument means we associate only with losers. When being right is more important to us than giving a little in a relationship, we most often end up the losers. Having the last word may, instead of settling something, intensify the problem. Here's a story by Frank Koch, taken from *In the Eye of the Storm*, that illustrates that point.

> Two battleships assigned to the training squadron had been at sea on maneuvers in heavy weather for several days. I was serving on the lead battleship and was on watch on the bridge as night fell. The visibility was poor with patch fog, so the captain remained on the bridge keeping an eye on all activities.
>
> Shortly after dark, the lookout on the wing reported, "Light, bearing on the starboard bow."
>
> "Is it steady or moving astern?" the captain called out.

The lookout replied, "Steady, Captain," which meant we were on a dangerous collision course with that ship.

The captain then called to the signalman, "Signal that ship: 'We are on a collision course, advise you change course twenty degrees'."

Back came the signal, "Advisable for you to change course twenty degrees."

The captain said, "Send: 'I'm a captain, change course twenty degrees'."

"I'm a seaman second-class," came the reply. "You had better change course twenty degrees."

By that time the captain was furious. He spat out, "Send: I'm a battleship. Change course twenty degrees."

Back came the flashing light. "I'm a lighthouse."

We changed course.[2]

Negotiation usually includes asking for what we need, listening to what someone else needs, and compromising so that each person is a winner. Building healthy relationships does not include manipulation. It involves being direct about what we need, being nonjudgmental and open to the needs of another, and being willing to cooperate as much as possible to meet the needs of everyone involved.

In discussing with another what we each need, we need not make the other person wrong; there may not be a wrong. Or if there is, it may not be all on one side. We can have an opinion without being judgmental toward another's opinion.

Once needs are openly expressed, each person should state honestly what he or she is willing or able to do to meet the needs of the other. Neither is obligated to give all that the other asks. Asking is not demanding. It is not a manipulation to push someone into doing what we want. As each gives the other the right to ask, each must give the other the right to refuse. Usually the most satisfactory resolution includes a compromise, each giving something mutually beneficial.

Exercise

Think about the situation between Celia and Tim in the story at the beginning of this chapter. Think of some ways Celia might have told Tim about her need to avoid seeing and smelling donuts before she has had her breakfast. Think of some ways that Tim might explain to Celia that he does not choose to give up everything that she excludes from her food plan. Then think of some compromises that can be made by each of them so neither is a loser.

Now think of a situation in which there is a conflict between your needs and those of someone you care about. Imagine yourself telling that person what you need and listening to what he or she needs. Imagine yourself saying, "Is there a way we can work this out?" Can you think of ways to compromise?

Forgiving

It is self-defeating to punish ourselves for what someone else has done. That is what happens when we cannot forgive what someone has done to hurt us. We let their past behavior destroy our present.

Forgiving frees us to change the hurt we have experienced into growth. It frees us from our resentments, our hurts, and our guilt. Forgiving goes beyond pardoning offenses. It is giving up judging and condemning another.

Forgiving means accepting. It means accepting the imperfections of others, allowing them to be human, as we allow ourselves to be. It means not seeing mistakes as failures. Acceptance of humanness allows us to learn from mistakes, whether they are ours or someone else's.

Forgiving also involves accepting differences. We forgive others for not being like us, for not thinking like us, for not behaving as we do. We recognize that we may be different one from another, but we are equally of worth.

When we are able to accept ourselves as we are, we become able to forgive. When we release ourselves from the need to be flawless, we can release others, too. The choice to forgive brings healing to the forgiver and the forgiven. Forgiving releases us to love and to be loved.

Exercise

Think of an experience in which someone has hurt you. When you are ready to let this situation go, imagine yourself standing by a moving stream talking to the person you want to forgive. Hold the hurt in your hand and show it to this person. Say you have carried the burden of this hurt so long that it is affecting your life in the present and you want to be free of it. Put the hurt in the stream and watch it drift away. Feel yourself free of this burden and see the other person forgiven.

Some of us may need to forgive our higher power. If you are angry about the unfairness of your lot in life, who do you blame? When we can't find a person or object to blame, we sometimes become angry with fate or our higher power for putting us into this position. Freeing ourselves from the burden of resentment includes forgiving a power outside ourselves.

Detaching

Sometimes we encounter situations in which someone else does not wish to hear what we need, does not ask us for what they need, and is unwilling to compromise or negotiate. In order to protect ourselves and our recovery, we may need to emotionally or physically detach from such people and allow them to have as little influence on us as possible.

This does not mean we stop caring for these people or that we refuse to forgive them. We accept their inability or unwillingness to give what we need. They may be under no obligation at all to support us. We allow them their choice, but we can also choose how we will respond. Our recovery is not dependent on what they do or do not do, nor is our serenity or peace of mind. If our serenity depends on someone else, we will never have any.

When we are unable to detach emotionally from people who do not care about us—or from people who do not value what is of worth to us or from people who do not choose to be cooperative or supportive of us—we tend to become defensive. We do not feel safe. For ongoing recovery we need people with whom we feel safe, and we may need to distance ourselves from those with whom we do not.

Toni and Linda had been friends for a long time. Once a week they got together to do something special. This frequently included eating, often getting some special treat, such as a hot fudge sundae. When Toni's self-care plan no longer included rich desserts, she stopped ordering hot fudge sundaes.

Linda was not comfortable with this change in Toni. She frequently said, "I don't understand why you can't have a sundae just this once." At first, Toni told herself that Linda's friendship was important to her and that she wanted Linda to be comfortable. Then she realized that if she acted on this belief she would be sacrificing her self-care to make Linda happy.

> *Toni had a talk with Linda and explained how hard*
> *it was when Linda encouraged her to eat rich desserts.*
> *Linda was offended and said, "Well, I guess we can't*
> *go out to eat together anymore if I can't be myself."*
> *Now Toni and Linda sometimes go shopping or to a movie,*
> *but they don't go out to eat. They are still friends. But*
> *Toni does not feel the need to make Linda comfortable*
> *and does not worry about Linda's opinion regarding*
> *hot fudge sundaes.*

We do not need approval or acceptance from everyone. Our recovery is dependent on *us*. When we give others the power to determine what we do, think, or feel, we give away our power to determine the course of our own lives and our recovery.

Exercise

Write a letter to someone with whom you want to mend a relationship. Express feelings about the painful situation and apologize for anything you have done to contribute to it. Describe what you need from this person and express your willingness to listen to what he or she needs from you. State your desire to work in a mutually beneficial way to mend the relationship. Keep the letter for a few days. Reread it; and if you think it can help improve the situation, give it to the person. If not, throw it away. Even if you choose not to give the letter to this person, maybe the exercise will help you figure out what you want to say should you choose to discuss the matter with this person at a later time.

MAKING AMENDS

Do you need to make amends to someone? Steps Eight and Nine of the Twelve Steps used by Overeaters Anonymous suggest that we make a list of all the people we have harmed, and make direct amends whenever possible (except when to do so would injure them or others). An important aspect of this process is that we are willing to take full responsibility for our actions, not excusing ourselves or blaming others. Taking these steps allows us to look directly at our own behavior and take action to restore harmony in our relationships. Making amends is more than saying we are sorry. It is taking action to make up for the harm done.

Exercise

Are you willing to make amends? If so, make a list of the people you have harmed. How were they harmed? What action could be taken to make amends?

These steps can get us off the shame hook. They allow us to take action to remove any shame that is a consequence of actions we have taken that have been harmful to others or to ourselves. Making amends means taking direct action whenever we can, going to people we have harmed and telling them how we believe our behavior has hurt them, telling them we regret our actions and stating what we are willing to do to make restitution. This does not mean that others must accept our amends or forgive us.

Do all you can to correct the wrong and forgive yourself, regardless of the response from others. You will probably find that most people will appreciate your efforts.

S.S.: My weight spiraling was of great concern to my caring family. During periods when I ate almost nothing, my husband and daughters worried that I might be seriously damaging my body from malnutrition. During times when I ate everything in sight, they worried that I would resort to purging with laxatives, even after I promised them never to do that again. A year into my recovery, feeling remorse for hurting my family, I asked my teenage daughter how I could make amends for the pain I had caused her. Her answer touched me deeply: "Mom, you have made amends to us by making amends to yourself. When I see you eating right and taking good care of yourself, I am so relieved and happy I don't need anything more."

Don't forget to make amends to yourself. You have probably hurt yourself more than you've hurt anyone else. Give yourself permission to forgive yourself and to treat yourself better in the future. If you can forgive yourself for not being perfect, it will be easier to forgive others. And when you treat yourself better, you may find that, at the same time, you are making amends to someone who loves you.

Exercise

List ways you have harmed yourself and ways you can make amends for those hurts. Are you willing to forgive yourself and treat yourself better in the future?

These steps, very sensibly, draw a line on actions that might relieve our own guilt but that could hurt others in the process. We cannot correct one hurt with another. When we cannot openly make amends because others might be harmed, we may be able to let them know by our actions that we are sorry. Perhaps we can do something quietly that touches their lives. There are some things for which we can never make amends, some people we can never repay. Maybe all we can do is say we are sorry. Apologies, as well as actions, can mend relationships.

NURTURE HEALTHY RELATIONSHIPS

Sometimes reconciliation requires more than restitution, an apology, or forgiveness. Some relationships need to be nurtured over time; they require an investment of energy. We may want to learn better or healthier ways of communicating with another person. We may need to learn to be more open and sensitive to someone else's needs and concerns. It may be time to stop protecting ourselves from exposure and allow others to know us as we are—with our imperfections and limitations.

We may need to learn that we can have relationships in which there is mutuality. The view that some people must be weak and dependent in order for others to be strong means that some are not free to be strong and others are not free to be weak. Having both strengths and weaknesses is part of being human, and healthy relationships allow the parties the freedom to be fully human.

Nor do most situations call for one person to be wrong in order for another to be right or for one to lose in order for another to win. Conflict is a normal part of life. It indicates that a problem needs to be solved, not necessarily that a battle needs to be fought. Battles have losers and winners; problems have solutions.

Exercise

List three relationships that are important to you. In what ways is each mutually supportive? In what ways is it not? What can you do and what are you willing to do to put more mutual support into each of these relationships?

RECONCILE WITH THINGS AS THEY ARE

We cannot always resolve the conflicts between the way things are and the way we want them to be, but we can re-orient life to what is. Maybe we can't change things, but we can learn to appreciate them as they are. You don't have a perfect figure even though you have lost weight? Neither do a lot of people who have never been overweight. Jicama doesn't taste like potato chips? No, but it tastes like jicama. Frozen sugar-free yogurt doesn't taste like ice cream? No, but it tastes like frozen yogurt.

We sustain a loss when we have a condition that limits how we would live. No one can change that. There are losses for us, but we can look beyond them and recognize the potential gain. Oriental philosophy contends that in every loss there is a gain and in every gain a loss. It is important to acknowledge the losses, but we can focus on the losses and never see the gains. In *The Physician Within*, Catherine Feste tells about learning that she had diabetes:

> I was ten years old when I got diabetes. Daddy had died suddenly of a heart attack ten months before I was diagnosed. When my mother came into my hospital room the doctor had just told me that I had diabetes. I asked her, "What does it mean?" With a big smile on her face my magnificent mother said, "Why, it means that you're going to learn so much about good nutrition. You're going to live such a healthy life that our whole family will benefit. And you will always be a stronger, more disciplined person because you have diabetes."[3]

We don't have a perfect world, and if we are angry about that, we are always going to be angry. Sometimes a shoelace is going to break. Sometimes the money machine at the bank is not going to work. Sometimes we are going to be put on hold on a long-distance call or be asked to punch in our social security number, date of birth, and mother's phone number before we get to talk to the person we are calling. We can choose to be at peace in an imperfect world, or not. Either way it will still be an imperfect world. As C. S. Lewis said, "We have to take reality as it comes to us; there is no good jabbering about what it ought to be like or what we should have expected it to be like."

The world today is fast paced, noisy, and stressful. Where is the peace? We have to create it. Do you need quiet? Find a park or go for a drive in the country. Listen to music. Go to an art gallery. Read a relaxing book. Do you need to be soothed? Talk to a friend, cuddle a baby, ask for a hug, get a massage, sit in a hot tub. Do you need stimulation? Talk to a friend, go to an amusement park, read a stimulating book, go on a safari. It's an imperfect world, but it has a lot to offer. And we only have one life to live. How do you want to live it? In turmoil or in peace?

RECONCILE WITH YOURSELF

It is important to acknowledge the conflict we are in but also to acknowledge our progress, to recognize the strength we have that has kept us from quitting before now. Letting up on ourselves is a good idea. As long as we are in raging conflict with ourselves, we will not be able to see that we do have many options. In order to see them, we need some peace and it must start within.

When Celia saw her scowling face in the mirror, she realized that most of the conflict she was experiencing was coming from within. "Nothing that is happening to me is as bad as what I am doing to myself," she said

out loud. *"My real conflict is with me." She became aware
of the discouraging things she had been saying to herself.
She got out a piece of paper and wrote down some of
the reasons she was discouraged. Then she wrote
down reasons she had for being encouraged. Daily
self-care had become a habit. Her health had improved,
and she felt better about her appearance. Even if she
never lost any more weight, she was pleased with
what she had already lost. My life is better, she
thought. I like myself more than I ever have. "I think
I'll go ice skating on my lunch break," she said to her
surprised secretary on her way to her meeting.
"Would you like to go along?"*

Restoring harmony with ourselves requires that we listen to
the part of us that won't give up on ourselves, that part that
has been telling us all along that we are worthwhile and courageous. Listen to that voice of wisdom that knows you are capable, strong, and worth loving; that knows you are special
and unique; that knows you have gifts and abilities to offer
and the courage to use them; that knows you are of worth.

There is a line in the song "Where Is It Written," from the
movie *Yentl*, that goes, "Why have the wings unless you're
meant to fly?" Look carefully and you will find that you have
wings. Listen to the voice within that knows you can fly.
Learning to fly means removing the restrictions that keep us
on the ground, that limit full expression of the part of ourselves that believes we can fly. Role restrictions, habits, old expectations, faulty beliefs, and shame tell us that we can't. We
will be in conflict within ourselves until we listen to that part
of us that gives us the courage to fly.

Exercise

Close your eyes and affirm to yourself: *I am open to the good experiences I am bringing about in my life.* Then listen to the voice of courage inside you that is saying you can succeed.

To interrupt regression at the point of conflict, we need to find ways to make peace with ourselves, others, and the world. Look carefully at your own situation. What kind of plans do you need to make that will help you find peace when you are feeling irritable, defensive, and lonely?

Exercise

Label a page of your notebook "My Plans for Resolving Conflicts." Complete these sentences:

My three most common conflicts are . . .

When I become aware that I am experiencing conflicts, I will . . .

Something that might interfere with my taking this action is . . .

Skills I can begin working on that will help me resolve conflicts when my recovery is in trouble are . . .

Three people I can turn to when I become aware that conflicts are putting my recovery in jeopardy are . . .

Chapter 11

Empowered to Choose

People who have a history of weight spiraling have experienced failure after failure. After a time they tend to doubt their ability to change anything, and may especially doubt that they can bring about change that is positive and reward producing.

When we feel powerless to make an uncomfortable situation better, we feel locked into pain—trapped, overwhelmed, overpowered, and defeated. When you feel that way, think about this story taken from *Parables for Today*.

Harry Houdini, the famed escape artist from some years back, issued a challenge wherever he went. He could be locked in any jail cell in the country, he claimed, and set himself free in short order. Always he kept his promise, but one time something went wrong. Houdini entered the jail in his street clothes; the heavy, metal doors clanged shut behind him. He took from his belt a concealed piece of metal, strong and flexible. He set to work immediately, but something seemed to be unusual about this lock. For thirty minutes he worked and got nowhere. An hour passed, and still he had not opened the door. By now he was bathed in sweat and panting in exasperation, but he still could not pick the lock. Finally, after laboring for two hours, Harry Houdini collapsed in frustration and failure against the door he could not unlock. But when he fell against the door, it swung open. It had never been locked at all. But in his mind it was locked, and that was all it took to keep him from opening the door and walking out of the jail cell.[1]

Believing Nothing Can Be Changed

When we are unaware of effective ways to bring about change, often we will apply the same would-be cures over and over again—more intensely, more diligently. The more ineffective our actions, the harder we try, despite our growing despair. If you are trying to pound a nail with a marshmallow, it won't help to hit harder.

As we come to believe that nothing can be solved, we lose hope of anything's getting better. We begin to make "absolute" statements to ourselves and to others: There is no possibility of improvement in our condition, we say in so many words. A common statement that shuts out the possibility of change is, "That's just the way I am." Another is "That's just the way I was raised." These are ways of saying, "Don't expect anything different from me; I will always be like I am."

Exercise

List some "absolute" messages you sometimes give yourself that may be keeping you locked in a jail of present circumstance.

Grab Hold of Today,[2] a motivational film about the rewards of living courageously, shows an interesting experiment with a pike. The fish, surrounded by minnows, is in a large tank. Of course, he is eating them very rapidly. The experimenters take the minnows out of the tank, put them in a large jar, and place the jar in the tank. The pike can see the minnows but not the jar. When he strikes at the minnows he bumps into the jar. Again and again he tries, with the same results. Finally, he gives up and swims to the side of the tank. The minnows are then released, but the pike doesn't try to eat them. They swim all around him, but he makes no attempt to catch them. He finally starves to death because he doesn't know food is available.

Because the pike believes there isn't anything he can do to change his situation, he dies with options all around him. He doesn't see them. If he knew he had a choice, he would eat those minnows in a second. He doesn't know he has a choice, and he dies.

The result of *believing* we have no options is the same as having no options: We are powerless to change anything. We feel trapped, hopeless. Without hope there is no joy. Giving up the power to change is swallowing the key to happiness.

> *So long as a man imagines he cannot do something, so long as he is determined not to do it, then it is impossible for him to do it.*   Spinoza

Overwhelming Deprivation

If eating is the only way we know to relieve the pain of our situation and we are deprived of that option, we may be overwhelmed by feelings of deprivation. All around us we see others who are able to eat the things we can't or who are able to find pleasure in other ways that we feel are closed to us.

As Doris walked into the coffee room during her break at work, it hit her like a barrel of bricks falling from the roof. As she put it, "plateful of junk after plateful of junk after plateful of junk." Someone was celebrating and no one had told her about it. People in her office were always celebrating something—birthdays, engagements, promotions, graduations. "No one ever brings anything I can eat," she said to herself as she viewed the food layout. "No one is sensitive to my needs."

Suddenly she was paralyzed by an overwhelming sense of deprivation, consumed by the thought that she would never be able to eat any of these things again. This certainty and this "celebration" couldn't have come at a worse time. Her weight loss had stalled; for some time, she hadn't seen any rewards for her self-deprivation. She had made so many changes recently. She was tired from spending so much time and energy planning meals and preparing food.

Doris looked at the chocolate mud pie and thought, "I used to eat that without thinking." It was not doing without the mud pie that bothered her; it was realizing that she could not eat whatever she chose. She was aware that whatever she did today would be painful and a burden. If she ate her veggie sticks while the others ate rich desserts, she would feel deprived. If she ate what her colleagues did, she would feel bad about giving up. Was there no way out for her?

Immobilization

When we feel powerless to get out of our pain, our feelings of hopelessness drain us of energy and sometimes we find it difficult to put one foot in front of the other. The more hopeless we feel, the more immobilized we become.

> *God has given us two incredible things: absolutely awesome*
> *ability and freedom of choice. The tragedy is that, for the*
> *most part, many of us have refused them both.*   Anonymous

When we reject the gift of choice, we automatically reject the gift of ability. If we don't believe something can be done, we are not likely to attempt it. The belief that we *can't* restricts us. Believing we *can* empowers us. This is not just the power of positive thinking. If we believe something is possible, we will invest more energy in making it happen than we will if we really don't believe it can happen. We have more energy to invest. Hope is energizing. It reinspires confidence; it fires imagination and creativity.

The "victim" beliefs we have about ourselves restrict us. Believing that our problems are beyond solution, we attempt to avoid blame for them. Believing our problems can be solved, we attempt to solve them.

> *Most of us have become so accustomed to the results of*
> *powerlessness, to the stress we must deal with as a result*
> *of that definition, that we no longer recognize the amount*
> *of energy it takes to handle the behavior or the conditions*
> *that powerlessness produces.*   Linda Moore[3]

We do have choices, even when we don't know what they are. Feeling powerless is, after all, not the same as being powerless. We can step out of the narrow, limiting, dark perception of our having no choices and see a bigger, brighter picture.

Exercise

Try keeping a log of "victim" thoughts. Write down instances when powerless thoughts go through your mind, thoughts such as *Just my luck* or *I don't stand a chance*. See if there are any similarities in the situations in which you feel a victim. Ask yourself what skills you can develop to help you handle such situations better.

Suggestions for Gaining the Power to Choose

We gain more and more control over our lives as we identify our options and make choices. When we feel trapped and hopeless we can say to ourselves, "I feel as though I have no choices, but I know I do. So I need to find out what choices I have." Here are some guidelines for rekindling hope and recognizing the power to choose.

ACCEPT RESPONSIBILITY

Realizing that life is not fair is painful. When we feel trapped by circumstances that seem beyond our control, we need a target. Who has done this to us? God? Society? Skinny people? The media? Somehow in our pain, it is all of the above. Life is persecuting us.

There may be some losses for us in giving up being victims.

There are some payoffs in being powerless to change. Some of us get nurturing from being helpless; most of us do, to some extent. The pain of our situation allows us to nurture ourselves in certain ways because we "deserve" it. After all, look at what we have suffered. We may believe we would have to give up nurturing ourselves if it was no longer a reward for our suffering.

Exercise

Are there some payoffs for you in being powerless to change? What would you lose by giving those up? Complete the following sentence seven times (even if you don't believe you see yourself as a victim):

If I were to give up being a victim, . . .

Are people with a weight problem victims? Well, in a sense we are. We are victims of our physiology. We didn't choose our bodies. We do gain weight more easily than some other people. If we were born that way, it certainly isn't our fault. And even those things we have done to contribute to the problem (such as rapid weight loss diets) we did in a sincere attempt, however misguided, to improve ourselves. So we are victims of incorrect information as well as of heredity. We are also victims of public opinion and prejudice.

But because this condition is not our fault does not mean we are not responsible for the choices we make as a result of it. It may be that heredity, our families, and society have contributed to our situation. But regardless of all the contributing factors, we are the ones who have to do something about it. It is not our fault, but we can choose what we do about it.

I, Merlene, have a condition, called fibromyalgia, that causes me physical pain in varying degrees, depending to some extent on my activities. Lack of exercise, lack of rest, and excessive stress contribute to increased pain. It is difficult for me to acknowledge the role my behavior plays in how I feel. If I take the credit for getting better because of something I do, then the implication is that when I get worse it is because of something I don't do. That means it is my fault. I would rather believe that I am a victim, and powerless over my symptoms; then when I don't feel well, people might sympathize with me instead of saying, "Well, have you been taking care of yourself?" It really is not my fault that I have this condition. I did not choose it. If something I did caused it, I was not (and am not) aware of what that something was. Nevertheless, difficult though it is to admit, my choices do affect how I feel and I am responsible for those choices.

That a condition is not our fault does not absolve us from our responsibility to make choices concerning that condition. Some people suffer from depression, epilepsy, or chronic fatigue syndrome. Other people have diabetes, dyslexia, attention deficit disorder, or the aftereffects of polio. It is not their fault, but they are still responsible for the behaviors they choose. So are we.

Life is not a matter of holding good cards. It is playing a poor hand well.   Robert Louis Stevenson

Many people think that if they acknowledge that changing their lives is their own responsibility, they are accepting blame for their condition. They aren't. This issue is not a "fault" issue; it's a responsibility issue. Accepting responsibility is accepting power, power we had given away when we placed blame only outside ourselves. Accepting responsibility gets us unstuck by giving us the power to change.

Exercise

What can you gain by giving up being a victim? What is the payoff for accepting the responsibility to change? Complete the following sentence seven ways:

When I am ready to use the power that I already have, . . .

APPLY THE SERENITY PRAYER

Earlier we discussed the Serenity Prayer. It is an excellent guide to identifying our options and taking steps out of our helplessness. Think about the words:

God grant me serenity to accept the things I cannot change, courage to change the things I can, and wisdom to know the difference.

The first step in living by these powerful words is learning to distinguish between what we can change and what we can't. We are healthy in acknowledging that we are powerless over some things. If we do not acknowledge that, we can spend all our time and effort trying to change what we cannot change, and our lives become unmanageable.

The Wisdom to Know the Difference

Education helps us to "know the difference." Our wisdom is increased by our openness to new information. Get new information from as many sources as you can. Learn from people who have had your struggles and have learned and grown from them. Learn from your own experience. Look back to a time when you were doing well; ask yourself what you were doing that was working. Look back to other times when you were not doing well; identify what you were doing that was not working. Look for patterns in your behavior and learn from them.

What can we change and what are we powerless over? The number one principle is that we cannot fundamentally change other people. We have very little power over the thinking, the feelings, and the actions of others. We can truly only change ourselves. Concentrated effort to change others can only result in losing control of our own lives. Certainly we can influence other people and we can work in cooperation with others to change the world—but not by taking responsibility for their thoughts, feelings, and actions.

> *When we quit trying to do the impossible, we are allowed*
> *to do the possible.*   Melodie Beattie[4]

So, what do we have the power to change about *ourselves*? Can we control our physiology, the way our bodies function? Can we control our feelings? Can we control our thoughts? Can we control our actions? To some extent, we can control all of them. We have the most control over our actions, a little less control over our thoughts, even less control over our feelings, and a little control over our physiology. Each affects the others, so when we change any one of them, we effect some change in them all.

William Glasser, in explaining his control theory,[5] uses a car to describe how all of these factors become part of our total behavior. The car can take us where we want to go if we get it on the right road. We get it on the right road by turning the wheels. The front wheels of the car are our actions and our thinking, the rear wheels our feelings and physiology (functions of our body).

Just as we can't turn a car by turning the back wheels, we

don't have direct control over our physiology and our feelings. Most people don't have the ability, by deciding to "just do it," to directly change their heart rate or their emotions. We change the direction of a car by turning the front wheels; we change the direction of our lives by changing our thinking and our actions. We can't go anywhere without thinking and acting. But all of the wheels work together. When we change our thinking and our actions, our feelings and physiology usually follow along.

Although we have little control over most of our physiological functions, we certainly do have control over how we care for our bodies. The quality of that care in turn influences how our bodies function. We are powerless over our genetic makeup and over our tendency to gain weight easily, but we can take actions that will improve the functioning of our bodies. Our thoughts and feelings also change the way our bodies function, by affecting brain and body chemistry. (The reverse is also true: Our chemistry affects our thoughts and feelings. Our "car" rides on a two-way street.)

Can we change our feelings? For the most part, our feelings are not under our voluntary control, but we can learn to recognize what we are feeling and choose how we will react to what we feel. We don't have to be at the mercy of uncontrolled anger and guilt. As we choose to react in ways that produce a better outcome for us, we may find our feelings changing, too. We change our feelings primarily by changing our thinking. As we change our beliefs and our perceptions by the way we think, we find our feelings changing. Many feelings are created and colored by the shame of our condition. We can change those feelings by changing our beliefs about ourselves. This is not a matter of twisting reality, of offering false comfort to ourselves. If we berate ourselves, we are misinformed (a correctable condition).

Exercise

Complete this sentence seven ways:
When I think of myself as attractive and capable, I feel . . .

Can we change our thinking? We use our thought processes
to compare and evaluate, to reason and figure things out, to
put together information in such a way that we can arrive at
a conclusion. We can change our thoughts. Of course, it is
easier controlling our thoughts in some circumstances than it
is in others. But we do not always have to be at the mercy of
uncontrolled thoughts.

We can choose to think thoughts that confirm our "shame"
beliefs or we can choose to think well of ourselves and give
ourselves self-affirming messages. Freedom of thought is a gift
no one can take from us, but we can give it away. In allowing
other people to make judgments and choices for us, we give
up our most precious possession. In accepting the messages
others give us without evaluating them for ourselves, we relin-
quish the faculty we have that most determines who and what
we will be.

Can we change our actions? We have more control over our
actions, what we do, than over our feelings or thoughts. We
choose many actions that we may believe are not a choice.
You may protest, "No, I don't choose to do this or that; I *have*
to do it: I *have* to go to a job I hate. I *have* to pay my taxes.
I *have* to fix dinner." It might help you to recognize how
much control you actually have over your life if you begin to
say "I choose" rather than "I have to" and to say "I choose
not to" rather than "I can't." When we say "I don't have a
choice," we usually mean that if we choose not to take this action there may be unpleasant consequences.

It is true that, should we choose not to pay our taxes, we may go to jail. But it is still our choice to pay them. There are people who do not choose to pay their taxes. Give yourself credit for choosing a responsible action rather than saying you have to do it. Drawing such distinctions will help you become aware of how much we choose the course of our own lives.

Sometimes when we say we don't have a choice we mean that we are not aware of a responsible option. Recognizing that we choose our actions may help us see options that, until now, we were unaware we had. There are alternatives to preparing dinner: asking someone else to cook, going out to eat, ordering in, eating leftovers, letting others fend for themselves. We can't think of many alternatives to paying taxes, short of quitting work (but that's an alternative to going to an unpleasant job).

But life is not made up entirely of responsible activities and a few alternatives to those activities. We are not limited to paying our taxes, going to a job we dislike, or fixing dinner. We may also choose to go to the circus or to play Sorry with the kids. We can choose to read a book, join the choir, or pick flowers. It is important for us to determine whether the actions we are choosing are getting us what we want out of life. If not, what actions can we change?

Exercise

Becoming aware that we choose our actions often changes our thinking and our feelings about those actions. Make a list of some of the activities that you feel you "have" to do. Then write them as "I choose" statements, such as "I choose to cook for my family." How do your feelings about that activity change when you acknowledge that it is your choice?

The goal of recognizing what we can change and what we can't is this: finding the road that will take us where we want to go and choosing behaviors that will help us stay on that road.

The Serenity to Accept What We Cannot Change

Serenity is a choice; it does not depend on circumstances. Serenity is the choice to be pleased with who we are and what we do. It is accepting the truth that our lives are imperfect and we are imperfect and that's all right.

Most of the time we think we will be happy *when*—when we lose weight and have the perfect body, when we get the right job, when we find our true love, when we get over the next hump. Most of us spend our lives preparing for tomorrow and never learn to live in today. Serenity means focusing on how things are instead of how we would like them to be. It means being content with less-than-perfect children, less-than-perfect mates, less-than-perfect jobs, less-than-perfect selves. It is accepting limitations in ourselves and others, and living fully with what we do have. This may mean changing our concepts of what we need to be happy.

In whatever state I am, I have learned to be content.

Apostle Paul
Philippians 4:11

Serenity requires our accepting those truths about ourselves that we would change but do not have the power to change; it requires our letting go of the shame connected with both the perceived defect and our inability to fix it. It is releasing the shame of *I am not perfect. I am not enough. I am not the best. I do not measure up.* It is accepting ourselves even when we are not the best and when we don't measure up. It is saying without shame: "I have attention deficit disorder" or "I am illegitimate" or "I have a weight spiraling problem."

Acceptance enables us to live in serenity. If we cannot accept that we are powerless over how our bodies react to certain foods and that we have the weight spiraling syndrome, then we will spend our lives attempting to change what we cannot and our lives will be unmanageable. There is freedom in acceptance. It allows us to stop trying to do the impossible. It frees us of the blame we have shouldered for an imperfection we can't change.

Acceptance creates the possibility of using limitations as assets. You have heard the old saying, "When life hands you a lemon, make lemonade"? Well, you can't do that until you accept that life has given you a lemon. When we stop trying to change our lemons into bananas, *then* we can use them to make lemonade.

Acceptance is difficult for some people because they feel that they are really giving up, or surrendering. They are. They are surrendering to the reality that some things are beyond their control. *Acceptance is giving up; it is not quitting.* It is giving up trying to make true what cannot be.

Our grandson Joshua was born handicapped. As any parents would, his parents wanted him to be "normal." For a long time they would not think about or talk about Joshua's being a child with a handicap. They thought of all kinds of reasons to explain why he was not doing what other babies his age usually did. As he grew, the truth became more and more apparent. They could not make him normal, no matter how hard they fought for it to be true. They began giving up the fight to prove he was normal. They saw a geneticist, who discovered that Joshua has a very rare hereditary disease (lactic acidosis) that damaged his brain before he was born. His parents grieved the loss of the child they had hoped Joshua would become. Then they let that child go—the child who never was and never could be—and let the real Joshua into their lives. Accepting him as he is allows them to experience the joys of having this special little boy. He goes to a school for handicapped children, where his teachers are specially trained to help him use the potential he has. When he learned to walk, at age five, it was the occasion for great rejoicing, because the people who love him were celebrating what Joshua is. They haven't given up on Joshua; they have just given up trying to make him into what they had wanted him to be.

Exercise

Name something beyond your control that you would change about yourself if you could. Tell yourself that feeling bad or worrying about that something is not going to help you. Then complete this sentence seven ways:

As I become more comfortable with accepting myself as I am, . . .

The Courage to Change What We Can

The ability to change is a skill. Skills have to be learned and practiced. Like someone learning to ride a bike, we must be willing to take a few falls.[6] As we learn from our falls, we can gradually develop skills we never had before. Even if we do take some falls, we can choose to keep at it. Commitment is not something we have; it is something we *do*.

Doris stood immobilized for some time looking at the table of food in the coffee room. Then she turned and walked out. She went into the restroom to give herself time to figure out what she wanted to do. For a minute she stood there wishing this wasn't happening, but wishing that didn't make the problem go away. "Well, I have

*a choice," she told herself. "I can pretend I can eat
anything I want and not suffer for it. Or I can look
at the big picture and choose an option better for
me." She thought about her recovery program and asked
herself a question: Do I really want recovery? She realized
that the rewards for choosing recovery might not be
immediate, but that didn't mean there weren't rewards.
She weighed the recovery rewards she had already experienced and the rewards she knew were still ahead
against the immediate rewards of eating chocolate
mud pie, and made her decision.*

*"Yes, I really want recovery," she said as she walked
back to the coffee room. "I want it more than I want
mud pie." Then she began praising herself for her
decision. "This takes courage and I have courage."
Instead of telling herself she was terrible for feeling so
deprived, she acknowledged that what she had faced was
difficult and gave herself a pat on the back. "Courage
feels better than mud pie tastes," she says.*

We can change. People change all the time. One of the most
difficult habits to give up is smoking; yet more than half the
people who start smoking eventually do quit.[7] Change is part
of life. Believing we can do something not only gives us hope,
it increases our chances for success.

Whether or not we believe we can do something often
makes the difference in whether or not we are able to do it—
not because of some magic that occurs because we believe, but
because if we believe it can be done, we put more effort into
doing it. It may still be difficult, but confidence enables us to
try harder to overcome the difficulties.

Recognize the strengths you have to make the changes you
want to make. We aren't weak victims. Those of us who have

been overweight have used our strength to survive prejudice, pain, disappointment, and rejection. We are strong survivors. We can also use our survivor strength to make the changes we want to make. We already have what it takes. If we go to the gym and work out, we are not creating new muscles. We already have the muscles, we are just making them stronger. The same is true for the abilities we need to change. We already have them; we just need to strengthen them.

The most essential ingredient in the ability to change is courage. We can have all the good ideas in the world and all the best intentions, but they remain just good ideas and good intentions if we lack the courage to carry them out.

Courage is the bridge between good ideas and action.

Tim Hansel[8]

The main reason most people do not take the steps to change what they would like to is fear: fear of failure and fear of exposure (people will find out my secret shame). Courage is not lack of fear. It is taking action in spite of fear. It is being willing to risk failure or exposure. Many people are so immobilized by fear of failure that they live timid, cautious lives. They cannot act because they are so afraid of what will happen if they fail. If you want to develop courage, give yourself permission to fail. Courage gives us the freedom to try.

Success is never final. Failure is never fatal. It is courage
that counts. Winston Churchill

Comparing ourselves with others usually does not help us develop courage. We aren't others. An act that is courageous for me may not be for someone else. In discussing courage in the book *Holy Sweat*, Tim Hansel says:

> What does it look like? For some people, courage may be just being able to shake hands with the stranger next to them. Sometimes it could be just getting out of bed in the morning. Often it is the guts to stand up for one's belief. Sometimes it's the guts to change careers, to stretch one's limits, to begin a new lifestyle, to simplify, focus, and get involved with life on a deeper level. Often, it is the courage to doubt or to ask hard questions. All of us can think of people we know who have this sort of gutsy courage. John Glenn, the famous astronaut, was once asked who was the most courageous person he'd ever known. Traveling in the circles he had, people speculated which famous person he'd pick—but they were to be surprised. His answer was stunning: "The most courageous person I know is my wife," he said without hesitation, "because she's demonstrated great courage by overcoming a speech impediment at the age of 46."[9]

Exercise
Complete this sentence seven ways:
    I am becoming aware that I have the power to change . . .

CHOOSE POWER WITH RATHER THAN POWER OVER
We usually think of power as the ability to affect or influence others without being affected by them. People are considered powerful if they are very often the person in control and seldom the person being controlled. Armies are considered powerful if they destroy without being destroyed. Rulers are thought to be powerful if they have the authority to get others

to do their bidding. The ability to endure is considered more powerful than the ability to be changed. Iron bars are thought more powerful than clouds because they are more resistant to change, because they have more capacity to endure.[10]

The power to affect others while resisting change is one kind of power. Let's call that *hierarchal power*. But the ability to be changed or influenced by something outside ourselves is another kind of power. Let's call this *cooperative power*. In cooperative power, we have not only the ability and strength to change things, but the ability to be changed. Having the power to be changed means we are open, vulnerable, accepting—characteristics not usually associated with power.

Being cooperatively powerful is being open and receptive to positive forces outside ourselves and being able to interact creatively with those forces to produce outcomes that we could not produce alone. We are not passively controlled by others; we are in charge of our own lives and we have the ability to be in powerful relationships.

For one person to have more power in a hierarchal relationship, another one has to have less. Cooperative power does not require one to be less for another to be more. To the contrary, it allows each to be all he or she can to strengthen the cooperative relationship.

To be powerful in a hierarchal relationship, we must do everything ourselves or manipulate others to do what we want them to do; we are responsible for the outcome of everything. In cooperative power, we are not responsible for everything; we don't have to control everything or do everything ourselves in order to be successful. This sharing of responsibility (and credit or blame for the overall results) lets us be diverse. There is no need to be alike. No one of us has to do it all. It frees us to be innovative and unique.

*Competition and comparison are two major stumbling
blocks to your creativity. Your uniqueness sets you apart
from all others. There has never been another person like
you since time began, so what is there to compare or
compete with? Comparison either makes you feel superior
or inferior. . . .*   Louise Hay[11]

To work, hierarchal power requires a pecking order. There is
always a hierarchy, descending from the most powerful to the
least powerful. The more this type of power we have, the
more we are valued by the hierarchal society, team, company,
gang, or army we are a part of. Victims are at the bottom of
the pecking order and those at the top are envied by the rest.
When there is a pecking order, relationships are shaped by
who is in control.

Pecking orders are efficient in the short run, but they work
against us in the long run. They are held together by fear—
fear that we will lose our place in the order. Cooperative
power tends to facilitate a sense of dignity for all rather than
fostering envy and power struggles.

Why are we talking so much about hierarchal and cooperative power? Because we want you to know that, if because of
poor self-image you have put yourself at a low position in society's pecking order, you don't have to compare yourself to
anyone to feel better about yourself. We don't have to place
ourselves above or below others to establish our worth. To
have the power to change our lives, we need to give up the
idea that our worth is determined by how we measure up. The
power to have dignity, control, creativity, recognition, or freedom does not have to be granted by someone else or gained
at the expense of anyone else.

We need both control and freedom. A life without control

is a life of chaos. A life without freedom is oppressive. If we give our power away by saying that we don't have any choices or that we don't have the right to have choices, we don't have any way to bring about our dreams. We become servants for someone else's dream.

Exercise

Complete this sentence seven ways:
   If I become a person of power, . . .

Hierarchal power means "power *over*." Cooperative power means "power *with*." The concept of power over is based on this idea: There is a limited amount of power available here, and if you have some, there will be less for me. Power with creates resources. When we combine our strengths and abilities, we have more. Cooperative power allows for the process of empowerment to occur between one person and another. Each strengthens the other. Each is empowered by functioning *with*—not against, for, or over.

Cooperative relationships can sometimes be a risk. We have to be willing to be open to another, to share heartache as well as joy and hope. We have to be vulnerable, sensitive, open. This may be risky, but to experience the fullness of life we must be open. We have to let the world in. Life is not only what we make of it but what we allow it to make of us. It is not only what we affect but how we are affected. A full life is one in which we can touch and be touched, influence and be influenced, empower and be empowered. Accepting yourself as a person of power (with other people of power) means you are a person who can.

Exercise

Label a page of your notebook "My Plans for Gaining the Power to Choose." Complete these sentences:

Three ways I act, think, or feel when I believe I am powerless to change anything are . . .

When I become aware that I am feeling or acting powerless, I will . . .

A skill I can begin working on that I can use when my recovery is in trouble because I feel powerless is . . .

Three people that can help me identify what my options are when I think I don't have any are . . .

Chapter 12

Constructive Behavior

Sitting in the OA meeting was getting more and more uncomfortable for Lorna. She had come because she thought someone might say something that would help her feel better, but she was not really listening. She was thinking about the bar exam she was going to take in a few days. The fear of failing a second time, as she had the first, was overwhelming. The need to eat to relieve her anxiety was growing stronger. And the messages in her head were running rampant: I will fail again. I will never succeed. What made me think I could be a lawyer? I need to eat to feel better. I am not capable of keeping my self-care going while studying for this exam.

As Lorna sat in the meeting without getting any relief from her anxiety, her self-talk messages were becoming blaming messages: No one gives me the support I need. Why doesn't someone say something worthwhile? People should know I am going through a hard time and give me some help.

When it came her time to say a few words, Lorna was unable to hold in her fear and anger any longer.

*"I don't know why I came to this meeting. It's a waste
of time. I have more important things to do." And
she got up and left the meeting. She sat in her car
for a long time thinking about what had occurred. She
knew right away she was wrong in what she had said.
She was blaming others for the struggle she was having that had nothing to do with them. After a while
she went back in the meeting.*

*"I would like to apologize," she said. "I was wrong.
I'm really uptight about taking my bar exam. I didn't
pass it the first time I took it and I'm really afraid
I will fail again. I should not have expected this meeting
to make my whole life better and should not blame any
of you because it hasn't."*

*A member of the group spoke up, "Lorna," he said,
"thank you for coming back. You have just demonstrated
the tenth step of this program. You have looked honestly
at yourself and promptly admitted that you were
wrong. As long as you keep doing that you'll be able
to see what you need to do to stay in recovery."*

S tep Ten of OA is: *continued to take personal inventory and
when we were wrong promptly admitted it.* This means that
we actually look for our mistakes, then admit them quickly so
we can do something about them. We can reverse the regression spiral when our behavior becomes self-defeating—if we
are willing to acknowledge that it *is* self-defeating. As long as
we are unable or unwilling to acknowledge that our behavior
is not working to make things better, we will be unable to
change it.

We are endowed with many faculties that help us change,
discover, grow, and evolve into better, more efficient beings.
Our thoughts, our feelings, and our behaviors are all part of

the system that allows us to choose different paths of growth throughout our lives. Examining our behavior and choosing appropriate actions allow us to become what we were created to be. As long as we are enmeshed in regression behaviors and unable to reverse them, we are not free to grow and change in order to live fully and creatively.

Deep down inside of us, in a place beyond words, is a dream, a vision of what we really want and really can be. In this place is a picture of ourselves as we yearn to be. This is not a picture of a skinny person or a fat person, a tall person or short person. It is a picture of a fulfilled person, a person who is healthy physically, mentally, emotionally, and spiritually. This is a picture of the person we were created to become. The behavior we choose is an attempt to get us what we think we need to become a happy, fulfilled person. For most of us, a fulfilled life includes finding purpose and meaning, having satisfying work, being a member of a loving family, taking part in caring friendships, and finding satisfaction in leisure and recreation.

Exercise

We all have ideas about what it means to live a fulfilling life or to be a fulfilled person. Describe yourself as a fulfilled person. What are you like? What characteristics do you have? Now that your life is what you want it to be, in what ways is it different?

Behaviors That Do Not Get Us What We Need

Self-defeating behaviors are those that do not get us closer to our dream of a fulfilling life. Constructive behavior helps us get closer to the vision, to become what we hope and yearn to be. Every time we change behavior successfully, we are able to see a little more clearly the dream inside us.

We usually do take actions we believe will get us closer to our dream. And when our actions don't meet our needs, we often continue to do the same things, not recognizing that what we are doing is not working. We think that if we do the same things harder or better, we can make them work.

We can choose to behave differently. We must first look at what we are doing and determine whether or not it works to meet our needs. If it does not, we need to find the courage to change. In order to prevent and interrupt regression, we need to learn to recognize when our behavior is self-defeating and to take action that will keep us on the road to recovery.

Many of us settle for what feels comfortable at the time and seldom if ever look carefully at whether our behavior is getting us where we really want to go. To get to the dream beyond our now-familiar life, we have to change our behavior—and that can be uncomfortable, even scary. If our dreams are obscured by thoughts that this is as good as it gets, we don't have to reach for the dream; we don't have to risk failure, or harm, or loss. The real risk is in our not attempting to reach our dream, and so missing an opportunity to live a more fulfilling life. There is something within that does not want to settle for that. This is the voice that keeps us searching and keeps us reaching.

Acting Out Our Beliefs

Our behavior is shaped by what we believe, how we think, and how we talk to ourselves. What we believe can change reality. If we continue to act as if something is true *despite contrary evidence*, often we can make it come true. If our beliefs and our self-talk are self-defeating, then our behavior probably will be, too.

> *Dawn had many experiences that convinced her she was discriminated against because of her weight. As a result, she developed the expectation she would always be picked last, hired last, fired first, and excluded from social activities. She regularly told herself, "No one will give me a chance because I am fat." She joined a singles group where people tried to accept her and make her a part of the group, but she made it very difficult for them. She came late and left early, then complained because no one spoke to her. People invited her to social activities; but when she came she kept to herself, then said she was not included. She finally stopped going and blamed the group, saying they had not been friendly.*

Because of some painful experiences, Dawn developed the expectation that *no one under any circumstances* would give her a chance, and she acted in accordance with that belief. In contrast, think of all the overweight people who have chosen not to let the restrictions that some people might put on them keep them from pursuing their dreams.

Oprah Winfrey is such a person. She is black, female, and overweight—all of which are facts used as a basis for discrimination. She once said that she knew when she was quite young that she would do something special in life. She has no doubt experienced her share of discrimination. But obviously, not any one of those incidences and not any number of them strung together have kept her from going after what she wanted to accomplish. If the belief that others will not accept us, will not hire us, or will not give us a chance causes us to

give up our dreams and fail to try, then the most harmful discrimination we experience comes from ourselves.

Your life is what your thought makes it.   Marcus Aurelius

Exercise

Write a story describing ways that your beliefs and self-talk
have influenced your behavior. Reading the story back, make
note of messages you have given yourself and the resulting
behavior.

You Can't Succeed if You Don't Try

Usually it is not so much the unhealthy things we *do* as it is
the healthy things we leave *undone* that most restrict and limit
our recovery. Most people feel worse about themselves every
time they lose weight and then regain it, or every time they
start a self-care program and then regress. These "failures"
keep them from trying again. It is certain that we can never
succeed if we never try. The things we believe about ourselves
and the messages we give ourselves lead many of us to give up
before we start.

If Lorna's belief that she is incapable of passing the bar
exam keeps her from taking the test, she will not pass it; her
belief becomes a self-fulfilling prophecy. If I tell myself I'm a
bad cook and, therefore, I seldom cook, the result confirms
what I have told myself: I *am* a bad cook. If I don't enroll in
college because I believe I can't get through, sure enough I
don't get through college. If I am so sure I can't get the job
I want that I don't apply for it, I won't get the job. Remember Elizabeth in the "For Better or Worse" comic strip? Be-

cause she believed that no one would like her, she did nothing to get acquainted. Consequently, no one liked her because they didn't know her, which confirmed what she already believed.

Our grandson Nathan showed a lot of natural athletic ability when he was very young. His outstanding performances and the resulting praise led him to believe he should excel the first time he tried any new sport. But when he first tried soccer he was only average. He believed he had to excel, but because he hadn't immediately excelled, he avoided playing soccer. Because of lack of practice, he did not become a better player. When he did occasionally play (with kids who had practiced) his performance confirmed what he believed all the time: He wasn't a good soccer player.

When Nathan joined a football team, he discovered that he wasn't an immediate superstar there either. But his coach encouraged him to stay on the team long enough to develop some skill for the game. With this support, Nathan found the courage to keep trying. He has become a pretty good football player and, most important, he loves the game.

There is no surer way to fail than by not trying. If our definition of failure is trying and not attaining as much as we would like, we are apt to give up before we start.

> *Throughout history, the most common debilitating human ailment has been cold feet.*   Anonymous

Exercise

Complete each of these sentences three ways:
Fear of failure causes me to . . .
If I didn't have to worry about failing, I would try . . .
If I knew I would get praise and appreciation just for try-
ing, I would . . .

The Need to Set Limits

If we are going to fulfill our dreams, we have to set limits. We can't do everything. We have to ask ourselves if something is going to help us achieve our goals or is going to slow us down. We need a certain amount of rest, a certain amount of play, a certain amount of work. Sometimes choosing to do one thing means we must give up another. The question is, which is going to get us where we want to go? Even when we don't know exactly what our dream is, it is there calling us, chal- lenging us. To be responsive may mean we *do not* do some things, we *do not* take some roads.

Trying to do everything is as harmful to recovery as doing nothing. No one can "do it all." In order to take care of our- selves and protect our recovery, we must decide what activities go at the top of our list. Some people never consider the pos- sibility that they do not have to do everything that is expected of them (or that they may expect of themselves). Often they have the faulty belief that everyone has to like them, all the time. Acting out this belief keeps them trying to make other people happy always (an impossible task), and when they don't make others happy, they feel they have failed.

Thelma is a loving and caring person, and through her many activities she has found an endless number of

ways to express her caring. As a child she discovered
that not only did she enjoy doing things for others,
she was valued and appreciated in return because
of her giving nature. Although she was overweight and
believed that the only way she would be accepted was
by doing good deeds, she did truly enjoy lifting the
burdens or brightening the lives of other people.

As an adult Thelma is very talented and has developed many skills that allow her to bring healing,
comfort, and uplift to others. She is a highly com-
petent nurse, a good musician, a busy mother, a loving
wife, a care-taking daughter. She is involved in her church,
PTA, community organizations. She teaches classes
for adolescents at risk for teen pregnancy and drug
use. She enjoys everything she does and believes she
is making the world a better place. People know if they
want something done and done well they can ask
Thelma.

Three years ago Thelma began recovery; over those
years she lost 100 pounds. For a while she was in a
recovery support group, but in order to keep up with
all her other activities she gave up the group. She
has been finding it harder and harder to follow her
nutrition plan and get regular exercise without her support
group. She has been noticing that now, for the first time
in her life, she has begun to feel burdened, stressed
by all she tries to do. Activities that once brought
her pleasure now add to the burden. She has come face
to face with the realization that it is humanly impossible
to do everything that needs doing or everything she
enjoys doing. She knows she has to make some
choices, but taking care of herself is now at the top of
her list of essential activities.

Do you feel responsible to take care of others? Do you believe you have to sacrifice your well-being for the sake of others? If so, you are probably setting yourself up for failure. No matter how hard we try, we cannot take care of everyone all of the time, nor are we responsible for doing so.

Exercise

Think of an activity or task you have been asked to do that you are not sure you want to agree to do. Check your body for indications of how you feel about doing it. Discuss it with a friend. Consider whether it will support or interfere with your recovery. If you decide that doing it is not within the boundaries you are setting for yourself but you don't know how to say that to the person who asked, practice saying no by role-playing with a friend. Then do the real thing.

Suggestions for Changing Behavior

Changing behavior is difficult, stressful, and uncomfortable if not downright painful. Some of us want to be surprised only by the familiar. It is important to know, however, that changes in habit get easier and easier. The first time we do something new, the effort may be difficult, the next time a little easier. Finally, the old habit is no longer part of our behavior pattern and has been replaced by the new and more effective habit. Recovery is impossible without change.

All change, however, is accompanied by some stressful feelings. Stress is not always a negative experience; some change is accompanied by excitement and pleasure. Whether we are excited or terrified (or both), change—even small changes—can be stressful. Careful planning for changes in our behavior can reduce stress and increase our chances of making those changes successfully. Making changes means taking risks, and that takes courage. We may make some mistakes in the process of changing our behavior. That is the risk we take. But mistakes are not failures; they are just mistakes. In making them we learn what works and what doesn't. A mistake is evidence that we did something. Here are some guidelines for changing behavior.

MAKE SPECIFIC PLANS

Make a deliberate choice to *take action*. It is easier to start doing something than to stop doing something. The quickest way to stop a behavior is to replace it with another. We are usually more successful in changing behavior if we make plans for what we are going to *start* doing rather than what we are going to *stop* doing. When we identify what we are going to change—what we will start doing—we need plans for doing it.

Plans should be specific: They should state when we will do something, where we will do it, with whom we will do it, how often we will do it, and what the action will include. We really don't know what our plan is if we just say, "I won't overeat anymore." We need to decide what we will eat, how much, how often; and we need to estimate how long a time we should eat this way. Specific plans give boundaries to the changes we want to make; perceptible boundaries make change seem less overwhelming.

Exercise

Think of something you need or want to do and set down a plan for doing it. Be as specific as you can. When will you do it? Where will you do it? With whom? How long? How often?

GIVE YOURSELF ENCOURAGEMENT
AND POSITIVE FEEDBACK

Just as our self-defeating self-talk turns into negative behavior, positive self-talk turns into positive action. We can choose to give ourselves the messages we need to hear. *Okay, I can do this. I am worth the effort.* Decide what you want to do and tell yourself you can do it, then give yourself encouragement all along the way.

One Step At A Time

Behavior changes are best made in little steps. Ask yourself if you are really going to do something: Are you really going to walk seven days a week? No? Then how about three? Small bites of change give success. Success reinforces change.

The growth process is made up of a thousand little steps, each creating its own feedback. Little achievements provide the fuel that energizes our motivation to keep going. In this way we can build on each success. Small, realistic goals let us feel successful.

Exercise

List ten things you are good at and ten things you like about yourself.

Celebrate the Successes along the Way

Failure and defeat are not the same thing. That we fail to reach a goal does not mean we are defeated. But if we tell ourselves we are defeated, we will not go on now and are not likely to try again later. Failure to meet a goal does not mean that we have not met with some successes in our attempt. A slip is not failure, failure is not defeat. Defeat is saying, "What's the use? I'm always going to be fat. No point in trying anymore." Temporary setbacks are inevitable. If we slip and we see the slip as a failure, we may give up altogether. If we fail to reach a goal and we see that single (and probably only partial) failure as defeat, we will never reach the goal. A negative outlook undermines the awareness of our accomplishments.

C.G.: In the past I never looked for the successes that were there right along with the "failure." If I wasn't perfect with my weight management plans, I had failed. Now, looking back, I can see there were positive changes every time I lost weight. I have continued to incorporate many of these healthy changes into my life—even during periods when I was regaining weight. I can see that I accomplished something of value from every weight loss experience. And those experiences are still benefiting me. From Weight Watchers I learned balanced eating, and I continued eating balanced meals even when I ate too much. Thanks to another program, I started incorporating high fiber. I have continued to do that whether or not I am losing weight. Until I became aware of what I had accomplished by my efforts, grandiosity kept me feeling like a failure. I thought I had to be absolutely perfect in my eating, that I had to get down to size ten (I never will, but I'm maintaining a fourteen pretty well). When I look at how many small successes I have had, I realize I have never been a failure.

Even if you have lost weight and regained it many times, you can feel good about your ability to lose it. Congratulate yourself on trying to change your condition. Congratulate yourself on the strength of character it took to lose weight and to maintain the loss as long as you did. It took courage, and you should feel good about that. It is not your failure that you have a body that causes you to regain weight easily. Nor is it your fault that an action you believed would help, not only did not help, but actually made the problem worse. Commend yourself for the courage you showed in acting for change. Give yourself credit for the pounds you have lost in your life. It took strength of character to get rid of them.

Exercise
List ten things you have accomplished and ten things you are glad you have done.

FAKE IT TILL YOU MAKE IT
When we act on a belief, that belief grows stronger; when we act against a belief, it becomes weaker. New behaviors may not always feel good. But when we do them anyway, our ability to do them grows—as does the belief that goes along with that behavior. We can make the choice to take positive action even when our self-talk is telling us otherwise. We can train ourselves to recognize when we are having self-defeating thoughts and to choose then to act as if those thoughts are false. We may be scared, but we *choose* to take action anyway. We act "as if," and "as if" can become fact. If we fail to attempt something because we are afraid, that situation will seem even more fearful the next time it challenges us. If we are afraid but act brave by doing the things we are afraid of, our fear lessens.

While we don't want to delude ourselves or deny situations we need to accept, a pair of rose-colored glasses can be useful when we need the courage to risk change. The belief that something can be different gives us the courage to act as if it is different. And our actions may just make it true.

For Reed, security has long been associated with food. He remembers an experience that occurred when he was eight. He usually felt afraid, because of the frequent turmoil and occasional violence that resulted from his father's alcoholism. One day his mother gave him money to go to the store. She included enough for him to get a candy bar. An apartment building next to the store had a concealed enclosure behind a stairway. With his candy bar in his hand, Reed made his way to the hiding place so he could be alone and savor the experience. He still remembers vividly the emotions he felt as he ate the candy. He had a strong sense of warmth and well-being. He felt secure as he snuggled into his oasis of calm, peace, and safety.

Because eating has been Reed's security blanket and represents safety, recovery has sometimes been frightening. Every change has been accompanied by insecurity and sometimes terror. Making the choice to move ahead with these changes—without the comfort and security of eating—has been a challenge. He began with relatively simple things and did them despite the fear. Pretty soon he was doing them naturally and was able to move on to something a little more difficult. Reed is amazed at how many new things he has done, without food for security, that are now a normal part of his life.

Exercise

Write down ten changes you are afraid to make. Put them in order from the least anxiety provoking to the most anxiety provoking. Now start practicing the first one. Fake confidence as you develop real confidence. This will give you confidence to try the next thing on your list—and the next and the next.

BUILD ON THE STRENGTHS YOU ALREADY HAVE

Many of the strengths we have used in the past to support ourselves through the pain and disappointment of the weight spiraling years can be used to support us in changing our behavior. Even if we have used these strengths in self-defeating ways, we can turn them around now and use them to support our healthy choices. As we reorient our life around health, we will see how the strengths we have always had can now be used for recovery and growth.

Do you have strengths you have used to deal with discrimination or some other pain of your situation in the past? Are there ways you took care of yourself that allowed you to binge or overeat? Perhaps you became very good at arranging your schedule when your eating behaviors were out of control so you could have time to be alone in order to binge without anyone knowing. You can use that ability for time management now, to give yourself special self-care time. The difference between stumbling blocks and stepping-stones is the way they are used.

Exercise

Earlier we asked you to make a list of strengths you have developed in order to survive weight spiraling. Now you might have a more complete list of what those strengths are. Review the notes you made and complete this sentence seven ways:

In order to survive having a weight problem, I . . .

Which of these methods of coping with weight spiraling are strengths that can be used to support recovery?

GET SUPPORT AND ASK FOR WHAT YOU NEED

In seeking community with others, find a safe place, one where change is expected, but in reasonable time. Be with people who reinforce your new behaviors and who do not support the old. Go where you will get endorsement for healthy choices. Ask the people around you for feedback on your behavior.

Role models help change our behavior. Find those people who have successfully done what was required for their behavior to change. There is an OA saying, *Stick with the winners.* Find people who are successful at what you are trying to accomplish and stick with them.

Exercise

Make a list of people who are good role models and who give you support. Put phone numbers by the names. Contact all these people to let them know you appreciate their support and ask if you can call periodically, when you need them. Keep your list handy and call when you need some extra support.

Sometimes the courage to change lies in asking for help, and that isn't always easy. None of us can live entirely by our own efforts. We need each other. Sometimes we just need to say, "I don't know *how* to do this. Will you show me?" Other times we need someone to hold our hands as *we* do it. Sometimes we are uncomfortable accepting help. Other times we can accept it (if others offer), but we don't know how to ask.

If we don't ask for what we need from others, we are not likely to get it. We may think that others know—or should know—what we need from them. But if we don't tell them, how will they know? This belief that others should know our needs without our telling them not only damages relationships but deprives us of getting what may be readily available if we just let someone know. *She should able to tell I'm upset and take care of me. He should know that it is difficult for me when he eats potato chips in front of me. If she loved me, she would clean up the house. If he cared, he would offer to watch the kids so I could go to an OA meeting.*

The behaviors that result from such beliefs are usually exaggerated to give an indirect message, but may not get the results we want. The expectation that others will read our minds from our behavior is faulty and self-defeating. When we act out our "loud" self-talk with "loud" behaviors—slamming doors, yelling—we may think that others should automatically know what our needs are and be sympathetic. When they respond in a "normal" way and move away from us instead of closer, we become indignant. We then feel more justified in demonstrating our self-defeating behavior because, after all, we think, they must not love us, or they would understand our needs.

This behavior further fuels the cycle, contributes to the distancing of others, and greatly reduces our chances of getting what we need. If you need help from others to make changes, ask them for it.

> **Words of wisdom from a child:** If you want to write something and you don't have anything to write with, you should ask for a pen or a pencil because if you just ask for a pencil and they don't have one, you won't have anything.

Exercise

Take a risk and ask someone for something you need. Start with a small request. Be direct and specific. Allow for the

possibility the person may say no. Give him or her that option. Give yourself credit for asking regardless of the response.

ADMIT YOUR MISTAKES AND LEARN FROM THEM

A mistake is not a failure unless we refuse to learn from it. If we look at a mistake as an opportunity to learn rather than as failure, it can just be a step in our success. We may need to change our definition of failure. We have not failed unless we fail to try. We have not failed if we use the experience to learn. *Most of us learn as much from what we do wrong as from what we do right.* We learn what works and what doesn't work. We learn what to do differently the next time.

Because most of us have grown up believing that mistakes are failures, we feel pain when we perceive that we are making mistakes. That is why most of us become defensive when a mistake is pointed out to us. We view it as evidence that we are defective, and we would like that not to be true. Seeing mistakes as steps in the learning process allows us to use them as assets.

Step Ten of OA (*continued to take personal inventory and when we were wrong promptly admitted it*) means we keep looking at ourselves: our thinking, our feelings, and our behavior. What do we need to change? What do we need to accept? Are we harming anyone? What do we need to correct? Are we harming ourselves? Are we building on our strengths as well as focusing on our weaknesses? Are we willing to admit we are wrong when we are wrong? Are we giving ourselves credit for positive steps we are taking? Are we forgiving ourselves for lack of perfection? Are we willing to be satisfied with progress?

Are we continuing to be honest with ourselves? *Promptly* is an important word in this step. Admitting our wrongs promptly is a necessary part of staying healthy. If we *promptly* remind ourselves that shameful beliefs about ourselves are faulty, those beliefs won't get a solid footing. If we *promptly* acknowledge that we are getting off track, we can more easily get back on. If we *promptly* admit our mistakes, we learn more easily from them.

We are all human. We will never be perfect, but an event that we may perceive as failure can be the first step in success. If we have shown the courage to try and we have learned something from the experience, we have already used that experience constructively.

Exercise

Label a page in your notebook "My Plan for Changing Self-Defeating Behavior to Constructive Behavior." Complete the following sentences:

Three ways my behavior is self-defeating when my recovery is in trouble are . . .

An action I can take to interrupt each of these behaviors when I become aware that I am doing it is . . .

Three people I can turn to for help or support when I become aware that my behavior is self-defeating are . . .

Chapter 13

Self-Empowering Self-Talk

Self-talk is a normal, healthy process. We do say things to ourselves in our minds, make statements and send messages; we may even stage whole conversations with ourselves, and sometimes (courtesy of imagination) with others. Self-talk helps us solve problems, remember, plan ahead, and make sense out of the world. It is very powerful, because the words evoke mental images, paint pictures in our minds. Whether positive or negative, the images are tied to emotional responses that contribute to the choices we make and to the behaviors that follow from those choices.

Self-talk can help us see situations more clearly and determine options for making changes. By talking things over with ourselves, we are better able to reconcile what is going on outside us with what is happening inside. Self-talk is a bridge between our perception of ourselves and our perception of reality. We need to see that things "add up," that they make sense to us. When we perceive a conflict between what we believe to be true and what is actually happening or seems to be happening, we use self-talk to make sense out of it all.

Self-talk is an echo of our beliefs about ourselves. We don't always know what those beliefs are, but self-talk consists of words we can actually hear ourselves saying. Sometimes we say them out loud and sometimes we say them only in our minds. The beliefs we have about ourselves are often buried deep within us, and we are unaware of what they are, but our self-talk messages give us clues to our real beliefs about ourselves.

Our self-talk can empower us or overpower us. It can be a productive process, one that helps us solve problems and make sense of our world, or it can be self-defeating. Self-defeating self-talk reduces problem-solving ability and leaves us less able to take constructive action. Instead of clarifying our options, it obscures them. It traps us into circular thinking, or thought regurgitation, in which thoughts cycle through our minds over and over again, creating negative emotions and images. Instead of motivating us to grow and move forward, self-defeating self-talk encourages us to run away from problems and to do things that are not in our best interest.

Most of us have a tendency to talk to ourselves in nonproductive ways when we are experiencing severe anxiety, but that is the time when we need most to give ourselves self-affirming and encouraging messages.

The Self-Talk Committee

The self-talk voices we hear form a committee in our heads. We need to learn to tell who on the committee is giving us overpowering messages and who is giving us empowering messages. A committee typical of the ones most of us carry in our heads includes a judge, a police officer, a teacher, a mother, a grandmother, and several other characters who invite themselves to the meeting.

The Mother says: *You must clean your plate because of all the starving children in India.*

The Grandmother says: *Come on, you can eat one more cookie. It won't hurt.*

The Police Officer might say: *You cheated, you're bad.*

The Judge says: *You're guilty; you ate all the cheesecake.*

The Teacher might say: *Why can't you get it right? Other people can do it. Why can't you?*

Mr. Perfect is another guy most of us have sitting in there. His shirt is neatly pressed, every hair on his head is in place, his shoes are shined, and he says: *You must be perfect. If you can't be perfect, don't try.*

Freddie Flak (the flakman) is the guy who is always putting us down, telling us we are defective. That basic message takes the form of: *You are incompetent. You can't do anything right. You're such a klutz. You aren't capable of keeping the weight off.*

The Preacher visits some of us, telling us we are unworthy: *You don't deserve anything good. It's your fault.*

The Victim is the guy with his hands tied. He says: *No one gives you a chance. No one supports you. No one understands.*

Exercise

Take a piece of paper and complete the following sentences:

The teacher in my head tells me . . .

The grandmother in my head tells me . . .

The mother in my head tells me . . .

The judge in my head tells me . . .

The police officer in my head tells me . . .

The preacher in my head tells me . . .

> The victim in my head tells me . . .
> The perfectionist in my head tells me . . .
> The flakman in my head tells me . . .
> Do you have some committee members we haven't mentioned? What messages do they give you?
> Now write the messages you would *like* to hear from each of these people.

Sometimes the voices in our heads form themselves into subcommittees, for such special purposes as rehearsing or rehashing situations that are past or that have not yet occurred. The Hindsight subcommittee is in charge of the reruns. This group replays situations that are past, adding editorial comments, of course: *You should have . . . , You shouldn't have . . . , Why did you? Why didn't you?* Without bothering to wait for any answer from you, they might add such favorite bottom-line pronouncements as *You never do anything right. You are guilty. You're such a klutz.*

The What-If subcommittee anticipates what is coming, and some of the committee members try to prepare us for it with the worst possible scenario. Using self-talk as a rehearsal for anticipated conversations is natural to us. It serves the useful purpose of helping us clarify and organize our thoughts. It can help us feel better prepared to state our position or express our views. But it can be self-defeating if we anticipate the reaction of someone else, blow it up in our minds, and play it over and over again, increasing our anxiety as we practice a confrontation that might never occur.

Say you're scheduled to make a presentation at work next week and you carry this awareness around, constantly thinking ahead to the presentation. You may be thinking of what you are going to say, how you are going to say it. Freddie Flak is usually on the What-If subcommittee and will have stuffed his flakpack full of self-defeating messages; after all, he has a whole week for bombarding you with flak. Anxiety increases as you-can't-do-this messages fill your mind.

Escalating Self-Talk

As anxiety increases, self-defeating self-talk becomes more rapid, more rigid, and less rational. You can alert yourself to the intrusion of self-defeating messages by picking up on their signals: "absolute" words such as *always, never, no one,* and *everyone.* Words like these usually indicate self-defeating messages because they do not allow for change or for new or alternative possibilities. If you hear yourself saying you can *never* succeed or you are *always* a klutz or you should *always* win or *everyone* is better than you, take heed. Those words almost *always* indicate a self-defeating statement.

The big question is: Who is the chair of your committee? Who sets the agenda, decides who can speak and when? Does everyone talk at once? Who is in charge? Who determines which member has the floor and when someone must shut up? You may not be aware that you can be the chair of that committee and you can choose whose voices you want to hear and what messages you want to listen to. The voices are, after all, in your head. You are the head honcho.

We are capable of hearing our inner dialogue. We can develop a sharp ear for its language. We can become mindful of our thoughts, much as we can become mindful of our behavior. One way to become aware of self-talk is to stop periodically and ask, *What am I saying?* We can bring the message into conscious awareness and evaluate it. Sometimes we can identify self-defeating self-talk by our behavior. Have you ever found yourself—perhaps while straightening the house or picking up at work—slamming drawers, moving rapidly, exaggerating your movements? If you stopped and listened to the voices in your head at such times, you would probably hear such messages as *No one does anything around here but me. Why am I the only one who cares how things look? Everyone takes advantage of me. It's not fair that I have to do this when I have so much to do. If I didn't do things like this, nobody would, and they would never get done.*

What is your self-talk telling you? Is it helping you or hurting you? Is it giving you a healthy message that you need to listen to: telling you that you are overcommitted (or overcommitteed) and need to slow down, that you need to take care of something you have been ignoring, that there is something you need to change? Or is it encouraging you to run away from something you need to face? Before we can do anything to change our self-defeating statements, we have to identify them.

Exercise

An activity that may help you identify your self-talk is setting aside a few minutes each evening to think back over your day. Make a list of the self-talk statements you heard yourself making. Were they self-defeating or self-affirming?

Once you have identified what some of your self-defeating messages are, try to become consciously aware of how much influence those messages have on your life. See if you can count the number of times a day you give yourself a certain self-defeating message, then identify some of the feelings you had when you were saying it to yourself. Were you angry, afraid, depressed, lonely, sad, ashamed? The negative emotional energy we put into our self-defeating messages drains

away the positive emotional energy we need to function in a
healthy way.

Suggestions For Creating Self-Empowering Self-Talk

Phil had successfully maintained his self-care plan for
six months when he decided to take a two-day mini-
vacation, driving wherever his car took him. A few
hours into his trip he began to realize that in the past,
being alone was his cue to eat certain unhealthy treats.
As his anxiety increased, he found himself doubting
his ability to refrain from that old practice. Soon some
of his old faithful self-talk messages began playing in
his head. You are all alone, no one will know. No one
could stick to carrot sticks under these circumstances. You didn't really believe you could keep
the pounds off, did you? You never have succeeded;
you never will be able to. Why not just give up now?

Phil realized that the anxiety of facing an old familiar eating situation was generating all his self-
defeating thoughts, but the faster the thoughts flew through
his head, the harder it was for him to do anything about
them. "My thinking was becoming more and more
exaggerated, and I realized that if I didn't do something to stop it I would be on a food binge in no time,"
he recalls.

Fortunately, Phil had been working on his recovery
long enough to learn a few things about stopping negative thoughts and to formulate some positive self-talk
to replace the negative. He had enough presence of mind
to say, Stop! as loud as he could. He repeated this

Stop! many times during the course of the next twenty
minutes, and slowly but surely the self-talk slowed
and he was able to interject some new, positive statements. He was able to affirm himself for taking control;
as he did, he thought of some positive options.

Phil pulled the car off the highway when he saw
a state park. He drove around until he found a quiet
bluff overlooking the river. He ate the nutritious sack
lunch he had brought from home and found it both appealing and satisfying. He stayed in the park for several hours, relaxing, meditating, and thinking back
over all the painful years of being stuck between radical
diets and bingeing behaviors. He knew that was not how
he wanted to live the rest of his life. He reminded
himself that he would rather have a healthy life than
a few hours of binge eating that he was sure to regret.
He focused on the beautiful day, the lovely view, and
the opportunity to be alone with his thoughts without
the necessity of overeating. He congratulated himself
for his six months of recovery and for interrupting his
self-defeating self-talk.

As Phil thought over what happened that day, he realized
that not only had he been able to recognize his self-defeating
self-talk and the anxiety that preceded it, he had learned some
bits of truth that added another dimension to his recovery.

1. He learned that he had the power to stop a furious cycle
   of self-talk.
2. He learned that when he took charge he could refocus
   and recover his ability to think more clearly, bringing
   positive options to mind.
3. He learned that overpowering thoughts do not dissipate

entirely until there are empowering thoughts to take their place.

Had Phil not learned about self-talk, he almost certainly would have had the disastrous experience most people have under those same circumstances. A typical response might have been, "Well, the weirdest thing happened. I was just driving along minding my own business when—you should have seen it—it was like that old Chevy came to life, acquired a mind of its own, turned right in at that convenience store, and when I came out of the spell, I was snarfing my way through three bags of jelly donuts!" Losing control can seem like a mystery when we are at the mercy of a process we do not understand. In coming to understand that process, we begin acquiring power over a seemingly mysterious and baffling phenomenon.

Phil's self-talk could have accelerated into a cycle of dialogue that could have led him very quickly into some harmful behaviors. But his recognizing the counterproductive nature of what he was saying to himself enabled him to stop that spiraling process before it reached an irresistible momentum.

SAY STOP TO SELF-DEFEATING MESSAGES

If the stress levels continue going up and we find ourselves cycling self-defeating statements, we can assert ourselves and tell the voices to shut up. As chair of the committee, we can take charge, bang our gavel, and say, "You are out of order. Stop."

Most people think they don't have the choice to participate in their self-talk. They think it is something happening to them that they cannot control. They think they have a choice about their actions, but not about what is going on in their heads. *Stop* is a powerful little word. Say it sharply and forcefully, out loud or in your mind. By saying it you are cuing yourself that your self-defeating dialogue has gone on long enough and it is time to assert control. It may take a while to stop the dialogue because there are many emotions flying around, but from the moment we begin to say "Stop!" we feel more in charge.

COMPARE SELF-DEFEATING MESSAGES WITH REALITY

Our goal at this point is to expose self-defeating self-talk for what it is. We must figure out who has the floor. Until we do, the self-talk committee will be able to convince us that our self-defeating self-talk is true. When these emotionally charged messages are exposed, we will be able to see how out of sync they are with present reality.

Remember, the goal is to stop the messages with the light of reality. Self-defeating dialogue can exist only in the darkness in which it developed, usually in faulty beliefs about ourselves. Bringing them out into the open allows us to compare them to our present reality. When we are caught up in a furious cycle of self-defeating messages, there is no other reality. But interrupting the self-talk barrage long enough to become objective and compare our internal talk with the external situation will allow us to expose the inaccuracy of our messages. The longer our self-talk goes on, the faster and more intense it becomes, the more firmly enmeshed with reality it becomes, and the greater risk there is that we will make choices as though the messages were true.

One way to expose self-defeating self-talk is through "mirror talk"—talking out loud as we look into a mirror. This allows us to face ourselves and confront our self-talk.

Exercise

When you find yourself feeling overly stressed and out of control of certain feelings and thoughts, look in the mirror and say to your reflection, "Okay, I feel anxious. What *is* going on? Am I really the not-okay person I feel I am?" Compare what the voices in your head are telling you with what is really going on. Remember, these emotionally charged, negative statements are connected to old self-defeating beliefs you have probably carried for a long time. As you expose them, ask your reflection if they are appropriate for the present circumstance. Your anxiety will probably decrease, resulting in less restrictive thoughts and an awareness that you have more options than you'd believed you had.

SUBSTITUTE SELF-EMPOWERING MESSAGES

After you tell your self-defeating messages to stop, immediately substitute a self-empowering message. When the victim voice says, "You can't trust anyone," correct that little voice with, "There are people I *can* trust." When you hear Freddie Flak say, "You can never maintain your self-care program," say, "I have maintained for six months, so I certainly *can* maintain." When you hear a voice saying you can't succeed, tell yourself there is no reason you can't. When your self-talk begins cycling around your weaknesses, replace it with self-talk accentuating your strengths. Praise yourself.

Who do you want on your committee? What characteristics do you want behind the voices in your head? The kind of people we think you should consider are people who are affirming, realistic, creative, courageous, kind, and patient—and who believe in your worth.

Exercise

Who do you want on your self-talk committee? Write down the names of people—living or dead, real or fictional—who meet your criteria. Form your own committee. If you have trouble thinking of enough people, create some people with the qualities you would like them to have and give them names. For each of the people you have listed, write their characteristics that caused you to choose them.

USE REGULAR SELF-AFFIRMATIONS

It is usually helpful to find some time every day to relax and be quiet in order to clear our heads of as much information as we can and begin to focus our thoughts and feelings on the new beliefs we are attempting to absorb. When we feel like the ugly duckling, we can say, "I am a beautiful person." When we feel bad about ourselves because we have been less than perfect, we can say, "I don't have to have it all together all the time. It is all right to make a mistake." When we feel defective we can say, "I'm okay."

Sometimes it is helpful to read positive thoughts to ourselves. Here are some self-affirming messages taken from *The Self-Talk Solution* by Shad Helmstetter:

I know that what I believe about myself is what I will become—so I believe in the best for myself.

If I have ever had any doubts about myself in the past, today is a good day to put them aside. It's a good day to throw out any disbelief that ever held me back.

I am practical and realistic, and I keep my feet on solid ground. But I also give my self freedom to live up to my fullest expectations.

No matter what it is that requires the very best of me, I can do it and I know I can.

Today is a great day. And I've got what it takes. So I choose to do it right, do it well. I choose to live today with joy and love.

Just look at what I can do today! I am incredible . . . and today is a great day to show it.[1]

We suggest that you write some affirmations of your own. You know what your strengths and limitations are, at least you are learning. You are identifying your self-defeating self-talk statements. You can write the self-affirming statements that you need to hear.

Exercise

Write messages from your new committee members on notes and stick them all over the place. Say them to yourself in the mirror. Look at yourself and say, "You are a beautiful person. You're okay." Even if you are uncomfortable, say those things anyway. Try to keep your face straight and take this seriously. (But if you laugh at yourself at first, that's all right. So did we.)

V.S.: When my counselor asked me to look in the mirror and say I was beautiful, I couldn't do it. She encouraged me to do it anyway. She said, "Do whatever it takes, but do it." The first week I just looked in the mirror and laughed. The second week I actually got the words out, but I still laughed. By the third week I was able to get serious about it and talk to myself like I meant it. And, guess what, I really did.

One way to help these self-affirming messages become part of you is to tape them. Use eight or ten statements and repeat each one several times. Play the tape several times a day. This technique will help you get comfortable with your new statements and make them your own.

CONTINUE TO CHALLENGE OLD SELF-DEFEATING MESSAGES

That we've fired some of our committee members and hired new ones does not mean they move out of our heads. As our new messages become a part of our perception of ourselves, we sometimes find the old messages coming back when we least expect them and least want them. Again: The only way to get rid of an old belief is to replace it with a new one. But that takes time and the old message will persist for a while. One part of us says, "You can never succeed." Another part will say, "I can succeed if I exercise my potential while acknowledging my limitations." One part of us will say, "It's no use. You have done *everything* possible and you can't make it." Another part says, "Maybe I haven't tried *everything*."

> *When one works at changing self-talk by becoming aware*
> *of it and then replacing it, an internal argument will develop*
> *with the new self-talk challenging the old.*   Shad Helmstetter[2]

There is evidence that once we get a message in our heads, it is always there. Even if we can't control *when* that message is going to pop into our minds, we can practice stopping the message and replacing it with a better message. The time it takes to recognize and change the message will become shorter and shorter. Self-talk that empowers us instead of overpowering us is strengthened by successful behavior and healthy outcomes.

Deciphering, understanding, and changing our inner dialogue is a discipline that will improve with time. Remember that our self-talk reflects our perception of ourselves, which has developed primarily from the messages we have received from other people. By the messages we give ourselves, *we* determine whether we'll keep or change that self-perception.

As we learn to interrupt our self-defeating self-talk, we will find that out of every success come more positive options. As we accumulate successful outcomes, our positive self-talk vocabulary will increase and we will have more and more control over our thought processes.

Exercise

Label a page of your notebook "My Plans for Replacing Self-Defeating Self-Talk with Empowering Self-Talk." Complete these sentences:

Three self-defeating messages I give myself are . . .

When I become aware that I am giving myself these messages, I will . . .

Messages I need to hear are . . .

Three people from whom I can receive these messages are . . .

Chapter 14

Using Anxiety as an Opportunity

S tress is a normal part of life. Anxiety is elevated stress. When anxiety is intense, we are in crisis. The word *crisis* is defined by Webster as "the turning point for better or worse . . . ; an emotionally significant event or radical change of status in a person's life; an unstable or crucial time or state of affairs in which a decisive change is impending." A crisis can be the beginning of regression, or it can be an opportunity for progression. It is a "turning point" when we either face the anxiety and progress in recovery or retreat into avoidance behaviors that prevent growth.

Anxiety is not necessarily bad. It can call our attention to a need for change, or it can make us mindful of something we've been unaware of. A crisis can be an opportunity. In fact, in Chinese the two symbols used together to make up the word *crisis* are "danger" and "opportunity." How we respond to a crisis determines whether it helps us or hurts us. Without the motivating force of anxiety, we probably would change very little.

The question is: Are we going to listen to what the anxiety is telling us or run from it?

Anxiety is a fearful reaction to change or anticipated

change. Fear causes the body to release adrenaline, which causes arteries to constrict, pulse and respiratory rate to increase, muscles to tense. Elevated blood pressure and sweaty palms are also common reactions. This is the "flight or fight" response. It is not bad; it is the body's natural way of enabling us to respond to a crisis. But this is intended to be a short-term response. Continuing anxiety can harm us physically and emotionally.

For many of us, anxiety triggers a desire to eat. Food soothes anxiety by releasing endorphins that help us relax. When eating has been our way of reducing anxiety and we choose not to use that method anymore, we need other ways to decrease anxiety. If we don't find them, anxiety continues to escalate.

Symptoms and Sources of Anxiety

Remember that anxiety can fuel and feed the regression spiral. If we do not respond to it constructively when it first raises its head, it can spiral into self-defeating ways of thinking and behaving, and, finally, into severe and debilitating pain that puts us at high risk of eating for relief.

We may not be consciously aware of anxiety, but the body still reacts to it. Until we recognize when we are experiencing anxiety, we cannot use it constructively—and we *can* bring symptoms of anxiety into conscious awareness, by paying attention to body sensations. We may feel tenseness in our shoulders, chest, or stomach. We may notice that breathing becomes shallow or rapid or that we are holding our breath. What happens to you when you are feeling stressed? Does your chest feel tight? Does your stomach feel queasy? Does your face get flushed? How would others describe you? What do you do?

Exercise

Complete each of these sentences three ways:
  A signal my body gives me when I am experiencing anxiety is . . .
  Something I do when I am anxious is . . .
  When I am anxious I think . . .
  When I am anxious I feel . . .

We also help ourselves by identifying situations that trigger anxiety for us. Does standing in line bug you? Does a messy house set you off? Does boredom make you anxious? How about going out to eat with people who do not have to watch what they eat?

Exercise

List ten situations that are major sources of stress for you.
List at least five people who are sources of stress for you.

We are not suggesting that you must avoid situations that cause anxiety; but knowing what they are allows you to prepare for them and take measures that will lower the stress or enable you to use it in a positive way. For example, Carolyn reduces the stress of eating out by eating a satisfying, low-calorie snack before she leaves home so she will not feel ravenous when the appetizers are served. She gives herself permission to ask waiters to have her food prepared as she needs it. She knows the places that are not cooperative about doing that, and avoids them. She asks for a take-home carton before her meal is served so that when it is put in front of her, she can put half of it into the carton to take home to eat the next day.

Anxiety often provides realistic feedback. Perhaps the anxiety connected with taking a test is pointing out to us that we didn't study. In that case, it is the behavior that needs to be changed. If a job is causing anxiety because of a lack of appropriate job skills, the anxiety should encourage action toward improvement in the needed skills. Learn to listen to what your anxiety is telling you: It may be telling you that a situation should change, or that your perception of the situation should change, or that your handling of the situation should change.

Fear of Exposure

Anxiety often points to what we really believe about ourselves. Anxiety arises when we fear that the shameful beliefs we have about ourselves may be revealed to the world. We who are ashamed of our bodies may go to great lengths to keep from being seen in a bathing suit or shorts, for fear others will see us as we really are.

Jane grew up in a family where there was nothing worse than being foolish. She heard the comment, "Oh, don't be foolish" so much that she was sure she was, and she carried that belief with her into adulthood. She says, "I knew I could not hide being fat, but I could hide the truth that I was a fat fool." She would not go swimming because she was afraid people would think, "Look at that foolish person trying to act as though she is size six." She made jokes about being fat so people would not think her so foolish as to pretend she was not fat. She avoided being friendly with eligible men for fear they would mistake her friendliness for the foolish

*notion that they could be interested in her. She would
rather be lonely than foolish.*

*Fear of being exposed as a fool kept Jane in a constant
state of anxiety and led her to avoid many opportunities to live a fuller and healthier life. She spent
a great deal of time alone.*

*As she began to recover, Jane started to look at the
ways her anxiety had put restrictions on her. Her fear
of exposure had caused her to deprive herself of opportunities to grow and to experience many of the good
things of life. She realized that she'd better be very careful
about the way she handled scary situations in recovery, to prevent the anxiety that might lead her into
regression.*

A seemingly minor incident can become a crisis and set us up
for regression when we do not feel good about ourselves. If we
see ourselves as unlikeable or uninteresting, we will fear a social situation where getting acquainted and talking with other
people is expected. If we lack confidence in our ability to
learn or remember, we'll experience high levels of anxiety
when expected to take a test or play a "thinking" game. The
shame associated with overeating or being overweight leads us
to approach life fearfully, and chronic shame and self-criticism
create chronic anxiety.

*People with low self-esteem are likely to misinterpret many
things in the light of their conviction that they are inadequate,
worthless, and unlikeable.*   Abraham Twerski[1]

If we believe we are incapable or undeserving, we will experience anxiety whenever that belief conflicts with expecta-

tions that we will accomplish something or try something new. If we believe we are really not capable of maintaining weight loss or staying on our self-care plan, we will live in ongoing stress because of the pressure to do what we believe we are incapable of doing.

We Respond to Our Perceptions

Whether something is really going on or we only believe that it is, our reaction is the same. If someone were to burst into your house with a stocking cap over his face and a gun in his hand demanding your money, what would your reaction be? Anxiety? Terror? Of course. If the intruder then pulled off the mask and you saw it was your next-door neighbor, the practical joker, with a toy gun, you would feel tremendously relieved. But as long as you thought he was a burglar, your reaction would be the same as if he really were. We react to what we *believe* is occurring.

We interpret events according to our perceptions. If we expect to be rejected, we may perceive that we are when in fact we are not. If we believe ourselves incapable of doing a good job, we may think we are doing a poor job when in fact we are doing well.

When bad things happen it is a pity, but that is all there is to it. However, if we are prone to self-deprecation, we are apt to interpret everything as an indication of our inadequacy.   Abraham Twerski[2]

Exercise

To explore the beliefs that help form your perceptions, complete each sentence five ways:

I believe people are . . .

I believe the world is . . .

To be okay in the world, I believe I must . . .

The Mistaken Beliefs of Others

Anxiety does not always mean something is wrong with our thinking, sometimes it means something is wrong with someone else's thinking. Healthy beliefs can be in conflict with unhealthy situations. Sometimes we experience anxiety when we are confronted by a person who does not recognize or support our worth. In such a situation we might choose to avoid the crisis by accepting the other person's belief, but we experience anxiety when we settle for less than we deserve or are capable of. This form of anxiety becomes unexpressed anger and even rage.

Those of us who are or have ever been overweight undoubtedly have met with occasions when we were treated unfairly. Being discriminated against because of our size creates anxiety. How we react to such a crisis will determine whether the anxiety triggers regression or becomes an opportunity to correct an injustice.

In the 1950s blacks were expected to sit in the back of the bus in the South. Rosa Parks believed there was nothing about being black that rendered her unworthy of sitting in the front of the bus. She listened to that inner voice that said, "You deserve better than this." She went to jail because she refused to continue to sit where others expected her to sit. She used this crisis as an opportunity to take courageous action, action that opened the way for other blacks to sit in the front of the bus.

An organization called the National Association for the Advancement of Fat Acceptance, which has about 3,000 members in the United States and Canada, fights against weight discrimination. NAAFA members believe that discrimination against fat people is a socially acceptable prejudice. This organization fights against all discrimination based on weight: job discrimination, insurance discrimination, health care discrimination, and fashion discrimination. Their aim is to spread the word that everyone, no matter his or her weight, has a right to be treated with dignity. Perhaps this is an organization you want to support if you believe people who are overweight are regularly discriminated against. (By the way, they use the term *fat* rather than *overweight* because the latter is a relative term—over *what* weight? However, we will continue to use *overweight*, since we believe it is a commonly understood term.)

We may also experience stress when we recognize our limitations but others do not. To accept what we cannot change takes courage, especially if others do not accept that we're unable to change that condition. When others expect us to perform as though we do not have limitations, we feel high levels of anxiety—until we are able to emotionally detach from their unrealistic expectations.

Most of us have felt quite stressed at some time by the expectations of people who do not understand why we can't just take off fifty pounds and keep it off like some other people can. "All you need is a little willpower," they say. We know that is not true, but the conflict between our belief and their expectation is stressful for us.

Even more difficult for some of us is others' denial that we need to take special measures to prevent regression. We go out to eat with them and they are embarrassed because we ask for our food to be broiled without butter. "Why do you have to cause such a fuss?" they complain. Or they invite us over and serve foods we choose not to eat. "Can't you eat it just this once?" they ask when we refuse.

Facing New Challenges

A perception of self that has been nourished and supported by our behavior, as well as by the reactions of others, will often continue until a crisis brings awareness that the perception may be faulty. It will take time for the new self-perception to replace the old, and meanwhile, there is some anxiety as the new belief and the old belief battle for control. As more and more positive outcomes result from the new perception, the old belief is replaced.

We cannot possibly continue to grow and develop without facing beliefs we have about ourselves. If we put restrictions on our abilities, we experience anxiety when we reach past what we believe we are capable of. How we react at that point determines whether we extend our boundaries or retreat to avoidance behaviors that allow us to hold on to our established beliefs.

We often look for confirmation that our perceptions of ourselves are accurate. If we challenge our beliefs instead of accepting them, we must do something different, and that means change. Most of us are uncomfortable with change and look for ways to avoid it. It takes courage to face new challenges and to develop the skills to turn our anxiety into an opportunity.

Exercise

Describe your greatest challenge connected with having the weight spiraling syndrome.

When Jane's recovery progressed to the point that she was ready to face some new challenges even if she had to risk looking foolish, she decided she wanted to learn to swim. For a while she thought she would wait until she had lost more weight, but she knew swimming would help her lose the weight. "I may never look like the girls at the health club in a bathing suit," she told her support group. "If I wait until I have a perfect figure, I may never learn to swim." So she mustered all the courage she could and bought a bathing suit. She contacted the Y because she knew they had a swimming class for people on a weight loss program. She laughs when she tells about getting into the water as quickly as she could. She has learned to swim and she loves it. "It's too bad I've missed the enjoyment of water all my life," she reported to her group. "And I am amazed how much easier it is to lose weight when I swim regularly. This has been one of the greatest challenges of my life, but doing it has helped me find the courage to try some other scary things."

Suggestions for Using Anxiety as an Opportunity

An effective response to stress and anxiety depends on what is creating the anxiety, on whether we can change the situation, and on whether taking action will make the situation better or worse. Sometimes the most appropriate thing to do is solve the problem creating the stress. Sometimes it is learning to relax despite what is going on. Sometimes it is taking action that will allow us to grow as a result of the situation.

LEARN TO RELAX

There are things we can do to reduce anxiety when we are unable to change a situation and we believe that the best thing to do is to wait it out. Deep relaxation helps us quiet body and mind. By stilling our thoughts and relaxing our muscles, we can reduce tension and anxiety. Deep relaxation rebalances the body and decreases the production of stress hormones. What happens when we relax is the opposite of the "fight or flight" reaction we ordinarily have to anxiety. When we relax, our muscles become heavy, body temperature rises, and breathing and heart rate slow down.

To experience deep relaxation, create a quiet place for yourself. Separate yourself from the world in that special place. Lie on your back or sit in a comfortable chair with your feet on the floor. Close your eyes. Release distracting thoughts. Breathe deeply.

With some relaxation methods, the focus is on the physical states you are trying to change—your muscles, body temperature, breathing, or heart rate. With others you concentrate not on your physical state, but on a color, a sound, or a mental picture.

If you choose to focus on physical states, begin with your muscles. Allow them to become heavy. Then concentrate on raising your temperature. You can do this by sensing a spot of heat on your forehead and allowing it to flow throughout your body. Think about your breathing. Let it become slower and slower. Feel your heart beating and concentrate on slowing it down.

You can relax by concentrating on something other than your body. Think of a color. Fill your mind with that color. Become a part of it. Or feel yourself in motion, floating, tumbling, or rolling. Or repeat a pleasant sound over and over to yourself. Or imagine yourself in a soothing environment, perhaps sitting beside a quiet lake or lying in the soft, silky grass of a green meadow. These are all relaxation exercises you can do by yourself, without the aid of a book or tape. The important thing is to find an exercise that works well for you.

You can also select a book that offers a variety of exercises you can choose from, or you can purchase tape-recorded exercises. Select a method that is relaxing to you and use it often. You will find it a helpful aid for reducing stress and creating peace of mind and serenity.

One relaxation exercise you can do without a tape recorder is the following: Get comfortable and close your eyes. As you breathe in say to yourself, "I am." As you breathe out say, "Relaxed." Breathe in, "I am." Breathe out, "Relaxed." "I am—relaxed. I am—relaxed. I am relaxed." As you continue this practice, allow your breathing to carry relaxation throughout your body. You can use this exercise whenever you feel the need for relaxation.

Another exercise you can do by yourself without a tape is this: Get comfortable and close your eyes. Select a word that is relaxing to you. It can be *flower* or *peace* or *meadow* or any word that has a pleasing sound to you. Repeat the word out loud a few times, whisper it a few times, then repeat it silently to yourself over and over again until you feel very relaxed. If your mind wanders and you forget to say the word, that is all right. Just gently begin the word again when you become aware you have stopped saying it. After about twenty minutes, stop saying the word and gradually allow yourself to become fully alert.

A technique based on the passive repetition of phrases focuses on feelings of warmth and relaxation. You can first listen to the following phrases, then read them aloud (or listen to them on tape) until you can repeat them in your mind without the aid of another voice. "I feel quiet . . . I am beginning to feel quite relaxed . . . My ankles, my knees, and my hips feel relaxed, and comfortable . . . My solar plexus and the whole central portion of my body feel relaxed and quiet . . . My hands, my arms, and my shoulders feel relaxed and comfortable . . . My neck, my jaws, and my forehead feel relaxed, they feel comfortable and smooth . . . My whole body feels quiet, comfortable, and relaxed . . . I am quite relaxed. My arms and hands are warm . . . I feel quiet . . . My whole body is relaxed, and my hands are warm and relaxed, my hands are warm, warmth is flowing into my hands, they are warm, warm . . . My hands are getting warm . . . My hands are getting warmer . . . My fingers are getting warmer . . . I can feel the blood flowing into my hands and fingers . . . I can feel the pulse in my fingers . . . My fingers are tingling with warmth . . . My fingers are growing and spreading out with warmth . . . My fingers are loose, limp, and warm."

This exercise uses emotionally cued words such as *warmth, relaxed, heavy,* and *quiet,* which tend to trigger a flood of stored memories from the brain; those memories, in turn, are accompanied by pleasant feelings of relaxation. In addition, you can imagine warm images, such as floating on a rubber mattress on a quiet lake with the sun and breeze gently rocking and warming you.

BREATHE DEEPLY

There is a connection between breathing and our emotional state. Fear and anger restrict breathing. Restricted breathing increases negative emotional states. A sense of well-being can be enhanced by proper breathing. When you calm your breath you calm your mind. As you breathe more normally, you will become more aware of your feelings. The level of oxygen in the blood is altered by the way we breathe.

Exercise

Try changing your outlook by changing your breathing. Several times during the day, notice your breathing. If it is restricted in any way, breathe deeply and notice any changes in how you feel.

Most of the time when we tense up, our breathing becomes rapid and shallow, or we hold our breath. Relaxing reverses this tensing by slowing and deepening our breathing. Deep breathing can be used alone or with other relaxation methods. It is something you can do for a few seconds whenever you feel yourself getting tense, without stopping whatever else you are doing. Or you can take a break and focus on your breathing for several minutes.

Try the following breathing exercise:

1. While sitting or lying down, place your hands on your stomach and chest.
2. Sigh (audibly) several times.
3. Slowly and fully inhale through the mouth, filling the lungs comfortably from the bottom to the top. Imagine you are bringing energy into your body.
4. Without hesitation, allow the air to be exhaled through the nose, emptying the lungs from the top to the bottom in a comfortable manner. Visualize yourself releasing your tensions as you breathe out.
5. Repeat this procedure for three to five minutes, working

up—in subsequent sessions—to ten or fifteen, until you are totally and pleasantly absorbed with the breathing process and alert but not focusing on any other thoughts or processes. You will feel a measure of peace and serenity just in focusing on your breathing.

SOLVE THE PROBLEM

One way to reduce stress is to solve the problem causing it. Start by naming and describing the situation that is a problem. List possible options for changing the situation. Evaluate each of them by looking at the consequences that are likely to result. Choose the solution that seems the best and take that action as soon as possible. The acronym SOCS may help you to remember these steps of problem solving: situation, options, consequences, solution.

Situation

Name and describe the situation that is the problem. Think about this carefully, it may not be as clear as it first seems. Be careful not to name something over which you have no control. For example, naming the weight spiraling syndrome as your problem will not get you anywhere, because that is not a problem to be solved. That is a condition that *is*. But you might name some problems that are related to having the weight spiraling syndrome, such as having clothes you can't wear taking up space in your closet, or experiencing conflict with your spouse because you want specially prepared food, or finding yourself too busy to go to OA meetings.

Exercise

Name and describe a problem you have. It may or may not have anything to do with weight spiraling.

Example: Lisa stated that her problem is being late for work because she has such great difficulty getting up in the morning that she turns off her alarm without even waking up.

Options

State some options for solving the problem. List as many as you can think of, even if some of them are not very realistic. When we let our minds go outside our normal boundaries for solutions, sometimes we end up with a creative and workable answer to a problem.

Exercise

List as many solutions to your problem as you can.

Example: Lisa listed putting the alarm clock across the room, putting it in a pan in the bathtub to make its message louder and more clangorous, having a friend call her every morning to see if she is awake, getting a wake-up service, going to bed earlier, and setting the alarm a half hour earlier to give herself a little wake-up time.

Consequences

Evaluate the consequences of each option stated. For each one ask yourself: What is the worst thing that could happen? What is the best thing that could happen? What is the thing most likely to happen? Weigh the worst possible outcomes against the best and think about how likely each of them is to happen.

Exercise

Write down the possible consequences of each of your options and evaluate them according to best, worst, and most likely.

Example: Lisa thought it would be inconsiderate to ask her friend to call her every morning. She couldn't afford a wake-up call (but if that turns out to be her only option, it is cheaper than losing her job). Setting the alarm a half hour earlier would just give her less sleep; this thought helped her to the further realization that she probably was not getting enough sleep, and going to bed earlier would take care of that.

Solution

Choose the solution that seems the best and put it into action. After considering all the options carefully, pick the one that seems the best and decide when you will start doing it.

Exercise

Write down the solution you have chosen and when you will do it or begin doing it.

Example: Lisa decided to go to bed earlier, as her inability to get up seemed a natural outcome of not getting enough sleep. It was her practice to go to bed after the 11:00 news on television. She started watching the 7:00 news instead and going to bed at 10:00. She started putting her plan into action the day she made the decision.

ACCEPT LIMITATIONS

Anxiety often occurs when we do not accept our limitations, when we fail to acknowledge there are some problems we can't solve. If we believe we always have to be great, we will feel anxious when we believe it might be revealed that we are average. The limitations that reality puts on us will be stressful. We cannot often be perfect. We cannot always be the best. We cannot pull off a pose that our real limitations somehow do not limit our behavior.

*Terri had polio when she was a baby, and the doctor
advised her family never to acknowledge that she
couldn't do anything that anyone else could do. Terri
lived up to those expectations and never used a wheelchair.
She learned to dance and to ski on crutches. Terri decided
she had truly created the illusion of self-sufficiency,
when a waitress in a restaurant, upon taking her
crutches, said, "I'll put your crutches up here out of your
way, but be sure not to forget them."*

*Terri believed it was not all right to acknowledge
the limitations that needing crutches placed on her.
As an adult she lives alone and takes very adequate care
of herself. But last winter Terri had a crisis. She was
feeling very stressed because of trying to get around
on the ice with her crutches. She was finding it especially difficult to carry groceries from her car. If she
were to ask for help, someone might find out that she
was not self-sufficient, that there were some things
she could not do as well as people who don't need
crutches. When Terri finally admitted that indeed there
were things she could not do, help was available, and
she realized she didn't need to live as though she had
no limitations. She even found the courage to admit
that skiing was not worth the effort just to prove she
could do it, and she doesn't ski anymore.*

*Doctors now tell Terri that she, like many other polio
victims, is suffering from postpolio syndrome. Her body
is deteriorating due to overcompensating for so long. Now
she uses a wheelchair as much as she can, and she enjoys
relief from the continual strain of walking.*

For many people, not recognizing limitations results in
their belief that they have a responsibility to be everything to

everyone. Not being able to do that is shameful for them. They come to believe it is not all right to set limits to protect themselves. If we believe that it is our responsibility to keep the world running smoothly, we will experience one crisis after another as that belief is confronted by the reality we've taken on an impossible self-assignment.

Beliefs that do not acknowledge limitations conflict with the real world. Do you believe you should have a perfect figure? Crisis, for you, will occur if you lose that last fifteen pounds and still your figure is less than perfect. When we believe we should never swallow anything sweet and then we do eat a sweet, we usually experience a great deal of anxiety about not maintaining self-care perfectly.

Exercise

Identify a limitation you have that cannot be changed. Write down some statements you have heard related to this limitation. What expectations have these statements communicated to you? In what ways are these expectations active in your life today? Are they realistic and reasonable? Do you need to change your response to them?

STRIVE FOR AN ACCURATE PERCEPTION OF REALITY

There is a difference between *feeling* bad and *being* bad: the difference between facts and feelings. It is important that we identify what our feelings are, respect them, and learn to express them in appropriate ways. But we also must realize these feelings may be based on inaccuracies. We may "feel" unlovable or invisible or unattractive. We may "feel" that we have no limitations or that we should be able to do everything. We may "feel" that we are going in circles in our recovery, when we actually are spiraling upward. We may "feel" that we are hopeless. Or we may "feel" that everything is all right because we are comfortably avoiding situations that challenge us. But to act on such feelings as if they were true will not get us where we want to go. What are the facts? Listen to your feelings, but make decisions and take action based on the facts.

> *A good adjustment to reality requires a correct perception of reality.* Abraham Twerski[3]

Exercise

Challenge yourself to complete this open-ended question seven ways:

I am beginning to realize . . .

Oftentimes, instead of changing our situation we need to change our perception of it. In order to do that, we must learn to tolerate discomfort long enough to figure out what the facts are and what action is appropriate. We may need to change our attitude about pain so that it becomes part of the process of opening up new opportunities, instead of being something to escape.

LOOK FOR THE OPPORTUNITY

We may believe that pain is proof we are doing something wrong. Pain is not always proof that there is a problem. Pain may mean that something wonderful is about to happen. But to get to the other side of the pain, we have to experience it and not try to make it go away. Pain can be our friend. If we face it, it can help us discover what we believe about ourselves, our situation, and our lives. Pain can motivate us to move toward our dream. But if the pain scares us so much that we turn around and retreat, we may miss the opportunity to reach for our dream.

All change includes loss. All loss creates grief. We may tend to look at our feelings of grief as proof that we have started down the wrong road. It may be that we are on the right road, grieving what we are leaving behind. It may feel like death, but if we move through the terror, the pain may bring about a birth.

> *... death of the old is birth of the new.*   M. Scott Peck[4]

If our goal is to make the pain go away, we can usually find a way to do that, temporarily. But if we can handle the discomfort without looking for pain control, we may find ourselves looking at a new opportunity. If we don't understand that we have this option, we will treat every crisis as a problem to be fixed, and never look for creative options that can open up new opportunities.

When I, Merlene, was a child I told my father that I was worried about going into third grade. He wondered why I should be concerned when I had never had any problems in school. I explained that I had seen my brother's third grade work and I didn't think I was smart enough to do it. He laughed and said, "Third grade isn't any harder when you are in third grade than second grade is when you are in second." It turned out he was right. I have never forgotten that, and it has given me courage to take action many times when I was fearful about what was ahead. Many fearful situations have turned out to be opportunities when I have taken them one step at a time, starting where I am instead of worrying about what was ahead.

Sometimes when we are uncomfortable, we may be breaking the shell around us; and if we are so uncomfortable that we have to stop the process, we risk interrupting the birth. If we find the courage to look at what we are afraid of and explore the creative possibilities, we treat fear as an opportunity.

L.L.: I always dreamed of the time I could wear regular sizes and stop shopping at the large women's store. When I was getting too small to get clothes at the large women's store, for a while I kept going there rather than risk the embarrassment of trying on regular sizes and have people look at me and think, what is this fat person doing looking at these clothes? So I kept buying clothes that were too big and taking them up. Finally, I decided not to let my fear stand in my way anymore. At first, I went in and looked at the jewelry. Then I went in and said I was looking for something for my niece. Finally, I got the courage to try on the clothes. At first, it was really scary, and it was embarrassing to find that most of the clothes didn't fit well. But it was wonderful finding something that did fit in a style I had never been able to wear before.

Exercise

Think about a situation creating anxiety for you. Ask yourself whether the anxiety is an indication that you are heading in the wrong direction or is, rather, a normal part of the growth you are experiencing. List the possible outcomes of going forward, or turning around and going back.

TAKE A RISK

Don't let your terror get you off the track from where you want to go, whether your goal is buying clothes in regular sizes or changing your career. Don't let fear block your dreams. The faith and courage we need to follow our dreams comes from the inner wisdom that *knows* what we need to do. We can deal with fear as a problem and turn around and go back, or we can walk through it to the dream that is on the other side. When we listen to the voice that says, "Escape, get out of this situation," we may miss the opportunity of our lives. When we listen to the voice that encourages us to go ahead, one step at a time, the anxiety lessens and we may walk into opportunities we thought would always remain just a dream.

Joan had never had a relationship with a man. It was her hope and her dream, but it was also her greatest fear. The possibility of having an intimate relationship was the scariest thing she could think of. She told her counselor, "I never learned about those things as an adolescent. How can I begin to learn the rules at forty?"

The first time Karl asked Joan if she would like to come to his house to watch a football game on a Sunday afternoon, she was so terrified that she refused. But realizing there was no way to her dream but through the terror, she went to her counselor for support. Talking about the dream and the fear helped her find the courage to say yes the next time Karl asked. She not only lived through the afternoon, but had a very pleasant time. He was not the man of her dreams, but he became a very good friend and she began learning some of the rules of interacting with the opposite sex so that she doesn't have to run away from the possibility of an intimate relationship.

Exercise

Complete this sentence three ways:
    If it were not for the fear, I think I would . . .
    Now list some people and resources that will provide support for you to do these things if you choose to do them.

Stepping out into unfamiliar and strange territory is risky. Initially, it offers only the hope—without concrete, objective proof—that things will be better. But to get where we want to go, we have to take that risk. Change demands risk, but change is an exciting part of life. There is this wonderful story in *There's a Lot More to Health Than Not Being Sick*, by Bruce Larson:

> On his twentieth birthday, our youngest son bought himself his first ten-speed bicycle with a tax refund from the Internal Revenue Service. The day after he bought his new bike, an all-Florida professional bike race was held in our town. Mark, along with two friends, decided to enter. I tried to discourage him. I told him bike racing was very sophisticated and he was foolish to try it with no training. "But it will be a good experience," he said.
>
> He returned that night with the first-place cup. Needless to say, we were astounded. I asked him what happened. "Well," he said, "I know long-distance bike racing is very tricky. You have to learn to pace yourself carefully and make your move at the right time. Since I didn't know exactly what to do, I just started out pedaling as fast as I could—and nobody ever passed me.[5]"

Taking the risk to try something new keeps life exciting and full of surprises. If we think we're too fat, too old, too young, too inexperienced to take a risk, we may miss the best and most exciting parts of life. We limit ourselves whenever we hesitate to reach for our dream because we feel inadequate or undeserving. When we retire from taking risks, we retire from living.

Painful situations will always exist in our lives. It is how we respond to them that determines the quality of our lives. We can feel sorry for ourselves or we can look for what we can use for good.

> G.P.: During my thirteen-year marriage, my husband never did anything special for me on holidays or on my birthday. As each year passed I collected hurt feelings around my birthday. When I divorced, I wanted to change the energy surrounding my birthday. The first year I gave myself a birthday party. The second year I telephoned my friends and wished them a nice day. The third year I wrote personal notes to forty of my friends. I wrote, "Dear Jerry, in celebration of my birthday I want to thank you for your gift of humor, your gift of laughter, your gift of friendship." With this third step I changed the negative energy around my birthday to positive energy. As I gave thanks for what I had and sent out my love, I forgave and released the hurts. Now I receive a lot of cards every year on my birthday.[6]

We have this day only once. Whether it is our birthday or just an "ordinary" day, we can live it only today. We have a choice how we live it. We can find pleasure in each day—in each moment—or not.

Exercise

Label a page of your notebook "My Plan for Using Anxiety as an Opportunity." Complete the following sentences:

Three situations that create anxiety for me are . . .

To use these situations as opportunities I can . . .

Something that might interfere with my taking this action is . . .

Skills I can begin developing that will help me take these actions when I need them are . . .

People I can turn to for support when I need courage to risk taking these actions are . . .

Part Four

There Is
More to Life
Than Not
Gaining Weight

Chapter 15

Balanced Living

All life has an intrinsic need for harmony in relationship; balancing our lives is living so that all parts are in harmony. While struggling with the weight spiraling syndrome our lives may have become chaotic and unpredictable. At times we may have felt the insecurity of living on the edge—the edge of despair, the edge of giving up, the edge of complete loss of control. We have felt the impact physically, mentally, emotionally, socially, and spiritually. We have been out of harmony with ourselves, others, and the world.

When we were focused on eating or not eating or on being a certain size, we were out of balance, trying to do the impossible. Like a top that can't spin when it is not evenly weighted, we have been drained of energy by our efforts to keep an unbalanced life in motion. When we are not getting as much energy from life as it drains from us, we are out of balance.

Balance *creates* energy. As we grow in recovery, we revitalize and rebalance all areas of our lives. We are released from attempting to achieve unattainable goals. Sickness and disharmony are replaced with wholeness and balance. We are revitalized, reconnected with healthy living.

When we are living a balanced life, we are living responsibly, with time for family, job, friends, and ourselves. Balanced living includes attention to health care with proper focus on nutrition, exercise, and rest; attention to personal growth with proper regard to attitudes, feelings, and actions; a healthy social network; an enriching spiritual life.

> T.R.: I began to understand how all aspects of my life worked together when I started having problems with my blood pressure and my blood sugar levels. Repeatedly losing and gaining weight had affected me physically, which affected my moods and my thinking. These affected how I thought of myself, which affected my behavior, which affected my relationship with others and my higher power. I realized that at any one time I was not just my body, my emotions, or my behaviors but was all of these working interdependently all the time. How they came together was vital for my health. My health was dependent on how these separate life parts worked together as a total system.
>
> I realize that I can't get healthier by just losing weight or by focusing on any one part of myself. As my life has become more balanced, the negative chain reaction I had created has been reversed. I have chosen to think better of myself, to take better care of my body, to improve my relationships, to accept what I cannot change, and to take some risks for the sake of a more harmonious life. For the first time in my life I realize I have the power to make decisions that will put my life more in balance.

At first, recovery may seem chaotic. So much focus and attention on self-care may seem to put our lives even more out of balance. It may seem that we are adding to an already-too-full schedule of activities, causing us to neglect other things that are important. But we cannot integrate good self-care into a balanced life until we learn the basic how-tos. Unavoidably, even in a life that is well balanced, special needs will arise and will cause us to focus on one aspect of living to the temporary exclusion of others. Beginning recovery is such a time. Learning good self-care habits and putting them into practice take time and energy, it's true, but after a while these practices become a predictable part of life.

As recovery becomes "normal," we move beyond basic self-care requirements—eating routines, exercise plans, meetings. We expand our recovery. We come to know ourselves better while we become aware of the balance between too much stress and too little, responsibility to ourselves and to others, time for work and time for play, time for activity and time for rest.

Balance of Body, Mind, and Spirit

To motivate themselves to watch their weight, Ellen and Arlene both start each day by focusing on their size. As a reminder that she never wants to be "like that" again, Arlene looks at a picture of herself when she was 100 pounds heavier. Ellen, who is still overweight, visualizes herself slim and beautiful. For both of them, the focus is on body image. In contrast, Carla starts her day with a quiet period during which she sees herself spending time in healthy, worthwhile activities. She sees herself as physically healthy—not just thin—as well as emotionally, mentally, and spiritually healthy.

We cannot look to any one aspect of life for all the answers. Because we are composed of many parts, we derive strength from many sources. Balanced living means we are healthy physically and psychologically and have healthy relationships. We recognize that each part of our lives impacts the others. We are no longer focused on only one aspect of life. We strive for and are motivated toward wholesome living.

Physical health allows psychological growth: When we feel good, we find it is easier to think about our attitudes and values and to work on eliminating shame, guilt, and anger. Psychological health allows us to do more easily those things that keep our bodies well. Healthy relationships support our personal growth.

But the whole is more than the sum of the parts. There is something more that is part of a whole person. Let's call it spirit. The spirit is more than just another part. It includes body, mind, feelings, behavior, and relationships, and it joins them all into a whole. The parts cannot be healthy until the whole is.

Balance Between Work and Play

The recovery process in the early stages may seem to be grueling work. As we progress, however, and expand our concept of self-care into life-care, we find that the "work" of recovery can actually be enjoyable. In fact, enjoyment can penetrate other aspects of our lives that we call work; whatever we do can include an element of fun.

Life is learning, and we learn better when we are having fun. For too many of us, fun is what we do when all the serious stuff (work) is done. Thinking this way keeps us imprisoned in the belief that we can "live" only on the weekends, on vacation, in retirement, or when we win the lottery.

Children do not make a distinction between work and play, they just experience life. Most adults have lost that ability. To

the extent we recapture it, we allow ourselves to enjoy whatever we are doing, whatever we call it. Of course, we can't
eliminate all activities that we do not especially enjoy; some
tasks will stubbornly resist being transformed from travail into
treat. That is part of life. But it is still possible to enjoy a sense
of accomplishment for doing them and to appreciate what we
learn from the experience—and equally important to give ourselves opportunity for the activities we do enjoy.

Balance Between Relaxation and Stimulation

Sometimes an unbalanced life means we need to learn to take
life easier; sometimes it means we need more activities that
stimulate and invigorate us. Rest is not doing *nothing*; it is enjoying the freedom to do *anything*.

We can be reenergized through both activity and inactivity.
Research indicates that we need a balance of brain chemicals
that stimulate us and those that calm us down. Some people
prefer activities that produce "upper" chemistry; others tend
to go for a "downer" chemistry. Both types of activity do promote feelings of well being. But while all of us have our pref-
erence, most of us need some mixture of both types in order
to live harmoniously with ourselves.

Many people who have struggled with the weight spiraling
syndrome have received a calming effect from food. In recovery we may need to find some alternative ways to feel calm.
Watching television or reading are good alternatives, but relaxation usually needs to be balanced by some activities that
are physically stimulating (such as dancing) or mentally stimulating (playing a game or engaging in meaningful conversation). Relaxing means more than putting our feet up, although

it certainly includes giving ourselves permission to do that. It also means experiencing stimulation.

> P.L.: I have become aware that not only have I preferred calming activities (mainly watching TV and reading), but these activities have been triggers to overeat. In and of themselves the activities I enjoyed were neither bad nor bad for me. But when they were my main activities I became bored, restless, and emotionally hungry— conditions that set me up to eat. I knew I should be more active, but the more inactive I was the harder it became to get myself moving. A turning point came just as I found myself beginning to regress because of my inactivity. I had a visit from a cousin I had not seen in a long time. During her stay I discovered she had a place in the country where she keeps horses. She invited me to ride. I decided to do it. It was not long until I was visiting often, had bought my own horse, and was spending most of my evenings riding in the open air and feeling much more alive than I had in a long time. I still enjoy watching television and reading, but balancing those activities with riding is more satisfying.

The balance of inactivity and activity also produces a balance of certain types of brain waves. When we are active, especially mentally active, we usually produce beta brain waves. When we are more mentally relaxed, we experience alpha and theta waves. Deep concentration produces a beta state; relaxation exercises produce an alpha or theta state. Biofeedback technology teaches that all mental states are essential to our total well-being, that to spend an inordinate amount of time in any one creates an imbalance. We create that balance with variety in our activities.

Balance Between Giving and Receiving

For many of us, the most difficult aspect of our lives to balance is fulfilling our responsibility to ourselves *and* our responsibility to others. Placing care of ourselves high on our list of priorities does not mean we do not also care for other people. Nor does giving to other people, even sacrificing for them, mean we should neglect our own recovery or our own growth. When we love ourselves, we take care of ourselves. When we love others, we allow them to take responsibility for their own lives as much as possible—but we support their growth, in whatever ways we can, without damaging ourselves.

As with other areas of recovery, our ability to provide for our own needs while responding to the needs of others expands as our recovery skills increase. At first, we may need to concentrate on our own needs as we learn to implement a nutrition plan, an exercise plan, and other components of a self-care program. As those activities become a normal part of life, we are able to become more involved in supporting someone else. Paradoxically, giving often comes back to us as a gift.

*As her recovery expanded, Marilyn found that giving
to others benefited her own growth. She put up in
her car a little sign that read PASS IT ON, and often
took people who did not have transportation to the doctor's,
or the grocer's, or to an OA meeting. She found time
to listen when others needed someone to talk to. When
anyone asked her what they could do to repay her,
she said, "Pass it on." Recently while a friend was in
her home, Marilyn mentioned that she was unable to
repaint her woodwork because she was allergic to
the paint fumes. The friend said, "I'll paint your*

woodwork while you are on vacation and will air out your house before you get back." Marilyn was deeply touched that someone would offer to do that for her. The friend, seeing Marilyn's reaction, said, "I'm just passing it on."

When we pass it on, we build a sense of community. When we just repay what has been done for us, we only balance the scales. The world is a better place to be when we are passing it on. A new energy is created that keeps on giving.

We need other people; our growth is dependent upon them. At the same time, we need to give to other people. We need to be concerned about others and contribute to their well-being. Through interaction with others we give and receive the feedback necessary for continuing growth. We cannot grow in a vacuum.

Many of us have not been able to achieve the balance of giving and receiving because we do not know how to love ourselves. Those of us who have lived in shame, who have felt defective and unacceptable, may feel unworthy of love and acceptance, from others or from ourselves. When our recovery enables us to accept ourselves as we are, we are better able to have mutually supportive relationships with others. When appreciation of ourselves is not dependent upon being a certain size, we are also better able to accept others and appreciate them as *they* are.

We need strong social networks to nurture us and provide a sense of belonging. We need reciprocal relationships in which we feel valued as we value others, and experience the satisfaction of giving and receiving.

Spiritual Balance

Spiritual balance means we are in harmony with ourselves, with our values, with others, and with God. Step Eleven of OA gives us guidance for achieving spiritual balance: *Sought through prayer and meditation to improve our conscious contact with God as we understood him, praying only for a knowledge of His will for us and the power to carry that out.* Just as we don't have to have any special concept of God to do this, neither do we have to use any certain definition of prayer or meditation.

But this step is not about trying to get our higher power to do what we want. It is about aligning our will with a higher will. It is about getting in touch with a power that will help us increase our understanding, our knowledge, our courage, and our willingness to live wholesome lives.

Prayer does not change God, but changes him who prays.

Sören Kierkegaard

Spiritual wholeness is living in harmony with what we believe and value. Shame and guilt result from lack of harmony between our values and our behavior. Conscious contact with a higher power, increased knowledge of that power's will for us, and the power to carry that out enable us to find harmony between what we believe and what we do. We are thus freed from the burden of guilt and shame to find spiritual fulfillment.

Exercise

Make a list of ten things you believe and ten things you consider important. What do your lists tell you about the kind of person you are and what you value?

Living in balance does not mean we do not have bad days. We still have our ups and downs; we still experience sadness, anger, fatigue, disappointment. We accept these feelings when they are appropriate. We don't have to be ashamed of them or feel guilty for having them. We allow ourselves to experience a whole range of feelings, but we don't let them control us. And we know how to take action that will prevent these emotions from triggering regression. A wholesome, harmonious life does not mean we never do things we regret or feel bad about. It means that we don't need to become discouraged by our inability to be perfect.

When we are living in balance, we accept our humanness and strive for progress. We seek to eliminate activities that cause us to go to extremes at the expense of other important parts of life. We give up the need for immediate gratification in order to achieve a lifestyle that is more fulfilling and meaningful.

Exercise

Make a list of actions you can take to begin to balance your life. Pick one you can start on today—then make that start.

Chapter 16

Joyful Living

Is there a voice within you, calling you to dream and to believe in your dreams? Listen to that voice. It is your creative spirit. It is calling you to live fully and passionately, to risk and to play. It is calling you to joy. As you listen to that voice and respond to it, it will become stronger. It is calling you to see yourself as a person of integrity and worth, one who has unique dreams and unique talents to offer the world. Responding to that special call leads us on a journey that goes beyond preventing regression, beyond just getting back to ground zero. Seeing the possibilities of life and seeing ourselves with the potential for attaining wholeness gives purpose and meaning to our journey. That sense of purpose and meaning is a result and a facilitator of healing.

As we replace self-defeating lifestyles with hope and meaning, the progression spiral takes self-care beyond maintenance and into abundant living. Abundant living means more than material abundance. It means lives that are rich physically, mentally, socially, and spiritually. Moving beyond the issues of eating or not eating, we replace artificial ways of feeling good with natural ways. The brain creates positive chemistry and generates positive thoughts and feelings, leading to an expectation of opportunities and new possibilities. Life becomes an adventure.

We do not become aware of the possibilities for abundance if our main interest in life is the prevention of weight gain. If we don't see something bright and new to move into, we can only long for what we are giving up. If we focus on an abundant life, and stay focused on it, then we will hope for that abundance, expect it, and seek it. If we feed our hopes, our fears will starve to death.

People who don't know how to live fully use temporary, artificial substitutes for the riches life offers. But we know that in the long run these substitutes only increase pain, deadening senses rather than awakening them.

People who have used overeating to produce pleasure or relieve pain and who don't know any other way to feel good or to relieve their pain, will eventually go back to overeating. If our emphasis is on not gaining weight, then we're focused on what we are *not* doing; we're saying *no* to life. It is time we say *yes*—yes to living fully and joyfully.

A Spiritual Awakening

Step Twelve of OA says: *Having had a spiritual awakening as a result of these steps, we tried to carry this message to others and to practice these principles in all our affairs.* A spiritual awakening occurs as we go beyond the struggle of controlling our weight and, having found meaning beyond ourselves, we discover the joys of *living*. We experience enriching pleasures that take us beyond just "not overeating." We actively participate in life rather than passively hoping life will offer us something good along the way.

A spiritual awakening occurs as we learn that spirituality is not separate from our daily lives, but encompasses life and brings new meaning to all our affairs. Although *spiritual* must be defined by each of us for ourselves alone, it is interesting to note that Webster's dictionary tells us the word is derived from *spiritus*, which means "of breathing" and "an animating or vital principle held to give life. . . ." Our spiritual awakening allows this animating force to be breathed into all areas of our existence.

Spirituality and religion are not the same thing. Religion is a set of beliefs about the spiritual and the practices based on those beliefs. Religion certainly is a means by which some people connect to the spiritual, but we may experience a spiritual awakening without being affiliated with a specific religion or religious denomination. A spiritual awakening is a personal experience that opens the door to meaningful and creative living.

Living Creatively

There lives a creative being inside all of us and we must get out of its way for it will give us no peace unless we do.

Mary Richards[1]

When creativity is blocked, the result is powerlessness and impotence. To live creatively is to give expression to our inner selves. A creative spirit calls us to create laughter, love, forgiveness, and healing in ourselves and others. Creativity may be expressed through cooking, gardening, caring for children, caring for elderly, writing, playing, making love, decorating, painting, dancing, journaling, teaching, counseling, repairing, designing . . .

The call to creativity is a call to joy, zest, and a sense of meaning and purpose. Are you listening to that call? Failure to experience life's meaningful pleasures creates a void that is often filled with destructive "pleasures." They offer no hope and no joy.

We need to sharpen our senses rather than deaden them. We need to wake up and see what is already around us. Someone has said boredom comes from lack of involvement. Get involved. Celebrate life. Celebrate people and animals and all creation. Celebrate yourself.

We must learn to reawaken and keep ourselves awake, not
by mechanical aids, but by an infinite expectation of the dawn,
which does not forsake us in our soundest sleep.

Henry David Thoreau

To live creatively and joyfully does not mean being happy all the time. Struggle is a normal and usually necessary part of creativity, just as labor is a normal part of giving birth. To live joyfully is to experience a fullness of life; it is to be open to suffering as well as to pleasure. Pain is woven into life's pleasures and comforts, and is even essential to them. When we turn away from struggle, we turn away from progress, and a deeper pain grows. To escape from normal pain and struggle is to escape from life.

Joys are our wings; sorrows our spurs.

Jean Paul Friedrich Richter[2]

Living in the Present

Our healing cannot be complete until the creative spirit is freed and finds serenity in the now. If we are to prevent life from passing us by, we must live it now, fully and completely—looking not only for meaning and purpose but also for fun, excitement, challenge, new experiences, and opportunities to smile at ourselves. Fun—play—enables us to live more effectively in the now. If you want to learn to live in the moment, watch children. They are masters of the art of living fully and joyfully. You will notice how effortlessly they savor each moment, unaware of the past or future, absorbed in the present.

Last summer when we were preparing to take him on a trip, we asked our grandson Jonathan where he would like to go. We expected him to say something like Disneyland. But he said he wanted to go where there were animals. "Like the St. Louis Zoo?" we asked. "No," he answered. "Someplace where there are chipmunks and woodpeckers and snakes." So we took him where there were trees and a lake. He was never bored. He caught chameleons and caterpillars. He watched butterflies and snakes. He found a baby bird that had fallen from its nest, and he became its "mother." He spent hours watching a locust come out of its shell. It was a lesson in awe and wonder.

Compassion

Our pain can never be erased without compassion—"an awakening of passion with all creation."[3] Compassionate living means maintaining creative relationships with the earth, the creatures of the earth, and other people. The reason we damage the earth, one another, and ourselves is that we are out of harmony. Harmony results from valuing all creation including ourselves—our bodies, minds, and spirits. Destructiveness comes from not honoring life. Compassion is reverence for life, including a reverence for our own specialness and our own beauty.

The most beautiful experience we can have is the mysterious.
It is the fundamental emotion which stands at the cradle of
true art and true science. Whoever does not know it and
can no longer wonder, no longer marvel, is as good as dead.

Albert Einstein[4]

Compassion brings responsibility, not out of prim "duty," but out of our wanting to care for what we cherish and value. What do you cherish? What are you enthusiastic about? The word *enthusiasm* means "spirit." Do you have life-spirit? Do you have self-spirit? Compassion is a call to courage. Discouragement kills faith and hope and spirit. Courage awakens and empowers. It empowers us to walk into our dreams with hope and enthusiasm.

An important aspect of recovery is giving to others out of compassion and concern. Our own wounds become a resource for healing: Out of our suffering come the wisdom and understanding to pass the healing on. Those of us for whom food and weight have been the objects and focus of life have the opportunity to give to others in recovery. Having lived through much anguish, we are survivors of a condition that has eaten the very center out of our self-esteem. Out of this struggle, we gain insight and compassion to give to and receive from others. Sharing these principles with others is important in keeping them active in our own lives.

Nothing renews commitment like sharing the joy that results from the commitment. . . . Sharing keeps the light on and the spirit high. Larrene Hagaman[5]

Sharing with others keeps the growth process going. Without it, we retreat back into ourselves and allow the old shames to creep in and take over. "Carrying the message" allows life to take on an "other" focus rather than just a "self" focus. As we give to others, we reflect their worth and see our own worth reflected in them. This sense of unity creates a deeper sense of the interconnectedness we have with others and with all living things.

Freedom

Freedom of choice is the greatest opportunity we have. We can choose life; we can choose to take a different path no matter where we have been. We can choose to use the resources we have to become what we were created to be. Or we can choose to hang on to feelings of inadequacy that keep us locked into dis-couragement.

As we become aware of our ability to use our own judgment and, through that exercise, to assert more control over our own lives, we begin to see our potential instead of our shortcomings. We stop seeing other people through defensive eyes as we learn to see them in the light of our empowering interaction with them. We see that we, as individuals working and playing together, can become more than we could in isolation.

We really do not grow or gain in self-esteem by adhering to the wisdom of the self alone. We need, ultimately, to feel a sense of belonging. We need to be involved with others, to exchange perceptions with them, to give and get support. We need others to help us stop the inner war that is fueled by shame and distorted pictures of ourselves.

Freedom comes from an emphasis on what we are seeking rather than on what we are avoiding. If emphasis is on the *not* (what we are *not* eating, what habits we are *not* engaging in), then we are always aware of what is lacking in our lives. Life seems to mean deprivation and restriction. But as we move into replacement activities our picture of life changes: We see and we expect abundance. Harmony in all aspects of life allows us the balance to go beyond the struggle of not gaining weight, and to enter into the experience of joyful living. We reach for an enriched life that is full physically, mentally, emotionally, socially, and spiritually. Armed as never before against regression, we spiral up now, into new aspects of growth.

Serendipity

A bonus on the recovery journey, serendipity is the good fortune of discovering something good while seeking something else. It happens when we compare what we have been seeking with what we have found, and decide that the thing we've found is even better than the thing we'd sought. Many people, out of their pain and acceptance, have spiritual experiences in which their insights and benefits far surpass their expectations of merely staying on track.

The person at an OA meeting who says "I'm a grateful overeater" is describing this experience of serendipity. She has found on her healing journey much more than she ever expected, more than only maintaining weight loss, more than "just hanging on." A new way of life has opened up for her. Expecting serendipity means living in a way that says, "Today

I can experience only the present. As I do, I expect the unexpected. I have a choice to truly experience today, as fully as I can."

A certain story has held particular meaning for us, and we wish to share it with you. We hope it will help light the path that you take in recovery.

There was once a young farm boy whose father was away and whose mother asked him to go to the barn in the dark to feed the animals. But he was afraid of the dark. His mother assured him that the lantern would furnish the light he needed to get there and back. "But the lantern only shines its light a short way in front of me," he said. "I can't see all the way to the barn." Then, handing him the lantern, his mother took him outside. "Now, Son," she said, "just take one step toward the barn." As he took one step the light moved ahead of him. "All you have to do," his mother told him, "is take one step at a time and the light will go before you all the way."

There is a light that goes ahead of us on our recovery journey. We can see as far as we need to see to live a full and joyful life. We don't have to wait until we get to the end of the journey to begin living or to experience the light. As you take your next steps into recovery, watch for the light that illuminates your path.

Notes

CHAPTER 1

1. Phillip A. Kern, et al., "The Effects of Weight Loss on the Activity and Expression of Adipose Tissue Lipoprotein in Very Obese Humans," *New England Journal of Medicine* 322 (April 12, 1990), 1053–1059.
2. Abraham Twerski, *When Do the Good Times Start* (New York: Topper Books, 1988), 23.

CHAPTER 2

1. See, for example, Claude Bouchard, "The Response to Long-Term Overfeeding in Identical Twins," *New England Journal of Medicine* 322 (May 24, 1990), 1477–1481; Phillip A. Kern, "The Effects of Weight Loss on the Activity and Expression of Adipose Tissue Lipoprotein in Very Obese Humans," *New England Journal of Medicine* 322 (April 12, 1990), 1053–1059; and A. J. Stunkard, et al., "The Body-Mass Index of Twins Who Have Been Reared Apart," *New England Journal of Medicine* 322 (May 24, 1990), 1483–1487.
2. Kern, op. cit.
3. Kelly Brownell, *The Partnership Diet Program* (New York: Rawson Wade, 1980).
4. Ibid.
5. Joseph C. Piscatella, *Controlling Your Fat Tooth* (New York: Workman, 1991), 107.
6. Kelly D. Brownell, *The LEARN Program for Weight Control* (Philadelphia: University of Pennsylvania School of Medicine, 1988), 19.

7. See, for example, S. F. Liebowitz, "Brain Monoamine and Peptides: Role in the Control of Eating Behavior," *Federation Proceedings* 45 (April 1986), 1396–1403; G. A. Bray, "Classification and Evaluation of the Obesities," *The Medical Clinics of North America* 73 (1): 161–184; R. E. Keesey, "Physiological Regulation of Body Weight and the Issue of Obesity," *The Medical Clinics of North America* 73 (1): 15–27; E. A. H. Sims, "Storage and Expenditure of Energy in Obesity and Their Implications for Management," *The Medical Clinics of North America* 73 (1): 97–110; and K. Blum, M. C. Trachtenberg, and D. W. Cook, "Effects on Weight Loss in Carbohydrate Bingers: An Open Clinical Trial," *Current Therapeutic Research* 48 (1): 217–233.

8. See Kenneth Blum and Michael C. Trachtenberg, "Addicts May Lack Some Neurotransmitters," *The U.S. Journal* (July 1987), 16; Joel C. Robertson, "Preventing Relapse and Transfer of Addiction: A Neurochemical Approach," *EAP Digest* (September/October 1988), 50–54.

9. Joel Davis, *Endorphins: New Waves in Brain Chemistry* (Garden City, NY: The Dial Press/Doubleday, 1984).

10. T. L. Neher, "Altered (Chemical) States, Insights into Neurochemistry," *Professional Counselor* 5 (March/April 1991), 31–35.

11. Ibid.

12. Piscatella, *Fat Tooth*, 18.

13. Ibid.

14. Judi Hollis, *Fat Is a Family Affair* (Center City, MN: Hazelden Educational Materials, 1985), 5.

15. Ibid., 4.

CHAPTER 3

1. Michael Cader and Debby Roth, eds., *Eat These Words* (New York: Harper Collins, 1991), 37.

CHAPTER 4

1. Charles Swindoll, *Standing Out, Being Real in an Unreal World* (Portland, OR: Multnomah Press, 1983), 51–52.

CHAPTER 5

1. Robert Hemfelt and Richard Fowler, *Serenity: A Companion for Twelve Step Recovery* (Nashville: Thomas Nelson, 1990), 30.

2. *Listen to the Hunger* (Center City, MN: Hazelden Foundation, 1987), 8.

3. Ibid., 20.

CHAPTER 6

1. Stanley Gershoff, with Catherine Whitney, *The Tufts University Guide to Total Nutrition* (New York: Harper & Row, 1990).

2. Martin Katahn, *The T-Factor Diet* (New York: Bantam Books, 1989), 19.

3. Joseph C. Piscatella, *Controlling Your Fat Tooth* (New York: Workman, 1991).

4. Larrene Hagaman, "Building the Temple Within," *Restoration Witness* (September/October 1990), 4–12.

5. Quoted in Piscatella, *Fat Tooth*, 103.

6. Ibid., 101.

7. Regina Sara Ryan and John Travis, *The Wellness Workbook* (Berkeley, CA: Ten Speed Press, 1981), 105.

8. Bill B., *Compulsive Overeater* (Minneapolis: CompCare Publishers, 1981), 208.

9. Quoted in Norman Cousins, *Head First* (New York: Penguin Books, 1990), 125.

10. Ken Alstad, *Savvy Sayins: Lean and Meaty One-Liners* (Tucson, AZ: Ken Alstad Company, 1987).

11. Ibid.

CHAPTER 7

1. Regina Sara Ryan and John Travis, *The Wellness Workbook* (Berkeley, CA: Ten Speed Press, 1981), 91.

2. M. Scott Peck, M.D., *The Road Less Traveled* (New York: Touchstone/Simon and Schuster, 1978), 25.

3. Judi Hollis, *Fat Is a Family Affair* (Center City, MN: Hazelden Educational Materials, 1985), 156.

CHAPTER 8

1. G. Alan Marlatt and Judith R. Gordon, *Relapse Prevention—Maintenance Strategies in the Treatment of Addictive Behaviors* (New York: Guilford Press, 1985).

2. Terence T. Gorski and Merlene Miller, *Staying Sober: A Guide to*

Relapse Prevention (Independence, MO: Herald House/Independence Press, 1986).

3. Ibid.

4. M. Scott Peck, M.D., *The Different Drummer* (New York: Simon and Schuster), 184.

5. Gorski and Miller, *Staying Sober.*

CHAPTER 9

1. Norman Cousins, *Anatomy of an Illness,* (New York: Norton, 1979).

2. Regina Sara Ryan and John W. Travis, M.D., *The Wellness Workbook* (Berkeley, California: Ten Speed Press, 1981).

3. Larrene Hagaman, "Building the Temple Within," *Restoration Witness* (September/October 1990), 4–12.

4. William Warden, *Grief Counseling and Grief Therapy: A Handbook for the Mental Health Practitioner,* 2nd ed. (New York: Springer Publishing, 1991).

CHAPTER 10

1. M. Scott Peck. M.D., *The Road Less Traveled* (New York: Simon and Schuster, 1978), 64.

2. Max Lucado, *In the Eye of the Storm* (Waco, TX: Word Books, 1991), 153.

3. Catherine Feste, *The Physician Within* (Minneapolis: Diabetes Centers, Inc., 1987), 63.

CHAPTER 11

1. Scott Norwood, ed., *Parables for Today,* Unpublished collection, 14–15.

2. *Grab Hold of Today,* 16mm, 28 minutes (Newport Beach, CA: Ramic Productions, 1977).

3. Linda Moore, *Release from Powerlessness* (Dubuque, IA: Kendall/Hunt, 1991), 18.

4. Melodie Beattie, *Codependent No More* (Center City, MN: Hazelden Foundation, 1987), 172.

5. William Glasser, *Control Theory: A New Explanation of How We Control Our Lives* (New York: Harper & Row, 1985).

6. David L. Watson and Roland G. Tharp, *Self-Directed Behavior:*

Self-Modification for Personal Adjustment (Pacific Grove, CA Brooks/ Cole, 1989), 5.

7. Ibid., 18.

8. Tim Hansel, *Holy Sweat* (Waco, TX: Word Books, 1987), 93.

9. Ibid., 97.

10. Thanks to C. Robert Mesle for his contributions to the ideas in this section.

11. Louise Hay, *The Power Within* (Carson, CA: Hay House, 1991), 170.

CHAPTER 13

1. Shad Helmstetter, *The Self-Talk Solution* (New York: Simon and Schuster, 1987), 138–139.

2. Ibid., 66.

CHAPTER 14

1. Abraham Twerski, *When Do the Good Things Start* (New York: Topper Books, 1988), 28.

2. Ibid., 29.

3. Ibid., 13.

4. M. Scott Peck, M.D., *The Road Less Traveled* (New York: Simon and Schuster, 1978), 74.

5. Bruce Larson, *There's a Lot More to Health Than Not Being Sick* (Waco, TX: Word Books, 1984), 101.

6. Thanks to Gayle Page for this story.

CHAPTER 16

1. Quoted in Matthew Fox, *The Coming of the Cosmic Christ* (San Francisco: Harper & Row, 1988), 5.

2. Quoted in Clyde Francis Lytle, ed., *Leaves of Gold* (Williamsport, PA: Coslett, 1948), 26.

3. Matthew Fox, *The Coming of the Cosmic Christ* (San Francisco: Harper & Row, 1988), 32.

4. Quoted in ibid., 47.

5. Larrene Hagaman, "Building the Temple Within," *Restoration Witness* (September/October 1990), 4–12.

Suggested Reading

"Addicts May Lack Some Neurotransmitters," by Kenneth Blum and Micahel C. Trachtenberg. *The U.S. Journal* (July 1987) 16.

Alcohol and the Addictive Brain, by Kenneth Blum, Ph.D. New York: The Free Press, 1991.

"Altered (Chemical) States, Insights into Neurochemistry," by T. L. Neher. *Professional Counselor,* (March/April 1991), 31-35.

Anatomy of an Illness, by Norman Cousins. New York: Norton,1979.

The Betrayal of Health, by Joseph D. Beasley, M.D. New York: Time Books, 1991.

The Carbohydrate Addict's Diet, by Rachael F. Heller, Ph.D., and Richard F. Heller, Ph.D. New York: DUTTON, 1991.

Codependent No More, by Melody Beattie. Center City, MN: Hazelden Foundation, 1987.

Compulsive Overeater, by Bill B. Minneapolis: CompCare, 1981.

Controlling Your Fat Tooth, by Joseph C. Piscatella, New York: Workman, 1991.

Dr. Bob Arnot's REVOLUTIONARY WEIGHT CONTROL PROGRAM, by Robert Arnot, M.D. Boston: Little, Brown and Company, 1997.

Endorphins: New Waves in Brain Chemistry, by Joel Davis. Garden City, NY: Dial, 1984.

Fat is a Family Affair, by Judi Hololis, Ph.D. Center City, MN: Hazelden Foundation, 1985.

Guilt Is the Teacher, Love Is the Lesson, by Joan Borysenko. New York: Warner Books, 1990.

Healthy for Life: The Scientific Breakthrough Program for Looking, Feeling, and Staying Healthy Without Deprivation, by Richard F. Heller, Ph.D., and Rachael F. Heller, Ph.D. New York: PLUME, an imprint of Dutton Signet, 1996.

Holy Sweat, by Tim Hansel, Waco, TX: Word Books, 1987.

The LEARN Program for Weight Control, by Kelly Brownell, Ph.D. Philadelphia: University of Pennsylvania School of Medicine, 1988.

Learning to Live Again, by Merlene Miller, Terence T. Gorski, and David K. Miller. Independence, MO: Herald House/ Independence Press, 1992.

Listen to the Hunger. Center City, MN: Hazelden Foundation, 1987.

The Partnership Diet Program, by Kelly Brownell. New York: Rawson Wade, 1980.

The Physician Within: Taking Charge of Your Well-Being, by Catherine Feste. Minneapolis: Diabetes Center, 1987.

Points In Your Favor, by Nancy Herring and Sandra Reichenberger. Wichita: St. Joseph Medical Center and Diabetes Treatment Center of America, 1987.

The Power Within, by Louise Hay. Carson, CA: Hay House, 1991.

Prescription for Nutritional Healing, by James F. Balch, M.D. And Phyllis A. Balch, C.N.C. Garden City Park, New York: Avery Publishing Group, 1993.

Protein Power, by Michael R. Eades, M.D. And Mary Dan Eades, M.D. New York: Bantam Books, 1996.

"Preventing Relapse and Transfer of Addiction: A Neurochemical Approach," by Joel C. Robertson. *EAP Digest* (September/October 1988), 50-54.

Release from Powerlessness, by Linda Moore. Dubuque, IA: Hunt, 1991.

The Road Less Traveled, by M. Scott Peck, M.D. New York: Simon and Schuster, 1978.

Self-Directed Behavior: Self-Modification for Personal Adjustment, by David L. Watson and Roland G. Tharp. Pacific Grove, CA: Brooks/Cole, 1989.

The Self-Talk Solution, by Shad Helmstetter. New York: Pocket Books,1987.

Serenity: A Companion for Twelve Step Recovery, by Dr. Robert Hemfelt and Dr. Richard Fowler. Nashville: Thomas Nelson, 1990.

The Slippery Slope, by Anne Barcus. Tustin, CA: Cornerstone, 1993.

A Spirituality Name Compassion and the Healing of the Global Village, Humpty Dumpty and Us, by Matthew Fox. San Francisco: Harper and Row, 1979.

Spontaneous Healing, by Andrew Weil, M.D. New York: Fawcett Columbine, 1995.

Staying Sober: A Guide for Relapse Prevention, by Terence T. Gorski and Merlene Miller. Independence, MO: Herald House/Independence Press, 1986.

The T-Factor Diet, by Martin Katahn, Ph.D. New York: Bantam Books, 1989.

The Tuffs University Guide to Total Nutrition, by Stanley Gershoff, Ph.D., with Catherine Whitney. New York: Harper & Row, 1990.

The Wellness Workbook, by regina Sara Ryan and John W. Travis, M.D. Berkeley, CA: Ten Speed Press, 1981.

Waking Up Just in Time, by Abraham J. Twerski, M.D. New York: Topper Books, 1990.

The Zone, by Barry Sears, Ph.D. New York: Regan Books, An Imprint of HARPERCOLLINS PUBLISHERS, 1995.

Resources

REVERSING THE WEIGHT GAIN SPIRAL WORKBOOK
by Stephen W. Emerick, Ph.D.; Lisa M. Havens, RN; and
Merlene Miller, MA
© 1997

The workbook is designed to give readers a comprehensive and guided process for self-assessment of their individual weight gain spiral. It includes structured exercises on managing food cravings and assists in the development of a detailed self-care plan. It provides tools for reversing weight gain and sustaining recovery.

Chapters include:
COMMITMENT TO HEALTH?
MORE THAN MIND OVER PLATTER: THE BIOLOGICAL BASIS OF OVERWEIGHT
THE ERROR OF OUR WEIGHS: WHY DIETING DOESN'T WORK
FOOD AND FEELINGS
CHOOSING RECOVERY: GAINING POWER THROUGH ACCEPTANCE
MANAGING CRAVINGS
SELF-CARE PLANNING
REGRESSION PREVENTION PLANNING OVERVIEW
REGRESSION PREVENTION PLANNING

TO ORDER:
Harrison Publishing
(937) 879-4324

WORKSHOPS, CONSULTATION, AND TRAINING CONTACT:

Stephen W. Emerick Ph.D.

Lisa M. Havens RN, NCACII

For information on training, consulting, or retreats contact
Stephen W. Emerick, Ph.D., CCCDIII
Life Development Centers, Inc.
337 North Broad Street
Fairborn, Ohio 45324
(937) 879-4324 SWELDC @ AOL.com
(937) 898-9977 (FAX)
or
Lisa Havens,RN, NCACII
LMH, Inc.
449 West Street
P.O. Box 303
Suttons Bay, Michigan 49682
(616) 271-5577

Index

HARRY BARTH

ABOUT THE AUTHORS

MERLENE MILLER coordinates the Addiction Studies Program at Graceland College. DAVID K. MILLER also teaches at Graceland and does private counseling, specializing in recovery from addiction, attention deficit disorder, and overeating. Together David and Merlene conduct workshops and relapse prevention retreats on these issues. Combining their professional knowledge and writing skills, they develop educational materials and have authored numerous books. Merlene and David are married—to each other—and live in Independence, Missouri.